HOW TO BECOME A SPY

The World War II SOE Training Manual

British SOE

Skyhorse Publishing

All inquiries should be addressed to Skyhorse Publishing, 307 West 36th Street, 11th Floor, New York, NY 10018.

Skyhorse Publishing books may be purchased in bulk at special discounts for sales promotion, corporate gifts, fund-raising, or educational purposes. Special editions can also be created to specifications. For details, contact the Special Sales Department, Skyhorse Publishing, 307 West 36th Street, 11th Floor, New York, NY 10018 or info@skyhorsepublishing.com.

Skyhorse® and Skyhorse Publishing® are registered trademarks of Skyhorse Publishing, Inc.®, a Delaware corporation.

Visit our website at www.skyhorsepublishing.com.

10 9 8 7 6 5

Library of Congress Cataloging-in-Publication Data is available on file.

Cover design by Rain Saukas
Cover photo credit: Thinkstock

Print ISBN: 978-1-63220-526-1
Ebook ISBN: 978-1-63220-901-6

Printed in the United States of America

Publisher's Note

This publication reproduces the basic syllabus used at the Special Training Schools (STSs) of the Special Operations Executive. The version reproduced here – to our knowledge the most complete and comprehensive of the surviving SOE training materials – was used at STS 103 in Canada, better known as Camp X. The lecture folders containing the syllabus are to be found in two files, HS 7/55 and HS 7/56, which may be consulted at the National Archives, Kew. The aim has been to reproduce the words, layout and appearance of the original documents as faithfully as possible. However, to keep the extent of this edition within bounds, the lists of library books, films and supplementary reading material have been omitted. Also, where necessary, lines and lettering have been strengthened in some of the illustrations; obvious typing errors have been corrected; and cross-references have been revised to conform to the pagination of this edition.

Primary Sources

SOE documents in the National Archives:

HS 7/55	Syllabus of Lectures at STS 103 (Camp X).
HS 7/56	Lecture Folder STS 103. Minor Tactics, Demolitions and Fieldcraft Lectures. Physical Training Syllabus.
HS 7/52	Group B Syllabus (in the Finishing Schools)
HS 7/51	*History of the Training Section of SOE, 1940-1945* by Major G.M. Forty.
CAB 102/649-52	*History of the Second World War: The Special Operations Executive – Britain and the Resistance Movements in Europe*, by W.J.M. Mackenzie, Fellow of Magdalen College, Oxford.

SYLLABUS OF LECTURES

---

* Not included in this book.

SYLLABUS OF LECTURES

* Not included in this book.

CAMP ARRANGEMENTS

NAME _____

COURSE NO. _____   ROOM NUMBER _____

1. DRESS.

On arrival in Camp you will be issued with Battle Dress (or Summer Drill) and the necessary accessories. This uniform will be worn during all working periods, for the following reasons:

a) <u>Security</u>. This is a military establishment. For the benefit of local inhabitants and visiting tradesmen, it is considered advisable for the military appearance of the Camp to be consistently maintained.

b) <u>Wear and tear</u>. Many of your activities on the course will be undertaken out of doors. By wearing your issued Battle Dress you will save your own civilian clothes and/or uniform.

There is no objection to your wearing whatever clothes you please for relaxation in the evenings.

You are not required to render military compliments to the officers of the Camp.

2. COMMUNICATIONS.

Any incoming mail may be addressed to you personally at:

> Box 55,
> Terminal A,
> Toronto 2, Ont., Canada.

Any outgoing mail will be handed in at the Administration Office. In view of the fact that the Camp's location is secret, this will be mailed in Toronto.

Therefore, NO mail will be handed to any member of the Camp Staff, other than the Clerks in the Administration Office who have been detailed to handle it.

For the same reason outgoing mail, though uncensored, will not contain any reference either to the Camp's location, appearance or activities.

Telephone calls from the Camp may be made outside working hours. NO incoming calls are permitted.

3. MESSING AND BAR SERVICE.

a) <u>Messing</u> will be charged at the rate of .50 cents per day. A service charge of .50 cents per week will be made to cover gratuities to the staff. It is asked that no additional gratuities be made, as this rate is in accordance with Canadian Army scales.

b) <u>Bar</u>. Within the limits of current rationing, beer, spirits and cigarettes are obtainable from the bar which will be open only between the following hours:

> 1215 - 1245
> 1800 - 1900
> 1945 - 2230

c) <u>Accounts</u>. All messing and bar accounts will be rendered and paid on the day previous to final departure. Subsequent purchases will be paid for in cash.

d) <u>Meal Times</u>.

Breakfast	0815	Hours
Lunch	1245	"
Tea	1630	"
Supper	1900	"

It is particularly requested that you observe these times. Kitchen accommodation and staff is limited. Considerable inconvenience can be caused through unpunctuality.

4. <u>INTRODUCTORY ADDRESS</u>.

You will assemble at ___ hours on ___ in Lecture Room, when the details of the Course will be explained in an introductory address.

5. <u>LEAVE</u>.

For Courses of over fourteen days' duration, weekend leave may be arranged from Saturday 1230 until Sunday midnight. A leave application form will be issued. This should be filled in and handed to the Secretary's Office in the Administration Building not later than the Wednesday previous in order to ensure the necessary hotel and transportation reservations.

6. <u>MISCELLANEOUS REQUESTS</u>.

Complaints, if any, and requests for interviews or general information should be made to the Secretary between the following hours:

> 0900 - 0925) Mondays - Saturdays
> 1215 - 1230)   inclusive

CAMP ARRANGEMENTS

1330 - 1410)

1000 - 1200 Sundays

C. Skilbeck, Lieut-Colonel,
Officer Commanding.

INTRODUCTION

OBJECTS AND METHODS OF IRREGULAR WARFARE

1. OBJECTS

In Europe and Asia the enemy seek to obtain from their own, from satellite and from occupied territories the maximum advantage:

(a) Politically.   For example by:

  (i) indoctrination.
  (ii) "Divide and Rule".

(b) Economically.   For example by:

  (i) Use of materials.
  (ii) Use of factories.
  (iii) Recruitment of foreign workers.
  (iv) Financial swindles.

(c) Strategically.   For example by:

  (i) Use of communications.
  (ii) Offensive and defensive bases.
  (iii) Use of quisling & satellite manpower.

But spontaneous resistance has occurred everywhere:

(a) Politically.   E.g. Norway's battle of Churches and Teachers.

(b) Economically.   E.g. France's resistance to labour-recruitment.

(c) Strategically. E.g. Mihailovic's guerrillas and abortive Haute Savoie rising.

Sporadic risings are useless. Necessity to co-ordinate where possible has produced tabulation of United Nations' fundamental objectives in the waging of Irregular Warfare:

(a) Politically.

  (i) To undermine enemy's morale and that of his collaborators.

  (ii) To raise morale of Occupied Territories.

4

(b) <u>Economically.</u>

    (i) To damage enemy's material.

    (ii) To improve and augment our own material.

        E.g. By infiltration of weapons, explosives, sabotage equipment.

(c) <u>Strategically</u>.

    (i) To damage enemy's man-power and communications.

    (ii) To improve our own man-power and communications.

        E.g. By infiltration of "organizers", radio sets and operators, etc.

2. <u>METHODS</u>

These, by definition, include all methods of attaining the above objectives <u>outside</u> the scope of regular warfare.

(a) <u>Informational</u>.

   – Espionage: The covert collection and transmission of information about the enemy to our own forces.

(b) <u>Operational</u>.

   – Propaganda: The art of persuasion with a view to producing a required mood or a required action.

   – Passive Resistance: Infliction of the maximum damage to the enemy with the minimum danger to oneself.

   – Sabotage: Covert destruction of material profitable to the enemy.

   – Secret Armies: Pre- and Post-invasion.

   – Politico-Military uprising.

3. <u>INTERDEPENDENCE OF METHODS</u>

All these methods are interdependent. Each one singly has its relation to our fundamental objectives; but, if each is used singly, the objectives can never be attained.

4. PRESENT SITUATION

There are two phases:

(a) <u>Pre-Invasion</u>. This phase, which in Europe is ending, consisted mainly in organizing the countries area by area – in a manner either simple or complex according to the country's physical geography, group-distribution and degree of contra-espionage control.

(b) <u>Invasion</u>. This phase is beginning. For you it will involve the attainment of (a, b or c) objective by the use of (a, b, c, etc.) methods

5. You will be a cog in a very large machine whose smooth functioning depends on each separate cog carrying out its part efficiently.
It is the objective of this course to clarify the part you will play and ensure the efficiency of your performance.

6

SELF PROTECTION

INDIVIDUAL AND COLLECTIVE SECURITY

1. DEFINITION.

Security: "Precautions taken by the individual for his own personal protection and the protection of his Organization from the enemy".

Without these precautions, it is dangerous to attempt regular and impossible to attempt irregular warfare alone or in conjunction with other people.

2. APPLICATION.

a) Apparent absence of enemy C.E. measures should never be allowed to engender over-confidence. (Cf. graph of agent's confidence.)

b) Insecurity by an individual may jeopardise not only his own safety but the safety of the organization with which he is in contact.

3. INFORMATION.

Basis of your self-protection is good information. As much as possible provided before departure, but you must check and supplement on arrival. Information required on:

    i) Local Conditions.
   ii) Local Regulations.
  iii) Enemy methods.
   iv) Enemy personnel.
    v) Your own subordinates.

4. INCULCATION.

a) Security cannot be taught by rule of thumb. It is a frame of mind attainable through self-discipline and self-training that will make the taking of precautions a "habit". (Cf. crossing a road.)

b) What is a habit? A single action committed so often as to become automatic. What precautionary actions must we practise so often that they become a habit?

5. <u>COMMUNICATION</u>.

The answer is "Communicatory Actions". Secret and confidential information can reach the enemy through our carelessness in:

a) Speech.

b) Writing.

c) Behaviour.

a) <u>Speech</u>.

Adoption of hush-hush attitude through vanity.

Confiding in friends to ease nervous strain.

Mentioning facts you are not "outwardly" supposed to know, or isolated facts which can be strung together.

Telling people more than they need to know.

Compromising telephone-conversations through misuse of conventions. (E.g. NOT "Three lambs with sweets and toys who need instruction in malaria" BUT "Three chaps with some goods for Harry who need instruction in my subject".)

b) <u>Writing</u>.

Commit as little as possible to writing. Memorise if you can.

If you must carry documents, select what you must carry.

Burn all secret waste and carbons.

c) <u>Behaviour</u>.

Be inconspicuous. Avoid all limelight by being an "average" citizen in appearance (height, clothes) and conduct (drink, women).

Be tidy. All engaged on secret work must be methodical in their habits - e.g. it is mainly knowing exactly where he has placed his belongings and arranged his room that an individual can detect disturbance by police search.

Have good "Cover" - the innocent activity undertaken or invented to conceal the secret aspects of his activity. Good cover must be consistent with necessary overt behaviour and non-compromising.

(For application to operational Agent see A.4.)

Be observant. Observe and deduce. (E.g. face or voice seen or heard twice suggesting you are being followed. Smell of

8

real coffee in France suggesting someone occupied in Black Market.)

Have foresight. See danger early. (E.g. axis agent in café, policemen checking papers.)

Plan for emergency. Alternative courses in case of accident (RV's) pre-arranged conversation when talking to colleague in case of sudden interrogation. Danger signs.

SECURITY FOR W/T OPERATORS

1. **INTRODUCTION**

   Lecture deals with special aspects of security for W/T Operators apart from general principles laid down in "Individual Security".

2. **CHOOSING OF PREMISES FOR WORKING SET**.

   a) **Choice depends on**:

      i) Security considerations.
      ii) Technical considerations.
      iii) Combination of i. and ii. and district.

   b) **Security**.

      Safer to have number of sets dispersed over wide area with owners or occupants of premises recruited (see further below).

   c) **Technical**.

      Avoid steel-framed buildings. Key click easily audible in next room or if radio receiver working off same circuit. Consider aerial camouflage.

   d) **District**.

      i) Thinly populated country districts, possibility for isolated buildings, e.g. farms, etc.

      ii) Towns - private house or place of occupation.

   e) In case of d) ii) above, consider following factors:

      i) **Accessibility**.

         Operator must be able to get to and from premises without arousing suspicions of neighbours or passers by.

      ii) **Cover.**

         Must have "genuine" reason for frequent visits (e.g. doctor). Use existing household.

      iii) **Facilities, defensive**.

         For concealing self and set.
         For escape (exits).
         Vulnerability to surveillance.

iv) <u>Control of Access</u>.

Limit to number and type of people with possible access to premises.

3. GENERAL SECURITY PRECAUTIONS

To be taken in any premise including place of residence.

a) Precautions against search during absence - tidiness, leaf in keyhole, hair, etc.

b) Minimum incriminating material, coded writings destroyed, etc. N.B.: Traces on blotting paper and writing blocks.

c) Hiding places prepared, particularly for set.

  i) Inside House - advantages and disadvantages.

  ii) Outside House - advantages and disadvantages.

  Possibility of working set from hiding places.

d) Preparation for destroying incriminating material.

e) Where possible room with 2 doors and light switch near while operating.

f) Guard while operating, e.g. possibility of hall porter.

g) All clear and danger signals, visual and/or oral.

h) Check on surveillance of premises, or when entering or leaving.

i) Alternative premises in case of emergency.

j) No casual visitors at premises - only possible ones are cut-outs.

4. CUT-OUTS

a) <u>Definition</u>.

Intermediary. Link between two agents. May only carry messages, knowing nothing about Organization, or act as liaison officer. Should undertake no other subversive activity.

b) <u>Reason for employment</u> (In case of W/T Operator).

  i) Dangerous for operator to be seen with Organizer.

  ii) May not want another member to know him.

  iii) Barrier between himself and authorities, e.g. telegram, official enquiry, hiring flat.

  iv) Transfer of suspicion, delayed or prevented.

c) <u>Cover</u>.

Must be able to contact inconspicuously people of different social positions, e.g. doctor, dentist, priest, waiter, postman, etc.

5. <u>SECURITY RULES FOR OPERATOR</u>.

a) Must never undertake other subversive activity. Danger of over enthusiasm.

b) Must not attempt to find out more about Organization than he is told, nor know one or two members.

c) Christian names only should be used. Numbering dangerous.

d) Never carry arms unless in situation for which no cover story (e.g. working the set).

e) Must report suspicious incident immediately, e.g. if followed.

f) Emergency measures, e.g. warning signals, hide-out, contacts to drop, how to re-establish contact.

INFORMANT SERVICE

1. INTRODUCTION

Without good information it is impossible:

(a) to protect oneself against enemy C. E.

(b) to plan or time operations (c.f. importance of "I" to "0" staff in regular army).

2. WHAT DO YOU REQUIRE TO KNOW?

(a) Local Conditions -

- unprocurable articles (e.g. danger of ordering wrong drinks or cigarettes).

- transport service (e.g. fewer trains, buses, taxis) and restrictions (e.g. reason for travelling).

- market days. Danger of search for "Black Market" goods.

- new slang or colloquialisms brought about by war.

- general temper of local population.

(b) Local Regulations -

- Identity Papers. Are yours in order?
(Compare yours with other people's and, if possible, procure genuine ones.)

- Ration Cards. Find out how to procure these.

- Movement Restrictions. What passes are necessary?

- Control Posts. Manned by enemy troops or local police?

- Evacuation from forbidden zones.

- Curfew hours.

- Blackout Regulations.

- Bicycles - licenses, restrictions, etc.

(c) Enemy Methods and Personnel.

- location of troops.

- location of nearest enemy police or Gestapo, with details or personnel; attitude of local police.

- names of civilian police spies, agents provocateurs.

13

(d) Operational Information

- possible targets: Enemy communications, H.Q., dumps, factories.
- bottle necks in enemy production and communications.
- internal working of factories, power station, railways, etc. e.g. type of machinery used.
- personnel employed in any of the above.
- means of entry: layout, guards, control system.
- documents: workers' passes, blueprints, etc.

3. HOW DO YOU OBTAIN THIS INFORMATION?

   a)   By direct interrogation.
   b)   By constant personal observation.
   c)   By reading newspapers and listening to radio.
   d)   By Informant Service:

   THE INFORMANT SERVICE:

   (a) Personnel

   (i) Very few should know that they are informants. The great bulk will be quite unconscious of it.

   (ii) Select from as many strata of society, trades, professions, etc., as possible.

   (iii) Best are types who constantly mix with all sorts
   -E.G.,

   Priests,
   Inn-Keepers,
   Waitresses, barmaids,
   Doctors, Dentists, hospital staffs,
   Postmen, telephone and telegraph operators.
   Bankers, shopkeepers.
   Railway Officials and workers, Servants,
   All grumblers and malcontents.

   (iv) In due course you may decide to approach a few of the more trustworthy informants with a view to recruiting them.

   (b) Methods

   (i) Journalists' technique of eavesdropping on the masses. c.f. - Ability to hear and separate two simultaneous conversations while ostensibly listening to a third.

14

SELF PROTECTION

    (ii) Taking advantage of other people's bad security –
e.g. –
- Careless talk
- Disgruntled enemy personnel.
- Affecting ignorance and thus encouraging others to air their knowledge.
- Making false statements to elicit correct reply.

    (iii) Do not discourage informants, however trivial the information. c.f. – reporter's maxim: "Never refuse a date".

COVER

1. DEFINITION.

Your cover is the life which you outwardly lead in order to conceal the real purpose of your presence and the explanation which you give of your past and present. It is best considered under the heads:

> Past,
> Link between Past and Present,
> Present and "Alibis".

2. YOUR PAST.

Before your departure, with the assistance of your Section Officers, you will probably prepare the story of your past life up to the time of your arrival. But you cannot always arrange a complete story before leaving; furthermore, you may have to change part or all of your cover story when you are actually in the field and know what your circumstances are to be. Nevertheless you must be able to give some account of yourself if questioned immediately after your arrival.

In inventing or amending your cover story, or that of another agent, the following points should be considered:

a) Identity.

    i) Your Own.

Advantages:	Your story will be mainly true. Only a limited period will have to be explained away. Records will confirm your statements.
Disadvantages:	The subversive part of your history may be known to the enemy or to persons who may give you away. This is usually the case with escapees.

    ii) That of a Real Person, Distant or Dead.

Advantages:	The story, being real, will be self-consistent. Records will confirm at least a part of it.

Disadvantages: People acquainted with the person whom you are impersonating may give you away. You may have incomplete information about this person's past life, so that your statements may be shown to be untrue. The person may be suspected without your knowing it.

iii) <u>Wholly Fictitious</u>.

Advantages: Less chance of entanglements and wider scope.

Disadvantages: Records will not confirm your story.

In some cases agents have to assume different identities in different places. This should be avoided as far as possible because it leads to contradictions.

<u>N.B.</u> The danger of two identity cards.

b) <u>History</u>.

i) Whatever your identity, your story must be <u>plausible</u> and not indicate any connection with subversive activity.

ii) It should be based, as far as possible, on the <u>facts</u> of your own life or that of the person whom you are impersonating. Do not introduce places or events which you do not know nor refer to knowledge which you have not. (Do not claim to know of engineering if you do not.)

iii) Pay particular attention to that part of your story which is linked with the details shown in your documents. These may be examined closely.

iv) Your <u>recent</u> history is of most interest to the police. It is also most difficult to invent satisfactorily. Particular care should be devoted to its preparation.

v) Although a complete mastery of details is essential in the preparation of the story, vagueness is often desirable when repeating it, especially in the case of more distant and less important parts.

c) <u>Documents</u>.

These are supplied by your Section and will be as nearly perfect as possible. The following points must be remembered:

i) You must know how you would have obtained them if they had been issued to you legally.

ii) All the documents you need cannot always be produced in this country, e.g. those which change frequently, such as ration cards in some countries.

iii) The falsity of forged documents is always ultimately detectable if counterfoils exist, especially if they are numbered consecutively. It may take a long time to establish this falsity.

iv) Perfect documents can only be obtained through official sources in the field.

d) <u>Clothes and Effects</u>.

i) Do not take anything with you which does not fit your story.

ii) Your effects can sometimes furnish valuable corroborative evidence of the "truth" of your background cover, e.g. unofficial papers, tickets, bills, local products, etc.

e) <u>Change of Appearance</u>.

i) To support assumed character (rough hands for workman).

ii) To avoid recognition if you are going among people who know you.

<u>N.B.</u> Application of disguise is dealt with in a special lecture.

f) <u>Final Search</u>

You must search your person and residence for traces which link you with your "other self":

i) Before your departure.

ii) Whenever you change your cover story

iii) If you wish to conceal some recent activity.

iv) If you are about to undertake some special subversive act.

3. <u>FROM PAST TO PRESENT</u>

As soon as you arrive you must adopt a cover life to account for your presence. Your cover story for your past must merge into this.

SELF PROTECTION

a) From the beginning start completing the details of the cover story of your past. Really do the things you say you have done. Really go to the places you say you have been to. This will serve a double purpose:

    i) You will obtain the information which you would have had had your story been true, e.g. see the towns, learn their recent history, etc. With this knowledge you can support and, if necessary, modify your background cover.

    ii) You can manufacture evidence confirming your background cover, e.g. make acquaintances in the places you go to, possess things coming from these places.

b) Build up also your present cover background by innocent and inconspicuous actions to which reference can be made later. It may be useful to make innocent acquaintances, etc.

4. <u>YOUR PRESENT</u>.

This is the life which you lead and the story which you will tell about that life to account for your presence. It may be planned with the help of your Section Officers before your departure. Or you may have to work it out for the first time after your arrival. In any case, your ostensible present must be consistent with your alleged past.

a) <u>Maintenance of Cover</u>.

    i) <u>Name.</u>

        Always sign correctly and respond to it immediately.

    ii) <u>Consistency in General</u>

        Your personality and general conduct must fit your cover background, e.g.:

        Expenditure must accord with ostensible income.
        Volume and nature of correspondence must fit your social circumstances.
        Character of friends and acquaintances must accord with your cover personality.
        Documents, clothing, possessions, etc. must be suitable.
        Manners, tastes, bearing, accent, education and knowledge must accord with your ostensible personality.

iii) <u>Concealment of Absence from your Country</u>.

Avoid foreign words, tunes, manners, etc.
Avoid slang which has developed among your countrymen in Britain.
Avoid showing knowledge or expressing views acquired in Britain.
Conform with all new conditions which have arisen, observe new customs and acquire the language which has developed in your country.

b) <u>Cover Occupation</u>.

It is advisable for you to have, or pretend to have, a cover occupation. (A real one is best, but sometimes their subversive activity does not permit agents to do other work.) An occupation is necessary:

i) To account for presence in locality.

ii) To explain the source of livelihood.

iii) To avoid, if possible, conscription for work in Germany or elsewhere.

In selecting a cover occupation, bear in mind the possibilities of having:

i) An unregistered job such as student, stamp dealer.

ii) An imaginary job. In this case it is an advantage if you have a real employer to vouch for you.

Your range of choice of occupation is restricted by certain factors. Some of these factors apply also to an imaginary job. Consider the following:

i) Some jobs involve special investigation of credentials and/or restriction of liberty.

ii) The job which you select should afford you cover and facilities for your activity. Consider hours, pay, movement, technical facilities, e.g. transport, storage, access, etc.

iii) You must have adequate technical qualifications.

c) <u>Conclusion</u>.

Good background cover is hard to build up and easily destroyed. It is essential to your relations with the general public. Never sacrifice such cover once acquired if you can possibly avoid it.

Remember, however, that a serious investigation is likely to break down your background cover by exposing the falseness of your documents or statements about your past life. Always, therefore, avoid trouble with the authorities. Have a ready story to account for everything.

In some cases an ostensible lawful existence is impossible. Then you must live underground. Be inconspicuous. Avoid officials. Vary your appearance, habits, haunts, routes, etc. Produce one story or another as the occasion demands.

5. "ALIBI".

a) Nature of "Alibi".

In addition to your cover background, you must have an explanation ready for every subversive act, however small, e.g. conversation, journey. Such alibis are more important than your background cover. If they are good no further enquiries will be made.

You may be questioned about your activity in many different circumstances and have to conceal its true nature, e.g. when obtaining permits, telephoning, by regular or snap controls, through infringing regulations or being called as a witness, through suspicious activity when under surveillance.

b) Construction of an "alibi".

Remember the following points:

i) Plausibility. If you give a plausible explanation of your conduct no further investigation is likely. An unplausible story will be investigated and must, therefore, be watertight.

ii) Detail. Decide on the "facts" which must be prepared in detail and those which can be left vague, e.g. people remember times of rendezvous, trains, etc., but not when they have finished meals.

iii) Self-Consistency. Your "alibi" must be consistent with your circumstances, especially those immediately ascertainable, e.g. clothes, general appearance, special knowledge, activity.

iv) Cover Background. For choice your "alibi" should be consistent with your main cover background, but you may have to manufacture special background for the occasion.

v) <u>Truth</u>. The "alibi" should be as near the truth as possible, provided that it is not suspicious. Time can be expanded. Dates of events can be transposed. Where the story is quite untrue the false parts can often be rehearsed. Cf. Build up of cover (above). It is dangerous to tell a story entirely untrue.

vi) <u>Dead End</u>. In so far as is possible the story should be closed. It should leave few openings for further investigation. Links with outside persons, events or places are dangerous.

vii) <u>Consistency with Others</u>. Persons called upon to corroborate your story must do so reasonably accurately. (Consider possibility of arrangement by which all questions of a certain kind are answered in the same way. E.g. "Describe a game of cards exactly as played yesterday" or "Initiative in any action always taken by A".)

viii) <u>Discreditable Story</u>. Consider the possibility of using as an "alibi" a discreditable story. Sometimes this can be used as an alternative upon which to fall back should the first story break down.

<u>N.B.</u> Provided that you have not been questioned about your alibi, you can change it freely; e.g. one to explain what you are going to do, a second to explain what you are doing and a third to account for what you have done.

SELF PROTECTION

MAKE UP AND DISGUISE

1. <u>DEFINITION OF DISGUISE.</u>

   a) It does not mean covering your face with grease paint and hair.

   b) It must have as its basis the art of being and living mentally as well as physically this new role. The important thing to remember is to be the person you are portraying mentally first and then afterwards physically. Therefore – EXTERNAL IMITATION BY ITSELF IS NOT SUFFICIENT.

   By this we mean imitating the external part of a character only, i.e. the walk, the voice, the manners and individualities etc. of the character. External imitation without proper mental preparation must mean you speak and do things mechanically without fully realizing who you are, where you come from, why, what you want, where you are going, what you are supposed to be and do when you get there, etc. You will therefore be nothing but an external caricature and easily caught out.

2. <u>OCCASIONS WARRANTING THE USE OF DISGUISE</u>.

   a) <u>Long Term</u>.
   When a well known personality is going back to work in his own home town and where, for the safety of himself and his organization, he must be unrecognized. (Example, done by plastic surgeon).

   b) <u>Short Term</u>.

      i) Your informant service has told you that the police are after you, they have your description and there is nothing for it but to get away.

      ii) Occasional contacting jobs. When you do not want to risk your own cover.

      iii) Special jobs, E.g. when you have to meet personally one of your collaborators arriving in the Country and for added protection, if you are seen, people will get a wrong description of you.

      iv) Leaving a building under surveillance (This will be more of a quick change and the mental side less important) (Example - Loise de Bettignies disguised as a maid).

3. <u>PRELIMINARIES TO DISGUISE</u>.

   a) Disguise must only be used in the case of emergency.

   b) Never allow yourself externally to portray anything that you have not inwardly experienced and which is not even interesting to you.

   c) Remember in a get-away the police will probably only have a description to work on, therefore work with a view to changing this description.

   d) The disguise should be chosen and thought out as long as possible before you have need of using it so that you can adopt it with the maximum of speed and confidence.

4. <u>POINTS TO BE CONSIDERED IN YOUR DISGUISE</u>.

   a) <u>Golden Rule</u>.

   Never come out of character. By this we mean not only from the clothes point of view but from the mental side also, E.g. if you are a workman do not wear a white collar and black tie, have clean hands and behave like an educated man.

   b) <u>Clothes</u>.

   Study in every detail the clothes you are going to wear not forgetting small items such as cut, socks, tie, handkerchiefs, etc. Different shapes and kinds of hats will alter type.

   c) <u>Personal Effects</u>.

   Cigarettes, type of newspaper, contents of paper, E.g. watches.

   d) <u>Hair</u>

   If it should be long or short, whether it should be tidy or untidy.

   e) <u>Your Face</u>.

   Whether it should be dirty or clean, whether it should be shaved or unshaved, whether it should be pale or sunburnt.

   f) <u>Teeth</u>.

   Whether they should be clean or not.

   g) <u>Hands</u>.

   Nails, dirty or clean, and your hands white or dirty or hard worked.

h) Feet.

Whether you wear shoes or boots, whether these should be clean or dirty.

i) Mannerisms.

Practice until your old mannerisms (such as playing with your right ear, etc.) are forgotten and your new mannerisms have become part of you.

j) Walk.

If you had any peculiarity in your carriage or your walk, practice until you have conquered the old ones and obtained new ones.

k) Handwriting

For signature or name if needed, educated or not. Whether you should sign as if you are used to signing it or whether you should handle your pen as though it were strange to you.

l) Habits.

Fit your habits to your character, E.g. don't play billiards in a cheap café if your new character is not the type of person who would.

m) Associates

Only associate or try to associate with people who fit in to your new life.

5. HINTS ON HOW TO CHANGE YOUR APPEARANCE.

a) Clothes.

These are more easily manipulated than the face. A simple straightforward change of clothes, provided that every detail is in character, will do wonders to alter your appearance, E.g. from your rough gardening clothes, to your best lounge suit. The types of clothes one can think out to change the appearance are endless.

Always make your clothes fit the character you are supposed to be, E.g. if you are supposed to be a merchant sailor do not have suede shoes on.

Stripes downwards with a single breasted suit make you look taller. Checks across with a double breasted suit make you look shorter and broader.

The position of buttons can alter apparent height and weight.

Round shoulders can be built up by cut, arms shortened by an added length of sleeve and vice versa. In general, get the reverse effect from your usual descriptions, E.g. if you have any deformity such as dropped shoulder, which is usually hidden by your tailor, then accentuate this etc.

b) <u>Hair</u>.

You should grow your hair longer than normal although there is no easy method of increasing hair growth, the appearance and shape of head can be drastically altered by cutting.

i) <u>To make dark hair fair or grey</u>.

<u>Preparations</u> – "Bitza" – ready for use. Peroxide – bought in small bottles. Max Factor hair whitener.

<u>Methods of use for all the above</u> – Pour into saucer and with small tooth brush apply to the hair, keeping the mixture away from the skin. Let it dry and as it dries it will lighten the hair. Apply again and it will be lighter still. If only the sides of the hair are done it will give a grey effect.

<u>Time needed</u> – 1 hour

ii) <u>To make silver or white hair go darker.</u>

<u>Preparations</u> – Black charcoal powder.

<u>Method of use</u> – Apply powder to hair with brush, rub in with the fingers, comb and brush. Continue this until the colour is satisfactory.

iii) <u>Forehead.</u>

Nothing can be done to change the shape of this except by wearing head gear.

iv) <u>Eyebrows.</u>

These can be easily bleached or darkened in the same manner as for the hair.

<u>Accessories</u> – Tweezers and oily substance.

<u>Method of Use</u> – If thick they can be cut, and if needed plucked. If plucked apply a little talcum powder to take away the redness. Apply a little oil to smooth them down.

If eyebrows meet, shave above the nose and apply talcum powder.

If thin and sleek, with the aid of a brown and black pencil, and by following the natural growth of the hair, pencil in lines and then smooth with finger. Then comb the eyebrows against their natural growth which will help to hide the pencil mark and give a rugged effect.

v) Eyes.

Accessories - Dark grey grease paint, coal dust or soot; Red make up pencil and Duo-liquid adhesive. Brown or black pencil. Grease.

Method of use - If eyes are very large and prominent shape the eyelids with soot or blue grease liner, shaping the eyelids and underneath the eye, following the usual bag line, and with a spot of grease blend in. Then with the red pencil work round the inside of the lower eyelid. This will give you a ready, bagged half closed eye. With your adhesive, fix the upper eyelids over your eyes, which gives a small squinting eye. To brighten the eye follow the natural eyelash line with the brown pencil and blend in.

vi) Ears.

Preparation - Duo-liquid adhesive.

Method of use - Apply this liquid to the back of your ear and hold your ear against your head for two to five minutes. This will stick the ear close to the head and will last approximately 24 hours. The same can be done with the lobe of the ear.

vii) Nose.

Accessories - End of fountain pen liner tube, two small round nuts.

Method of use - Bore holes in the nuts and place them inside the nostrils. This will give a very squashed tipped nose and it is possible to breathe quite freely.

viii) Moustaches.

If students are growing moustaches before leaving it is advisable to grow very large and very thick ones, as by cutting or shaving different shapes can be obtained.

Moustaches can also be darkened or bleached. For quick work we can have made-up moustaches of any shape and size on hair lace. This, with the aid of a little spirit gum can be stuck on in a minute and removed if needed in two seconds. The effect of a different shaped moustache on a face is quite staggering.

ix) <u>Teeth</u>.

If a student merely wants to discolour his teeth, iodine is very useful.

x) <u>Cheeks</u>.

Rubber pads can be inserted in the cheeks which alter the shape completely of the lower half of the face. These can be made by the student himself from sponge.

xi) <u>Cleft Chin</u>.

A little wax applied, mixed with a little rouge and worked into the cleft takes away the cleft.

xii) <u>Whole Face</u>.

For an unshaven appearance, with a small piece of porous sponge apply brown and dark brown make up. This gives the desired effect by merely dabbing the make-up on to the side of the face. Soot or coal-dust, if used with a porous sponge gives the same effect.

<u>Lines all over the face</u>. Deep lines can be applied to the face by simply using a soft black pencil in your own lines. Care must be taken only to use the natural lines.

Dr. Middleton, the Research specialist for Max Factor, has been experimenting with skin for a number of years and it is thought that he would have small bottles of skin colours to alter the colour of the skin as required.

xiii) <u>To cover Scars</u>.

Collodian bought at any chemist and found in every hospital, can easily be used.

<u>To make Scars</u>

Collodian (flexible). Apply to the skin with a brush. The skin must be held for a minute and a half to the required shape and when the collodian dries the effect of a scar remains. As many as needed can be made.

xiv) <u>To make a Face Younger</u>.

A very close shave, apply hot towels, then apply alum all over the face. This tightens the skin considerably and when talcum is applied afterwards gives a fresh young appearance.

xv) <u>To make a Face Older</u>.

Experiment with all the foregoing hints.

xvi) <u>Hands</u>.

These can be made rough by oil and dirt on the hands, and cuts. To get them to look well cared for, have them manicured and put ladies' face powder or hand powder over them.

6. CONCLUSION.

Long term disguise will be an integral part of cover, thus to employ it will require careful study and the assistance of experts long before the subject leaves for the field.

Short term disguise should be considered together with the system of alternatives that is always urged for the agent (i.e. means of communications, H.Q., reputation, hide-out and appearance). As a security measure to be employed in an emergency requires study and practice in advance if to be successful.

Sit down quietly and think out your new character mentally, not forgetting characteristics such as walk, stance, etc. When this is done experiment with your face so that not only is it changed but so that it fits in to your new character.

<u>APPENDIX</u>

During a sea voyage, Colonel H. had the opportunity of examining the growth of 64 beards, all of which were started on the same day. The beards were examined on the 19th day, the results being as follows:

1 true beard and moustache; growth about ¾" from face covered with good strong moustache well shaped and altering face entirely.

4 promising ones, little alteration to character of face.

1 bad beard but entirely altering lines of face giving an Elizabethan appearance.

30 growths that promise to be good beards in a month's time.

19 very poor, doubtful if they will ever develop into beards at all.

9 N.B.G. ever.

The best age groups: 23 - 48
The worst age groups: 17 - 20 and 41 - 53

Generally speaking, men on regular watch on deck are in advance of engine room staff (with one exception, a man who has a good crop of hair, none on his chest.)

1 totally bald man is in the group containing 4 promising beards.

2 totally bald men are in the 30 group.

7 baldish men in the 30 group.

1 totally bald in the 19 very poor group.

1 baldish in the 19 very poor group.

In view of the foregoing, it is suggested that the lecture on hair should be amended to read "Moustaches 15 - 25 days, beard 25 - 40 days."

OBSERVATION

1. GENERAL.

One of the most important ways of being well informed (See A.3.) is to be observant.

Just as information has been described as both a defensive and an offensive weapon, so observation can be used defensively and offensively.

2. DEFINITION.

For the agent, observation means: "A general awareness of what is going on around you without the appearance of being inquisitive."

Observation is not confined to seeing but includes hearing, smelling and feeling and also includes the power of deduction brought into play by the facts that have been noted.

3. POWERS OF OBSERVATION.

These are:

a) Inherent.

Young children are naturally extremely observant. They have not, however, developed their power of deduction.

b) Acquired.

Powers of observation are lying dormant in every one of us and can be revived by practice.

There are various methods of improving one's power of observation according to the type of memory which one may possess.

E.g. Some people have a photographic memory; other people can remember better by sound and others by numbers. The following method is recommended as being suited to all types of memories.

4. OUR METHOD.

a) Things.

i) Take the things that please you - your eyes, touch, smell and hearing. Try and express in words why

31

they please you. Such an effort will cause you to
observe the object more closely.

  ii) Take the things that you dislike and repeat the
process.

  iii) Take the things that are neutral to you and repeat
the process asking yourself why you have no
particular feeling towards them.

b) <u>Human Beings</u>.

  i) Apply the same three processes to the general
appearance and voice of the person observed.

  ii) Study the person's actions, asking yourself the
reason for such actions.

  iii) You will have observed by now a lot about a person.
Try and judge his character.

5. <u>CONCLUSION</u>.

This method requires a conscious effort to begin with and
systematic practice. It is, however, interesting and has the
following results:

  i) You will obtain a greater knowledge of the people
in your area.

  ii) You will have obtained a greater knowledge of
objects round about you.

  iii) You will be able to notice the presence of
strangers, the absence of people you know, and
anything unusual which might previously have
escaped you.

OBJECTS AND METHODS OF COUNTER-ESPIONAGE

1. INTRODUCTION.

A Counter-Espionage Organization is a Service or Governmental Agency designed to protect a particular country or area from all forms of subversive activity or irregular warfare that "the enemy either intends to carry out or is carrying out in that area".

Counter-espionage is a combination of the activities of various Governmental Agencies and is usually concentrated into one controlling service, e.g. police, immigration, customs, treasury, government security service, radio security, military security -the various departments being combined as under M.I.5, Deuxième Bureau, Abwehr, F.B.I.

2. OBJECTS OF A COUNTER-ESPIONAGE ORGANIZATION.

   a) To prevent agents of the enemy, engaged in any subversive activity, from entering a country.

   b) In the event of not achieving this, at least to ensure that the agents are rendered conspicuous and thereby detected.

   c) In the event of failing to achieve the first two objectives, so to control the country and its population that the activities of the agents are neutralized and therefore harmless.

   All counter-espionage activity is constantly subject to the political and economic influences present in the area concerned. Thus, there will always be a conflict as between the desire to achieve maximum security through efficient C.E. activity, and the need for the economic and politic life of the country to continue in as efficient and satisfactory a manner as possible. Recognition of this conflict is essential in order to evaluate the strength or weakness of counter-espionage in any country under review.

3. COUNTER-ESPIONAGE METHODS.

   In order to achieve the three above mentioned objectives, counter-espionage practice combines these main activities:

33

a) Control regulations. Systems of control exercised over the whole population to make an agent's work more difficult and to render him conspicuous.

b) Detective measures. To detect those persons who have contravened regulations and made themselves conspicuous, and to follow up any activities which are not entirely consistent with normal life.

c) Penetration. Counter-espionage will constantly endeavour to penetrate the enemy underground organization and activities. It can therefore be regarded as a bridge between a) and b).

4. <u>DETAILED COUNTER-ESPIONAGE PRACTICE</u>.

   a) Control Regulations Preventive.

      i) Identity.

      ii) Movement.

     iii) Communications.

     iv) Publications.

      v) Finance.

     vi) Action.

   b) Detective Measures.

      i) Security lists.

     ii) Snap controls.

    iii) Informant Service.

    iv) Agents provocateurs.

     v) Censorship and d/f.

    vi) Surveillance.

   vii) Searches.

  viii) Interrogations.

   c) Penetration.

     Likely to take one or more of the following forms:

      i) Getting members of counter-espionage organization recruited into the enemy underground organization. Cf. Police method dealing with the Communist Party.

     ii) Member of C.E. to work in the enemy country or in neutral country to endeavour to locate and contact personnel of the enemy organization by the use of bad security, mislaid documents, jealousies, overhearing conversations on the part of the enemy.

iii) Use of double agents. The capture and subsequent turn round of a member of the enemy underground. Using the means of communication either to plant misinformation on the enemy, or alternatively, to obtain through this channel any information concerning the enemy's requirements or probable future plans.

iv) Use of agents provocateurs to provoke persons into making indiscreet or revealing statements. Cf. German methods in occupied Europe; and ref. 4.b).

5. LOOPHOLES IN COUNTER-ESPIONAGE PRACTICE.

a) Political and economic conditions previously referred to. Cf. Foreign workers in Germany; neutral seamen in the U.K., World War I and World War II.

b) The human element. All C.E. practice is subject to the human element and therefore to the weaknesses accruing. E.g. bribery, slackness, low intelligence.

c) Shortage of personnel. Cf. Deterioration of German C.E. personnel in Occupied Europe.

Thus, on the one hand the enemy agent will endeavour to locate loopholes in a counter-espionage system since that is the only way that he can succeed in evading the attentions of the C.E., and on the other hand C.E. will always seek to cover such loopholes and to prevent, as far as possible, the enemy agent from knowing exactly the methods being employed. Cf. Criminals know the existence of detectives but a good detective does not reveal his methods.

POLICE METHODS & COUNTER MEASURES

DESCRIPTIONS

1. GENERAL.

   You may be called upon to -

   a) Describe a person so that a third party can recognize him from your description.

   b) Yourself recognize a person so described.

   c) Extract (innocently or not) such a description from a third party.

2. POLICE METHODS.

   We have no time for a Bertillon system - photographs, finger prints, limb measurements. We want a system that is reliable and quick.

3. CONVENTION.

   Quick recognition of a person in a crowd depends upon quick elimination of unrequired persons.

   A person's features should, therefore, be described in the following order and under the following headings:

   a) Features ALWAYS Described.

      - Sex
      - Apparent age
      - Height (measure by your own)
      - Build (slight, large, stocky or medium)

   b) Features only Described if DISTINCTIVE.

      i) Permanent, e.g. shape of eyes, Adam's apple, nose.

      ii) Impermanent, e.g. moustache, spectacles, hair, clothes and effects.

      A few (2 - 4) of these features is all that is necessary.

4. DETAILS.

   The following is a fairly comprehensive list of features, both permanent and impermanent, and if distinctive should be observed and described methodically.

Abnormalities such as hunchback or crosseyes will of course always be described.

No account is being taken, in this lecture, of a deliberate disguise.

a) Head.

Small, large, round, long, high crown, flat at the back, bulging at the back.

b) Face.

Round, chubby, broad, long or cadaverous, narrow, thin, oval.

c) Complexion.

Fair, dark, black, brown, yellow, sallow, sunburnt, red, purple, freckled, fresh. (Under this might also be included race.)

d) Forehead.

Receding, bulgy or prominent, broad, high or low.

e) Eyebrows.

Arched, straight or oblique, thick or bushy, meeting, lack of, thin, plucked, sandy, red, black, grey, white. Colour to be mentioned only if different from colour of hair of head.

f) Eyes.

Only rarely describe their colour, but give size, shape or position, i.e. large, piggy, almond, sunken or protruberant.

g) Ears.

There are four points about ears.

   i) Size - whether large or small.

  ii) Fold - pronounced or lack of.

 iii) Lobe - attached, unattached or lack of.

  iv) Sticking out of head or pressed close into the head.

h) Nose.

Straight, convex or concave, base elevated or depressed. Nose long in proportion to the face should be mentioned. Very wide nostrils might be mentioned.

i) Cheeks.

Prominent cheek bones, fat or flabby, jowl, hollow, dimpled.

j) <u>Mouth</u>.

Large or small.

k) <u>Teeth</u>.

Prominent, false, missing, discoloured, white, gold.

l) <u>Lips</u>.

Length of upper lip, thickness, overhanging upper lip, pendent or protruding lower lip.

m) <u>Chin</u>.

Receding, protruding, small or pointed, large or square, double, dimpled.

n) <u>Neck</u>.

Long or short, thin or thick, Adam's apple.

o) <u>Shoulders</u>.

Broad, sloping.

p) <u>Arms</u>.

Long or short in relation to body.

q) <u>Hands</u>.

Artistic or workers.

r) <u>Legs</u>.

Long or short, bowed or knock kneed, no ankles (women)

s) <u>Gait</u>.

Slow or quick strides, long or short, pigeon toed or splayed feet, limp.

t) <u>Bearing.</u>

Stooping or straight.

u) <u>Voice</u>.

Soft or loud, accent.

v) <u>Mannerisms</u>.

Any peculiarity of manner or habit should be described.

5. <u>ADDITIONAL POINTS</u>.

   i) Always describe the <u>circumstances</u> under which the subject was last seen, e.g. in profile or full face, at table or standing up, wearing hat, drunk.

ii) Always give <u>date</u> when subject was last seen to allow for possible alteration in appearance due to lapse of time.

iii) Never use <u>similes</u>, e.g. face like a ferret, unless conversant with workings of recipient's mind.

SURVEILLANCE

A. Following

Successful surveillance requires:

1. SUITABLE TYPE OF FOLLOWER.

   - Inconspicuous. (Always under medium height.)
   - Tenacious.
   - Intelligent and resourceful.
   - Observant.
   - Experienced in the work.
   - Possessing first-class knowledge of district.

2. INFORMATION ON SUSPECT.

   - Character and habits. (E.g. smoker, drinker, lazy, sociable.)
   - Business and private addresses.
   - Normal movements in business and leisure.
   - When and where surveillance is likely to take place.
   - What is required to be found out about suspect.

3. PLANNING.

   a) Cover.

   Following is rarely done by single person, more frequently by combination of several with various types of cover, E.g.:

   - Taxicab driver with vehicle. (Largely "blown".)
   - Tradesman's van with driver.
   - Tradesman or messenger with bicycle.
   - Shoppers, house or apartment-hunters.
   - Man with girl.
   - Woman with baby carriage.

   b) Method.

   Must be carefully worked-out in advance. E.g.

   - Whether by one or more persons.
   - Division of labour in emergency.

- Sign to denote whether or not you have lost the
suspect.

4. **EQUIPMENT**.

In general follower requires this personal equipment:

- Dark, inconspicuous clothes which appearance fits
relevant locality.
- Waterproof raincoat.
- Quiet shoes.
- Money with plenty of small change.
- Watch.
- Pencil and notebook.
- Food.
- Cigarettes and/or pipe. (Stopgap for awkward waits and
cover for looking around.)
- Reading material. (To be read _only_ in suitable
environment.)

Hints on equipment:

a) Always go to the toilet before starting surveillance.

b) It is possible discreetly to alter your appearance
during surveillance. E.g. start with hat or raincoat
on and later take it off; start with dummy package and
later leave it at check-room.

5. **EXPERT MANOEUVRE**.

a) _In the street_:

- Vary distance between yourself and suspect according
to density of crowd.
- Use as much physical cover as possible. (E.g. keep
street-lamps or other people between you and suspect;
walk with other people, especially when crossing
street.)
- Never stop or start, break into run or slow down at
same time as suspect.
- If alone, better to follow on opposite side
of street to suspect; as this is not only
less conspicuous but gives better field of
vision. (E.g. through shop windows and around
corners.)

41

b) <u>In public vehicles</u>:

- Sit on same side as suspect, rather than opposite.
- Where no flat-rate fare exists, sit in front of suspect and let him ask for fare first.

c) <u>In cafes, restaurants. etc.</u>:

- Choose seat where suspect has his back to you.
- Order short meals and short drinks.
- Anticipate his departure by paying check straightaway.

d) <u>At all times and places</u>:

- Never catch suspect's eye. Use reflections in windows and mirrors; look at him when either you or he are drinking.

B. <u>BEING FOLLOWED</u>.

1. <u>ASSUMPTION OF SURVEILLANCE</u>.
Whenever you are going anywhere with subversive intent assume that you are being followed. E.g. here is how a successful criminal, whom we interviewed, stated he would move with criminal intent from Point A to Point B:

a) Take a taxicab - but not the first or second that presents itself. (Note numbers and descriptions of first and second cab and of their drivers, in case they pass you again. If they do, you are probably being followed.)

b) Give your cab-driver wrong address first for benefit of any "innocent" bystanders. Change your mind when inside.

c) Take cab to innocent place in direction of but not at Point B. E.g. stores, church or park.

d) Leave cab and take following precautions to throw-off any possible surveillance:

- Spend some time in large stores, using elevators.
- Get into crowds.
- Walk up side street and take sudden turn.

e) Again take taxicab, repeating precautions above. (<u>Note</u>: Do not look directly out of the rear window. Use reflections, or don't look.)

f) Again go to innocent place near to, but not at, Point B.

g) Complete journey on foot.

2. <u>CHECK FOB SURVEILLANCE</u>.

If you are suspicious of definite surveillance, check by following methods:

a) Walk up comparatively empty street and see who follows.

b) Cross street and see who does likewise.

c) Enter cafe, restaurant, bar, and see who follows.

d) Enter small store and see who hangs about outside, especially if he attempts to conceal himself.

e) Leave innocent article (e.g. newspaper, stick) in small store, walk away, turn round suddenly and go back for it.

3. <u>COUNTER-MEASURES TO SURVEILLANCE</u>.

If you know that you are definitely being followed, two alternative courses are open to you:

a) <u>Shake follower off by</u>:

 - Suddenly running to catch public vehicle. (Fail or succeed)

 - Boarding public vehicles naturally but with good timing.

 - Using elevators in big stores with many exits.

 - Making for open place and move quickly to crowded one.

b) <u>Lure follower on by</u>:

 - Abandoning all subversive activity and acting innocently. E.g. carry on innocent conversations with innocent persons; write, mail and/or deliver innocent letters to innocent persons; leave harmless articles in innocent places; go to the movies, etc.

4. <u>GENERAL WARNINGS</u>

In the performance of all security precautions listed under Sec. B., the following warnings must be scrupulously heeded:

a) Never give any sign (either by sudden, undue haste or looking round) to show follower that you suspect you are being followed.

b) Have good cover for all "shaking-off", "luring-on" and "check" manoeuvres. (E.g. look at watch before running;

utilize pretty girl, undone bootlace, cigarette-lighting and such odd street-noises as backfiring car, for looking round.)

c) If possible ensure that descriptions of all followers are circulated among your organization.

PERSONAL SEARCHES

1. <u>GENERAL</u>

You may sometimes have to carry secret or subversive material. Hence the use of searches by C.E. personnel as an important detective measure.

2. <u>TYPES OF SEARCHES</u>

(a) <u>Routine Searches</u>:

Usually a quick frisk for arms, currency, food, taxable or dutiable goods, often carried out at or just before arrival.

(i) At fixed places such as frontiers, demarcation lines.

(ii) At fixed times such as market days (occupied countries) or before visits to important personalities (all countries).

(iii) Irregular - anywhere and at anytime - as a snap control.

(b) <u>Special Searches</u>

Usually only undertaken in case of definite suspicion.

Here, in chronological order, is an outline of a perfect body search as it <u>should</u> be undertaken by a completely efficient police force.

If you are going to conduct a body search, this is the model to be aimed for. If you have to undergo a body search watch for lapses from this standard.

(i) Suspect may be taken unaware - either by sudden arrest or by the pretence that routine search only is about to take place.

(ii) Suspect may be kept under close observation, not allowed to see friends, leave nothing behind or throw anything away, not permitted to eat, drink, smoke or go to the toilet.

(iii) Suspect may be left ostensibly alone to see if he tries to destroy or dispose of anything.

(iv) Baggage may or may not be searched in suspect's presence.

45

(v) Hands up against wall with feet well apart is good method for one individual alone searching another.

(vi) Search carried out methodically by working from head to foot.

Body:

Assistance of doctor sometimes required for physical examination.

Clothes:

Unsearched clothes on one table - searched clothes on another.

(vii) Suspect kept under observation throughout by non-searcher to note reactions - e.g. anxiety or (often more dangerous) relief.

(viii) Suspect usually not interrogated until after search but police may try to trip him into indiscreet remarks in casual conversation.

(ix) Suspect once searched is not allowed to regain contact with unsearched persons; even though released he may be kept under surveillance for a considerable time.

3. COUNTER MEASURES

In general an agent must not attract attention - e.g. by wearing or carrying anything conspicuous or inappropriate. Best never to carry incriminating materials; but if it cannot be avoided, note the following:

(a) Advance Plans:

Most important for agent to decide before hand between two alternatives:

(i) That he will try to get rid of the article if searched.

(ii) That he will conceal it as thoroughly as possible and not try to move it.

(i) In the first case he must leave it readily accessible (e.g. in hand or pocket) for disposal (e.g. by dropping it or planting on an innocent person).

Note:

Use edible or soluble paper for messages.

In the case of a bulky article (e.g. radio set in suitcase), you may be able to abandon or disown it - in which case it is necessary to see that it cannot be traced to you in anyway.

(ii) If article is thoroughly concealed, it will probably not be found in a routine search, but remember:

- Use silk paper or cloth for messages to avoid rustling.

- Use dummy padding to give clothing similar appearance in similar places.

- Police should know the method of search in which one feels both sides of a coat, both lapels, etc. simultaneously.

- If message is sewn into clothing, appropriate type of thread must be used and stitches must be similar to those already there.

All possible hiding places have already been used. But:

Try to choose one that is as difficult to get at as possible - e.g. by mixing article with anything of which you have a quantity, such as tobacco shreds, potatoes.

(b) Counter Measures During Search

(i) Find out if possible the object of the search and act accordingly.

(ii) Your attitude must be consistent with your cover (e.g. indignation, resignation, indifference, nervousness.)

(iii) Your reactions will be watched. Therefore never show anxiety at critical moments or relief when they are passed.

(iv) It may be possible to confuse the methods of the searcher (e.g. by putting unsearched article amongst those that have already been searched).

(v) It may be possible to put police on wrong scent, either simply by showing anxiety when they are examining some innocent article or (better still) by letting them find some minor incriminating article (e.g. currency or liquor) and ignoring real article.

HOUSE SEARCHES

1. GENERAL.

    A search, if properly carried out, will meet with success
    in finding the article being searched for, or will at least
    obtain the knowledge that the article is not there. If the
    search is carried out in a "slipshod" manner there is always
    a doubt as to whether it may not still be there.

    There are two distinct types of House Searches:

    a) The search of a building whilst occupied.
    b) The search of a building in secret, unknown to the
       occupants.

2. SEARCH OF A BUILDING WHILST OCCUPIED.

    a) Preparations.

        i) Information required.

            - Premises: As complete a plan as possible of the
              house, surroundings and such items as telephone,
              sewers, electricity, gas, etc. should be obtained.
              It may be necessary to do this by personal
              reconnaissance, seen or unseen according to the
              circumstances.

            - Occupants: All possible information concerning the
              occupants including dogs, cats, geese or other
              domestic animals should be obtained.

        ii) How Obtained.

            - Official information.

            - Informant service.

            - Personal reconnaissance.

        iii) Personnel.

            The searching party should be very carefully chosen,
            possibly for their knowledge of the house or district
            and especially for their powers of observation and
            inquisitive natures.

iv) <u>Plan</u>.

> Know what you are looking for. Decide on the size of the search party and make sure that each man knows what he is looking for and exactly what he has to do. The exact time of the raid is probably best kept secret from the members of the raiding party until the last possible moment.

b) <u>Entry</u>.

It is necessary to consider methods of entry for either one individual or a party, and to adjust them to requirements along the following lines:

i) The approach should be unobserved and unexpected.

ii) If more than one entrance is used they should all be entered at the same time.

iii) All entrances should be covered.

iv) Measures should be taken against alarm being raised.

v) Speed in taking up positions is essential.

vi) The search both of persons and premises should be begun as quickly as possible.

c) <u>Actual Search</u>.

i) Occupants should first be searched and placed under guard in a room that has been searched.

ii) Each room must be searched methodically. E.g. Ceilings, walls and the floor, and the latter in a clockwise direction or perhaps in sections.

iii) In searching a room note the following points:

- Measure inside walls and see that they agree with outside measurements.

- Sound all inside and outside walls.

- Measure articles of furniture and see that the inside and outside measurements agree.

- Test all woodwork to be sure it is solid.

- Remove all drawers completely.

- Remove rugs, carpets, linoleum, etc. and examine the floorboards carefully.

- In basements, sound all rafters and beams for hollow places.
- The simplest and the most inaccessible places are generally used for hiding places, depending on the nature of the article to be hidden.

3. <u>SEARCH OF A BUILDING IN SECRET UNKNOWN TO THE OCCUPANTS</u>.

a) The above observations in general apply to this type of search. It is more difficult to carry out as every article that is searched must be put back in its proper place and in the same condition as it was originally. It may have been placed deliberately in a certain way in order to inform the occupant whether or not it has been disturbed.

b) Members of the searching party should be chosen particularly for their powers of observation.

c) The person directing the search must exercise strict control and also make sure that one room is not searched twice and another forgotten.

4. <u>CONCLUSION</u>.

The success of all searches will depend on careful preparations, careful plans, surprise and methodical searching.

BURGLARY

1. DEFINITION.

The secret entry by an agent into premises for the purpose of:

a) Examining, photographing, stealing documents or articles profitable to your organization.

b) Reconnoitering interior of a building for any subversive purpose - E.g. assassination.

2. GENERAL WARNINGS.

a) If possible, above objectives should be attained without incurring enemy's knowledge or suspicion.

b) Burglary with subversive intent is best not carried out by leader himself but by subordinates - preferably local people who, if caught, can use cover of "normal" burglary. (Where necessary, objects of value may be removed to substantiate this cover.)

c) If a genuine burglar is hired or recruited for the job, greatest care must be taken that he will not give away organization to enemy.

3. METHOD.

The following information has been obtained from police and very reliable criminal sources:

a) INFORMATION NEEDED.

　　i) Number of occupants.

　　ii) Habits of occupants.

　　　　- Meal-times (Especially evening).

　　　　- Normal times of departure and return.

　　iii) Silent and covert lines of approach and retreat.

　　　　- Use lawns and grass-borders.

　　　　- Avoid gravel, flower-beds, dust, dirt and mud.

　　iv) If dog present, discover situation of kennel.

　　　　- Naturally noisy dog not so dangerous as normally silent one.

　　　　- Use of aniseed for decoy, or poisoned-meat for killing.

v) Situation and state of windows, doors (impression of key) and ladders.

b) <u>HOW OBTAINED</u>.

i) Best obtained from "insider" - E.g. maid, gardener, janitor, clerk. But risk of subsequent interrogation by police.

ii) "Outsider" can be useful - E.g. tradesman, plumber, carpenter.

iii) If no informants available, watching by a stranger should not exceed 48 hours.

iv) To establish whether occupants are out or away:

- Call from pay-station telephone. If someone answers, enquiry must be made for person of different name from occupants, followed by apology for wrong number.

(NOTE: This trick is well-known and should be used with care.)

- If house has no telephone, approach front door and ring door bell. (Knocking on door of empty house is dangerous as it attracts attention.) If door is answered, ask for fictitious name and back up story with fake letter.

c) <u>EQUIPMENT</u>.

Reconnaissance as outlined under 3. a). and b). will show which of following items are necessary:

i) Chamois leather gloves.

ii) Dimmed flashlights.

iii) Key or skeleton-keys and shaped thick wire for turning keys left in locks - all carried in black cloth to avoid jingle so that they may covertly be thrown away without noise in emergency.

iv) Newspaper for obtaining key from reverse side of door.

v) Glass-cutter and gummed cloth or paper for breaking windows.

vi) Pair of old, large socks for silent climbing of ladders.

    vii) Length of light-proof material.

    viii) Jemmy or garden shears (Only to be taken when other method of entry impossible).

NOTE: Only take what is necessary from above items.

d) <u>ENTRY</u>.

    i) <u>Personnel</u>.

       - Maximum number for operation is three. Two said to be best.

    ii) <u>Doors</u>.

       - Best method is by key, either made from impression (demonstrate) or stolen.

       - Skeleton keys. (Demonstrate)

       - Key left in lock, turned by wire or pushed out and pulled under on newspaper. (Demonstrate)

    iii) <u>Windows</u>.

       - Find one left open.

       - Cut and break (Break first time. One crash merely wakes occupants; two crashes gets them out of bed.)

       - Jemmy or garden shears.

e) <u>PROCEDURE AFTER ENTRY</u>.

Dispose your available personnel as follows:

    i) One man standing well back from window, watching probable line of approach by police, occupants or other interrupters. (To identify returning occupant, see if he searches for his keys.)

    ii) One man to make certain of alternative exits in case of alarm. Having made sure of these, he watches opposite side of house to "window-man", or, if burglary takes place at meal-time, he watches for possible interruption by occupants.

    iii) Leader searches for what is required.

Communication among members of the party should be by agreed sounds and there should be NO talking and no smoking during the operation. No cigarette ends should ever be left anywhere in the neighbourhood of a burglary as chemical analysis of saliva helps very much to identify persons.

f) <u>METHOD OF SEARCH</u>

i) Before search starts, arrange delaying action to prevent surprise:

- If light is on in the room, leave it on but lock the door or place table against it.

- If light is not on, remove bulb and do not block the door. If a light must be put out, the silent method is to take out the bulb instead of turning the switch, which will make a click.

ii) In general, do not alter any existing dispositions. If something must be taken away, consider possibility of leaving a similar-looking object.

iii) Search systematically, starting with some definite object in the room and working in one direction round the room, one man only doing the search; another may assist, E.g. by holding the torch and tools, but should not interfere, so as to avoid any confusion.

g) <u>GET-AWAY</u>

i) <u>If no alarm</u>.

- The party should leave one at a time and not join up again.

- A gang of burglars would have to meet to share proceeds. It is interesting to note that their practice in arranging personal meetings and danger signals agrees with teaching in lecture A.18.

ii) <u>If disturbed and alarm given</u>.

- If running away, pretend there is some joke by bursting out laughing and shouting to some imaginary friend.

- If one member of the party is left in house and is hiding while owners have returned, others who have got away may break a fire alarm and give the address of the house opposite or one near, so as to cause a diversion. (This method of diversion is often used by burglars to cover entry in the first place.) 50% of the fire alarms in London are said to be due to burglaries.

- Man left in house may nip into toilet and lock door.

- If a dog is set on to you do not run. Imitate the owner and repeat what he says to encourage the dog to search for the third party.

- If you encounter someone unexpectedly always have story ready and speak to them before they address you.

h) <u>PRECAUTIONS AGAINST BEING FOLLOWED</u>.

(See A.8.)

i) <u>BORROWING CARS</u>.

If it ever happens that borrowing a car is possible:

- Numbers should be changed by means of shaped pieces of white and black gummed paper. (N.B. red and white in Belgium). Letters of the registration should not be changed, nor should the number of figures be reduced or increased. After the job the car may be left stranded somewhere.

- When waiting by a car for an accomplice, pretend to be pumping up the tyre rather than doing anything to the engine. It is suspicious if you have to leave in a hurry immediately after feigning engine trouble.

INTERROGATION

1. <u>GENERAL</u>

Interrogations can be divided into three classes:

a) Carried out by <u>Local Police</u>. Generally on account of infringement of minor regulations. Usually confined to four simple questions.

- Who are you?
- Where do you come from?
- What papers have you?
- What are you doing?

<u>NOTE</u>: Immediately after arrival, you should be prepared to answer plausibly these questions:

- Who are you?
- Where do you come from?
- How did you come?
- Where are you going?
- Who is and where is the last person you spoke to who knows you personally?
- Give details of this locality.

If able to satisfy the police on all above points, suspect is generally released. In the event of any discrepancy he will be subjected to further interrogation.

b) Carried out by <u>Specialist Police</u>. To find out whether a person is definitely suspect, e.g. through having failed to satisfy the local police in the preliminary interrogation. Suspect will have to satisfy the police that his "story" and papers are genuine. His replies will probably be checked. Attempts may be made to catch him out by producing facts which he thinks the Gestapo does not know.

c) Carried out by <u>Gestapo</u>, or equivalent authority, after arrest. For a person seriously suspected, e.g. because he has failed to satisfy local police and Gestapo in previous interrogations. This interrogation may last from 24 hours to many months. Methods are manifold but aim is single — to extract a confession. No rules; nothing barred; "all in".

2. INTERROGATION METHODS.

   a) Before Interrogation.

      i) Exhaustive enquiries about suspect's life and activities in order to collect as much evidence as possible before interrogation.

     ii) Two types of arrest:

        - Sudden and violent arrest at midnight or in small hours when vitality is at its lowest.

        - Sudden but polite arrest on pretext of unimportant inquiry, followed by indefinite detention to prevent warning of associates.

    iii) Complete personal and house search (See A.9 and A.10.)

     iv) Treatment in prison, all part of interrogation plan, e.g. bad food and good food alternately; comfort and discomfort; comparative liberty and solitary confinement; promising visits from friends, etc. Object is to break down morale before actual questioning.

   b) During Interrogation.

      i) Discomfiture of Prisoner.

        - Prisoner facing strong light; unable to see examiner properly.

        - Prisoner with back to examiner, arms above head.

        - Prisoner seated on uncomfortable chair. Not allowed to eat, drink or smoke while examiners indulge all three.

        - Single interrogation may continue indefinitely so that prisoner becomes exhausted.

        - Examination may be carried out by two or more persons acting simultaneously or, more usually, in sequence, e.g.:

        First Interrogator usually the "bully" type who tries to make prisoner either angry or frightened; impresses on him the terrible power of the Gestapo ("Wir wissen alles!"); threatens, throws things about.

        Second Interrogator puts clear, concise, sharp questions. If results are unsatisfactory, prisoner may be "beaten up."

<u>Third Interrogator</u>: friendly, offering food, drink,
cigarettes and apologising for rough treatment; will
try to lull prisoner into indiscretion. Probably
most dangerous type.

ii) Tricks of Questioning.

- Long silence in which interrogator appears to forget
  prisoner; this is intended to produce unsolicited
  remarks.

- Long silence in which prisoner is discouraged from
  talking. "Don't answer yet. Just think. Just try
  to remember what happened – and then tell us the
  truth."

- Continually referring back to the same question with
  a different method of approach.

- Reconstruction of offence exaggerating prisoner's
  share in it.

- Reconstruction of events by interrogator who gives
  half the circumstances in great detail. Later the
  prisoner is ordered to repeat what he has been told.
  If he was, in fact, present when the events took
  place he may easily include details which were not
  given by the interrogator.

- Suggestion that prisoner has been let down by his
  friends or is shielding someone else.

- Showing prisoner a "confession" signed by a colleague.

- Firing squad used as bluff.

- Threats to family.

- Use of other to soften prisoner's will-power.

- Giving prisoner papers to sign after exhausting day
  of interrogation

3. <u>COUNTER-MEASURES</u>

a) <u>Before Interrogation</u>.

- If in same prison cell as other members of organization,
  say nothing; danger of microphone.

- If allowed to mix with other detained persons, say
  nothing; danger of "stool-pigeons".

- Beware of "friendly nurses" sent to see if you need anything.

- Beware of mirrors in your cell. Observers stationed behind cell-wall can observe your actions through "two-way" mirror.

- Be careful of your actions when released, either before or after interrogation; release may only be temporary in order to watch your movements.

- Always try to appear clean, neat and, if possible, well dressed.

b) <u>During Interrogation</u>.

- Speak slowly, clearly and firmly. Do not answer simple questions immediately and hesitate with the more difficult ones.

- Do not be clever or abusive. Create impression of being averagely stupid, honest citizen, trying his best to answer questions intelligently. Interrogators are not impressed by tears or heroics.

- Avoid replies that lead to further questions. All your answers should end in a cul-de-sac.

- Deny everything you cannot explain. Do not attempt to get round difficulties by altering or embellishing your stories.

- Arrange for code sign in text or signature on any statement extracted by force.

- Do not express personal affection or interest in anybody.

- Beware of apparently foolish interrogator of whom you think you have got the better. This may be a trap to tempt you to boast of your cleverness in circumstances where your boastings will be reported.

- Do not be bluffed by the interrogator who pretends to a knowledge of your British connections. It is likely that over a period of time the Germans may have learned some facts about this Organization, e.g. location of H.Q., Schools, etc., or names of personnel. By referring to these they may hope to persuade you that they know much more. Insist upon your complete ignorance of all facts referred to.

- If subjected to ether, start counting to yourself. When questioned you will answer only with the numbers that are passing through your mind.

4. <u>CONCLUSION</u>.

If you <u>are</u> arrested by the Gestapo, do not assume that all is lost; the Gestapo's reputation has been built up on ruthlessness and terrorism, <u>not</u> intelligence. They will always pretend to know more than they do and may even make a good guess, but remember that it <u>is</u> a guess; otherwise they would not be interrogating you.

AGENT MANAGEMENT

MOTIVES

1. INTRODUCTION.

   The success of the organization is going to depend on the quality and work of the individual members, therefore it is impossible to over-estimate the importance of picking the right people. No good rushing the job, every single potential helper must be carefully studied and the question of security considered before any approach is made.

2. WHAT TYPES OF HELPERS WILL BE REQUIRED?

   a) Regular agents and sub-agents of all kinds (see lecture on Organization).

   b) Individuals from whom some special service may be required (e.g. overlook some infringement, or persuading someone to do so, obtaining papers, providing refuge, abstaining from denunciation, etc.)

   c) Information contacts.

3. HOW TO MAKE PEOPLE WORK FOR YOU.

   a) Sum up your quarry and judge what motive is most likely to appeal to him.

   b) Dress up your story to fit in with the motive you have selected.

   c) Make the suggestions come from him if possible.

4. LIKELY MOTIVES AND HOW TO APPEAL TO THEM.

   People usually act from a complex of motives, but there is generally one that is uppermost.

   a) Patriotism.

   There are plenty of genuine patriots willing to take risks for anyone working against the enemy. The danger here is that in order to persuade such a person to do the service for you it may be necessary to disclose information about your organization and activities. Therefore, while patriotism is possibly the best motive to work on when recruiting agents it is dangerous when requiring isolated services.

b) <u>Religious or Political Motives</u>.

Also more suitable for recruiting agents than for obtaining isolated services. Possibility of influencing the activities of religious or political groups or individuals - but danger of disagreements over policy.

c) <u>Need</u>.

The ruling motive with many because of privation suffered by themselves and by their families. In enemy occupied countries it is often extremely difficult to obtain an adequate livelihood. Therefore a regular wage (which is quite different from bribery, and is merely a reward for time or services given) may prove a great attraction, either as a whole time job or to supplement an insufficient income from another employment. This can be used to reinforce either a). or b).

Sometimes it is not money that is needed so much as certain articles or services. The agent must find out what is needed that he can offer, e.g.

<u>Products:</u> Food - tobacco - petrol - medicine - clothes - etc.

<u>Services</u>: Communications - employment - escapes - payment of fines - lodgings - etc.

The fulfillment of such a need may stimulate gratitude on the part of the recipient; or the whole transaction may be regarded as a regular exchange of services.

d) <u>Hatred of Germans</u>.

Many people have a purely personal hatred of the Germans, having suffered much at their hands. An agent can appeal to them by showing that the service required will spite or inconvenience the Germans, without disclosing the subversive nature of his activities.

e) <u>Love of Adventure</u>.

Especially among young people. Comparisons may be drawn between those fighting in the front line and those left at home.

The above are all good motives as a basis for recruiting conscious collaboration. Certain other motives can also be used as a lever for obtaining services or restraining dangerous elements.

   i) <u>Personal Sympathy</u>. Especially from women. An agent can represent himself as persecuted, hungry, victimised by the Germans, etc.

  ii) <u>Greed</u>. There are many people who are not in need but whose greed will respond to bribery whether by money or in kind.

   <u>N.B.</u>

   The agent must take note of the customs of the country, the recipient's profession and class and his personal character. If open bribery is unsuitable there are many methods of covert bribery (e.g. putting the man in a position to receive money in an incidental way, at cards, in business transactions, by presents to his wife, thus "preserving the decencies"). Obviously a man who is bribed is untrustworthy.

 iii) <u>Sex</u>. Procuration in one form or another may be useful in some cases. The services of someone outside the organization should be employed in order to avoid any dangerous consequences.

  iv) <u>Self-importance</u>. E.G. a local official who dislikes Nazi supervision. An agent may be able to flatter him by giving him a good reputation to live up to and may persuade him to take his own decisions irrespective of the Nazis; or the same result may be achieved by taunts.

   v) <u>Snobbery</u>. Titled people can sometimes be used to attract the attention and goodwill of snobs.

  vi) <u>Fear</u>. Although it is wisest to avoid blackmail as far as possible, it may be useful in an emergency, and for that reason any information about people's private lives and weaknesses should be remembered.

RECRUITING

1. INTRODUCTION

Having considered the general question of what types of
agents are required, and the kind of motives which are likely
to appeal to them, we now come to the question of actual
recruiting.

At first the organizer will want to recruit his principal
subordinates himself. Later on best for his chief sub-
agents to recruit their own subordinates. This process
may be carried still further down the scale, or, as
an alternative, special agents may be appointed as
recruiters.

Since recruiting is the most dangerous part of subversive
activity the utmost care must be exercised, and the following
three principles adopted:

a) Go Slow.

Quality must come before quantity (although certain types
of subversive activity need large scale organization to
be effective). The necessity for maintaining the utmost
security by only recruiting reliable men is particularly
important during the early stages, when the organizer is
selecting men to be his principal assistants and creating
the nucleus of his organization.

b) Retain the initiative.

Persons who offer their services to the organizer should
always be looked upon with suspicion, as this is a
favourite method adopted by agents provocateurs.

c) Man should be recruited for the job - not vice versa.

The organizer may make a note of people who may be useful
to him later on but he should not recruit them until he has
work for them to do, as otherwise there will be a dangerous
period of hanging about. Incidentally, recruiting the man
for the job will, in most cases, eliminate difficulties of
finding cover.

AGENT MANAGEMENT

2. <u>QUALITIES OF THE GOOD RECRUITER</u>.

   a) He must inspire confidence, both nationally and personally.

      i) <u>Nationally</u>. The mission he is about to propose may involve considerable risks, and it is therefore essential that the person he approaches should regard him as completely above suspicion.

      ii) <u>Personally</u>. Even though the recruiter is regarded as above suspicion on national grounds, the person whom he approaches (who may be a family man) may still regard him as being too young and inexperienced, or may doubt his discretion.

   b) Whatever his walk of life, the recruiter should be a man of the world, capable of talking easily to comparative strangers, and, better still, of handling men. This involves taking an obvious interest in the contact and giving him a certain sense of importance, being a good listener, etc.

   c) It is often a good plan to do some small service, or to ask for one, as this creates a certain sense of obligation on either side.

3. <u>METHODS OF FINDING AGENTS</u>.

   This will depend entirely on the kind of area allotted to the organizer, to the tasks he wishes to be performed, and to the types of agents he has set himself to find. The following are some general hints:

   a) Table groups which are likely to provide a good field for recruits. Such might be: Ex-soldiers' organizations, trade unions, professions, societies (e.g. freemasons), religious communities, etc.

   b) Table likely individuals. Consider their character, integrity and intelligence, their known opinions. Those who have suffered themselves or whose families have been persecuted are potential recruits.

   <u>Caution</u>. Beware of those who air their grievances too loudly.

   c) Collect all the information you can about the potential recruit. All information is useful, particularly concerning his weak points (both of character and of position - e.g. if any members of his family are in the hands of the enemy); such information may avoid prejudicing security

65

and may also afford a useful hold on him later. It is also important to find out what motives are most likely to prompt him to action against the enemy. (See A.12)

In recruiting women, information about their personal attachments is most useful. These may prove dangerous; and on no account should a woman be recruited who is motivated solely by sentiment.

d) Do not touch anybody whom you know (or suspect) to work for another organization. If anything ever happens to that organization, the whole of your own may be involved in the disaster.

e) Beware of the professional agent who is prepared to work for several organizations. Some agents in the last war sold their information to as many as five different intelligence services.

4. APPROACHING THE POTENTIAL RECRUIT.

Security is the main consideration and the recruiter should be as certain as possible of his man before approaching him.

a) Introduction.

If the recruiter can be introduced through a third party this will save time and may make a quicker judgment of his suitability possible - provided that the third party is himself a reliable judge.

If the recruiter has to introduce himself he should try to do so in such a way that the other man feels that he himself has made the first move. Use of the confidence trick.

b) Getting down to business.

Should always be done in such a way that the recruiter does not commit himself and is able to withdraw if the results are likely to be unsatisfactory.

If possible concrete suggestions should always come from the recruit. The conversation may be directed in such a way as to make this possible.

The recruiter should watch his reactions to any remarks about opposition to the Germans and subversive activities in general.

The recruiter may ask questions or make hypothetical remarks which do not commit him but may elicit a definite statement from the recruit, e.g. "I wonder how they organize these sabotage attacks... It must be very dangerous to carry out subversive activity ... The trouble is reprisals - family ties, etc."

The recruiter should never over-persuade the man. On the contrary he should show him all the difficulties and dangers of the job.

He should create the impression that he belongs to a big and efficient organization.

He should disclose no real information about the organization. It may be best to pose as an intermediary whose knowledge is limited. He should not reveal his own identity or address.

5. INITIATION.

In some cases some kind of initiation ceremony may have a useful effect on the recruit's attitude and conduct (e.g. oath of secrecy): the opportunity may be taken to impress on him his responsibilities. The recruiter must be careful, however, not to employ this kind of thing on people who would be unfavourably impressed by it.

6. TESTING THE RECRUIT.

He should be given something harmless to do (e.g. conveying an innocent message). This will not only test his reliability but will tend to make him feel that he is committed to the organization.

When the man is finally recruited it may be best for the recruiter to fade out and an intermediary to be introduced with whom the recruit will in future deal.

HANDLING

1. <u>PAYMENT.</u>

Payment should be put on a business footing from the start. Although patriotism is the best motive to seek when recruiting agents, it is usually best to pay agents as well (they may need it; and it affords an additional means of controlling them).

a) The Organizer should institute regular salary scales. An Agent should not be paid too highly at first as it is bad to reduce the amount at a later stage, but useful to be able to increase the amount. Payment of a regular salary is a more satisfactory method than making irregular payments for services rendered. The latter method encourages the making of claims which have to be carefully investigated and may lead to disputes. The payment of bonuses for especially good work is, however, permissible.

b) The organizer should look after his agents in the same way that a good employer looks after his employees. If possible, assurances should be given to the agent, when he is recruited, of assistance to him or his dependants, in case of illness, danger (possibility of organizing escapes), or arrest.

c) A clear distinction should be drawn between salary and expenses. It may be necessary to demand evidence of expenditures but the need for security must be borne in mind. If an agent is unwilling to accept a regular salary it may be possible to see that he does not lose, by paying him generous expenses.

d) Payment should always be made punctually and if possible in advance. If the organizer is unable to make a promised payment he should tell the agent about it quite frankly, and, if possible, state when he expects to be able to pay.

e) The best way of actually making payment is in cash at a personal meeting (See Communications). This opportunity may be taken to warn the agent of the dangers of spending too freely. No receipts to be given.

f) No financial disputes should be allowed. If any agent claims more than seems reasonable, the organizer should talk the matter over with him and pay him what he asks on the first occasion but should make it quite clear that he will not do so again.

g) It is sometimes more useful to make payments in kind rather than in money.

h) Do not let one man know what another is being paid.

2. Training.

Any newly recruited agent should receive a certain amount of training, either from the recruiter or through a cut-out. There are two main aspects:

a) Security.

If the agent is recruited for a particular job he should not have to find a new cover story; but he must be instructed in the importance of maintaining his cover at all times and of having a good reason for everything he does.

He must be instructed in the other rules of individual security, particularly in inconspicuousness, discretion, knowledge of Enemy C.E. methods and planning for an emergency. He should be encouraged to train himself in taking the usual security precautions and to develop his powers of observation and memory. He should also be instructed in the security rules of the organization. (See Planning an Organization).

It may be useful to test a new recruit's security as early as possible and to check up on it from time to time.

b) His Job.

If the agent is recruited for a particular job he will need the training consistent with this job and he will need a certain amount of technical instruction, e.g. in sabotage methods. It may be necessary to rehearse with him the particular method that he is going to use.

3. PROMOTION.

On the whole the Organizer will want to select his chief subordinates when he is starting to create his organization, rather than promote them at a later stage. Questions of promotion will, however, arise from time to time and the following points should be remembered:

a) A man should seldom be put in authority over men among whom he has worked as an equal. It is better to transfer him to another department.

b) Seniority in cover occupations may have to be taken into consideration.

c) Even the organizer's chief subordinates should be checked from time to time from the point of view of security.

4. DISCIPLINE.

This will depend, above all, on the personality of the organizer. The following points should be noted:

a) The organizer should impress on each agent the power of the organization to protect those who are loyal to it and to punish those who betray it. This point should be introduced tactfully as a safeguard to the agent's own security.

b) He should also impress each agent with the efficiency of the organization. He can best do this by being efficient himself; by being punctual and discreet, by his ability to make decisions, and by his reliability in the matter of promises, etc. He should always prepare very carefully before interviewing an agent, especially early interviews.

c) Attitude to results. The organizer will show that he expects any job to be successfully achieved. He should show confidence without minimising dangers and difficulties. He should give credit to successful agents but never carry praise too far. In the case of unlucky failure, he should show sympathy and encouragement.

d) Attitude to inefficiency. It is important to discover the real cause of inefficiency by checking the agent's statements, having him watched etc. If the organizer is satisfied that a particular agent's inefficiency is due to over-work or nerves, he should talk to him frankly, give him a rest and continue to pay him. If it is due to stupidity, the organizer may either give him an easier job in future or tell him that he is suspected by the enemy and must lie low.

e) Attitude to double crossing. If after checking and testing a man it is clear that he is a traitor, the organizer can either frighten him or pay him off (both risky) or kill him. The same courses are open if a man pretends that he is being blackmailed by the enemy.

The best method, however, is to <u>prevent</u> double crossing taking place by stressing the ruthlessness and long arm of the organization at an early stage. Although the agent only knows a few people that he can betray, his superiors are well aware of his activities and can always take vengeance.

November 1943.

RECRUITING

1. <u>INTRODUCTION</u>.

   The strength of the organization depends on the individual, whether for undercover work in the field or at the base.

2. <u>SECURITY</u>.

   We are most vulnerable when we recruit owing to the danger of penetration. Therefore the utmost precaution must be taken.

   a) Retain the initiative - people must not be foisted on us. Consider what types are needed, then find them - avoid picking up people who come readily to hand.

   b) Use of Security Check <u>and</u> individual judgment.

3. <u>CONSIDERATION OF TYPES NEEDED</u>.

   a) <u>Undercover</u> agents to work into occupied or enemy territory singly or to make contact with existing nets.

   b) <u>Semi-Undercover</u>. Operational groups for short term operations, e.g. pre-invasion.

   c) <u>Para-Military</u>.

   d) <u>Propaganda</u>.

   e) <u>Radio Operators</u>.

   f) <u>Operators for Neutral Countries</u>.

   g) <u>Home base executives</u>.

   h) <u>Instructors - home or field</u>.

   Natural Cover will often determine selection. Many good men with NO cover.

4. <u>MOTIVES FOR RECRUITMENT</u>.

   People act from a complexity of Motives, therefore consider combination of the following:

   a) Patriotism.
   b) Political or Religion.
   c) Love of Adventure.
   d) Need - (in the field)

also

a) Self importance.
b) Greed.
c) Fear - Blackmail.
d) Revenge.

It is necessary to determine which motive will appeal most to the recruit, and subordinate subsidiary motives to the main one.

5. PROCESS OF RECRUITMENT.

a) Good rule for security - often has to be broken: Always try to find the man for the job, rather than find a job for a man. Disregard of this rule allows the enemy to penetrate by placing an attractive but vague proposition before you. Attention to the rule helps the morale problem in case of the man not being employed.

b) Quality first.

c) Go slow - hurry may risk other agents or whole organization.

d) Inspire Confidence.

i) Nationally - recruit must feel full backing of the country.

ii) Personally - recruit must feel he is dealing with high-grade men.

6. POINTS.

a) Face the recruit with the least attractive side of the work.

b) Do not persuade or buy - rather dissuade if in doubt.

c) Study his character - weaknesses especially important, e.g. wine, women or inability to lie.

d) Give him a face-saving let-out. Therefore it is not wise to tell him too much.

e) Try and get him to work as quickly as possible.

7. CONCLUSION.

A chain is as strong as its weakest link. Everything depends on the individual. We must have the best for the particular job to be done.

ORGANISATION

TYPES OF AGENTS

PART I

1. INTRODUCTION.

   In order that subversive activity may be effective it must be organized. The type of organization will depend on the nature of the activity, local conditions and the requirements of general policy (see Opening Address). This lecture deals with the question from the point of view of an agent who is sent to organize a new region.

2. SURVEY OF AREA.

   The organizer's first step must be to survey his area in relation to his projected activity. It is essential to carry this out before plunging into operations. He should consider the following:

   a) Geographical areas.

   b) Groups (economic, social, political, national, religious, subversive).

   c) Opinions – e.g. Anti-Axis feeling, rivalry among groups.

   d) Individuals – especially leading personalities.

   e) Enemy C.E. forces.

   This survey will enable him to decide where and how to organize subversive activities – e.g. propaganda is best organized by groups; a military organization must be formed on a geographical basis; the presence of low morale or strong enemy C.E. may preclude any activity in a certain district.

3. PLANNING THE SECTIONS.

   The next step is to decide what sections are needed to carry out the projected activities. They can be considered under two headings – Operational and Support Sections.

   a) Operational might include some of the following:

      i) Propaganda. For this section an organizer might wish to recruit writers, printers, copiers, distributors.

74

ii) <u>Passive Resistance and Minor Sabotage</u>. These two activities require much the same kind of organization -i.e. on a fairly large scale, which may involve the formation of cells inside particular targets (see later) with the aid of "insiders".

iii) <u>Major Sabotage</u>. This requires a totally different kind of organization - i.e. the formation of small sabotage squads, highly trained and well equipped, either local or mobile. "Insiders" may also be needed. Engineers are obviously very suitable.

iv) <u>Para-Military Section</u>. For the formation of special paramilitary units, or liaison with existing organizations, professional soldiers may be needed.

b) <u>Support</u> might include some of the following:

i) <u>Internal Communication</u>. Responsible for all communications within organization. This will include:

- <u>Couriers</u>. People who have cover for traveling within a specified area, e.g. commercial traveller, engine or lorry driver.

- <u>Boites-aux-lettres</u>. People in charge of places frequented by all classes, e.g. shops, kiosks, etc. which can be used for depositing letters.

- <u>Accommodation Addresses</u>. People who receive regularly through the post a large correspondence, e.g. business men of all types.

ii) <u>Security Section</u>. Responsible for watching and reporting on enemy counter-espionage, procuring papers, passes, etc., security of the organization and of individual members.

iii) <u>Reception Section</u>. Responsible for meeting and looking after personnel and supplies from abroad, e.g. farmers, peasants and estate owners. Cover for moving about at night, flashing torches, etc. must be arranged.

iv) <u>Storage and Distribution</u>. Responsible for storing goods and equipment belonging to the organization and for distributing them when required. Ironmongers, builders, warehousemen, carpenters, priests and farmers are examples of types used in this section according to the type of stores to be accommodated.

Only a few main storage places advisable, supplemented by a number of distribution centres; as far as possible these should remain unknown even to those who will use them.

v) <u>Transport</u>. For this purpose men connected with transport services, and firms using trucks, vans, etc. are necessary, or even farmers with carts. Accumulation of petrol in preparation for zero hour may be handled by this department.

vi) <u>Finance</u>. Particularly necessary in a large organization, e.g. cashiers, bookkeepers and accountants are useful in this connection. Responsible for the payment of agents and other disbursements.

vii) <u>Recruiting</u>. It may be necessary if and when the organization becomes large to recruit men capable of "spotting talent" and themselves doing the recruiting.

viii) <u>Medical</u>. Doctors and hospitals will become necessary especially in the case of para-military activities.

ix) <u>Emergency Measures</u>. A special section should be responsible for hide-outs, safe houses and escape facilities, and for accumulating first rate knowledge of prisons, routes, etc.

These sections may comprise a large number of agents or only one or two, the main thing is that each should be organized separately.

4. <u>FORMING A NUCLEUS</u>.

Having decided on what sections he will need, the organizer must now recruit a small number of "Staff Officers". These will form the nucleus of the organization. They will be in charge of one or more of the sections, and will be instrumental in enlarging the organization.

Provided their safety remains unimpaired, the organization will be able to survive misfortunes.

They must not be too many in number because the organizer must limit the number of people with whom he is in contact. Therefore, in a large organization where there are many sections, one staff officer may take charge of several activities and have several section leaders under him.

Most organizers will have a limited mission and will only need to set up a small organization; but the same principles apply, and the nucleus is always all-important.

5. PRINCIPLES OF LAY-OUT.

Before enumerating the principles to be followed in planning the lay-out of an organization in order to achieve the maximum security, it should be pointed out that there is always a conflict between security and efficiency.

Security is best achieved by the use of water-tight compartments, whereas efficiency depends upon close liaison. A balance must be struck between the two. As it is always possible to reduce security but very difficult to improve it once it is weak, it is best to aim at the maximum security from the outset.

a) Do not make the organization too large. Much work (especially passive resistance, minor sabotage and propaganda) can be done by people outside the organization at the instigation of its members.

b) The organizer should deal with only 4-6 subordinates, who will normally be his "staff officers".

c) Leaders of groups or sections will normally do their own recruiting, but should furnish full details (except names) to the organizer for approval.

d) Each section must have a clearly defined function and stick to it.

e) The organizer must determine the minimum number of contacts necessary between sections, and prohibit any others.

   N.B. Over-centralization is to be avoided, as well as too much lateral communication.

f) Individual agents should have the minimum number of contacts within the organization

g) Individual agents should have as little information about the organization as possible.

h) Men must be held in reserve to fill key positions in the event of an emergency.

i) There should be the maximum use of cut-outs (see below).

PART II

6. CUT-OUTS.

   a) Definition.

   A cut-out, or intermediary, forms the link between two
   agents or between an agent and the outside world. He may
   know very little about the organization and just carry
   messages, or he may be a liaison officer who is able to
   answer questions and make decisions; but the important
   thing is that he should not undertake any other subversive
   activity.

   b) Reasons for Employment.

      i) It is dangerous for two important agents (particularly
         from different sections of the organization) to be
         noticed together.

      ii) One agent may not want another, with whom he
         communicates, to know him.

      iii) An agent wants a barrier between himself and any
         authorities – e.g. when sending a telegram, making an
         official enquiry, hiring a flat.

      iv) The use of a cut-out prevents, or delays, the transfer
         of suspicion and the linking up of activities.

         N.B. The value of a cut-out must be explained to
         subordinates. It does not show a lack of confidence in
         them.

   c) Cover

      i) A cut-out should be able to contact inconspicuously
         each of the two agents between whom he is the link.
         If they are of widely differing positions, his range
         of contacts must be correspondingly wide. Special
         opportunities are open to men who work in one milieu
         and live in another – e.g. waiters, taxi-drivers,
         postmen – and also to professional men who are used
         to being consulted by members of all classes -e.g.
         priests, lawyers, doctors, bank managers, etc.

      ii) A cut-out should be able to disappear quickly, cutting
         short police enquiries.

CELL SYSTEM

PART III

1. <u>CELLS</u>.

For many types of subversive activity – e.g. propaganda,
passive resistance, etc. – and with all large organizations,
it is necessary to organize on a basis of cells; this
strengthens security.

a) <u>Definition</u>.

A cell is a small group working subversively inside some
existing group of individuals – e.g. factory, party, union,
group of workers going into Germany.

b) Expansion.

i) One of the most important functions of a cell is to
recruit other cells. Best method is for one member of
each cell to have the duty of recruiting a man outside
who will organize another cell. Similarly, another man
in the new cell will recruit a further cell, and so on.

ii) As the recruiter in the first cell is the only man to
have contact with the organizer of the second cell,
security is maintained to the highest degree. The
value of this is that in the event of one agent coming
under suspicion, police will take a long time to
trace others, and even if part of the organization is
discovered it does not necessarily reveal the whole.

iii) An alternative method is by radiation, whereby the
members of a cell recruit the organizers of more
than one new cell. Quicker expansion and more direct
communication, but security reduced.

iv) Chain system is most suitable for simple activities
not requiring complicated orders or exact timing –
e.g. propaganda; radiation system best where speed and
coordination are essential – e.g. secret armies.

c) <u>Control</u>.

i) Policy must be laid down from the top and carried out
uniformly throughout the organization.

79

    ii) No cell is superior to others; orders are simply passed on from above.

   iii) Field of recruitment for each chain of cells should be limited - e.g. one department in a factory - so that each group of cells is kept separate from the others and under the control of the agent appointed to look after it.

    iv) The organizer should limit the number of cells to be formed in each department or group. The cell members will be the "shock troops", influencing outsiders to undertake subversive action also (cf.A.15, 5. a).)

d) Internal Working.

    i) Number. A cell should contain only a small number of individuals (3 - 8).

    ii) Distribution of Functions. All members carry out the activity for which they are recruited. They must also collect any useful information and pass it back. They must also maintain security; anything suggesting that security is menaced - e.g. absence of cell member from work - should be reported up and down the cells at once.

    The organizer responsible for the foregoing also maintains liaison with the cell above, collates information, passes on orders, maintains security. The agent who has recruited the organizer of a new cell liaises with him.

N.B. It may be advisable to appoint one man in charge of supplies, stores, etc.

e) Plans for Emergency.

Plans must be laid in advance for the possibility of a break in a chain of cells which would leave some cells isolated. Possibilities are:

    i) General directives on the policy to be pursued in that eventuality.

    ii) The linking of the last cell in the chain with the organizer of the whole chain, thus making it circular.

   iii) Emergency address - e.g. to appear in an advertisement in an agreed paper.

f) <u>Conclusion</u>.

    i) The cell system has obvious disadvantages - **viz.** slowness, inefficiency, remote control.

    ii) Nevertheless, it is the only system of large-scale organization that affords the necessary degree of security.

    iii) It is particularly suitable for a continuous campaign of simple activities - e.g. propaganda, passive resistance, minor sabotage, strikes - and also for ground work preparatory to an armed revolt. It may also be used for penetrating existing organizations and influencing their policy and activities.

2. <u>PREPARATIONS FOR ZERO DAY</u>.

a) The organizer must plan the lay-out of his organization, not only for operations during the present period of the war, but also for operations to take place contemporaneously with an Allied invasion.

b) He may organize a special section to deal with this or may plan to switch his normal organization over when the time comes - or both.

c) He must arrange for more rapid lines of communication to be substituted for the slow methods necessitated by security during the first phase. Cut-outs may be eliminated and key men put in direct touch with each other.

d) He must have men in reserve to take over key positions. It is always possible that the enemy knows more about his organization than he thinks and will leave it until the approach of zero day before making a swoop.

e) He will have to arrange action and recognition signals for use **on** zero day.

f) He will have to pay particular attention to the collection of material - viz. weapons, ammunition and explosives - and information about zero day targets.

3. <u>SECURITY RULES FOR MEMBERS OF THE ORGANIZATION</u>.

a) Every member must receive training in self-protection and the security rules of the organization.

b) Each member should have a special function and should be prohibited from undertaking any other. Danger of over-enthusiastic trying to do too much work, or work to which he is not suited.

c) No member must attempt to find out more about the organization than he is told.

d) Every member must know what names are to be used in the organization and stick to these. (Christian names are safest and are adequate for a small organization; if numbers are used, they should not be consecutive.)

e) No member may carry arms unless he is in a situation where he can have no cover story.

f) No member may contact a member of another organization without special permission.

> <u>N.B.</u> The dangers of contacting other organizations which may have been penetrated by the enemy have already been shown. If it is absolutely essential to contact another organization, it should be done in the most cautious way through a cut-out, and it may be wise to plant a man inside it to investigate its security.

g) Every member must report any suspicious incident immediately, e.g. if he himself is followed or if a fellow member fails to appear.

h) Every member must know what to do in case of emergency. This involves:

> i) What warning signals will be used;
>
> ii) What other members he must warn himself;
>
> iii) Where to go (hide-out, cover story, etc.);
>
> iv) What contacts and activities he must drop;
>
> v) How to re-establish contact.

4. <u>ORGANIZER'S ACTION IN EMERGENCY</u>.

As has been shown, the organizer must prepare plans for an emergency as far as possible in advance. If an emergency arises -e.g. an agent finds that he is under surveillance, or is arrested – the organizer must:

a) Decide what contacts, plans and places are affected;

b) Warn the contacts to take their pre-arranged measures;

c) Postpone or drop any activities that are affected;

d) Clean up any places that are affected - i.e. destroy or conceal material and documents, cease to use R.V.'s;

e) Possibly send a message to H.Q. in this country;

f) If an agent has been arrested, find out the reason for his arrest and whether he has talked;

g) Help the arrested agent to escape if it can be done without prejudicing the security of the organization.

USE OF PREMISES

The use of premises brings with it special security problems.

1. GENERAL.

   a) No H.Q. should be established until organization has been organized.

   b) Premises should be used as little as possible at first. Plans and records should be kept in organizer's head and agents contacted in many different places.

   c) As organization grows use of H.Q. for above purposes will be necessary. Organizer may use residence or place of business.

   d) Additional premises may be required - E.g. for storage, printing, courier termini, safe houses.

   Recruit owner or occupier of an existing organization rather than set up a new establishment and instal new personnel.

   e) Principle of dispersal most important. Too many activities concentrated in one place is bad - E.g. do not keep documents at a place where agents meet.

2. CHOOSING PREMISES.

   Choice will depend on the particular country or region. In thinly populated country districts there may be opportunities for using isolated buildings - E.g. hiking or ski-ing huts. In a densely populated country a private house or commercial establishment in a town may have to be used. In selecting the latter, the following factors should be considered.

   a) Accessibility. It is important that strangers may be able to find their way without arousing suspicion by making enquiries or by their appearance being out of tune with the district.

   b) Cover. Wherever possible an attempt should be made to utilize an existing concern; any new business is very likely to be suspect and subject to enquiry. The usual office hours should be kept, bills paid normally and genuine business in every way conducted.

It must fit into the background - E.g. if it is a shop it must be of the appropriate class for the district.

It must provide cover for agents who come to visit it - suitable cover both for regular cut-outs and for irregular visitors or complete strangers - E.g. from abroad. Visitors must have "genuine" reason for coming.

Its cover must be built up. If possible, genuine business should be carried on before subversive activity is started.

c) Facilities. Some attention should be paid to the suitability of the premises from a defensive point of view - i.e.:

- Facilities for concealing persons and articles, E.g. thickness of walls.

- Facilities for escape (alternative exits)

- Vulnerability to surveillance.

d) Control of Access. There are three degrees of access available in a town:

- A "general" shop, where it is impossible to prevent the entry of police spies.

- An establishment with individual attention for the clients -E.g. tailor, doctor, lodging-house.

- A private office which is confined to a specific group of clients. This creates the maximum of difficulty for police infiltration, both because of the need for an adequate story and also because of the possibilities offered by waiting-rooms. Safes and records may also be kept here. The professional man, whose office fulfils these conditions, can combine the functions of H.Q. and cut-out, acting as a representative of the organizer.

It will be seen that the degree of security will vary in inverse proportion to the facilities for providing cover.

3. SECURITY PRECAUTIONS.

As many as possible of the following precautions should be taken in connection with any premises, including agent's own place of residence.

a) Agent must always be able to tell whether a room has been entered and searched during his absence. The best precaution is tidiness. Additional methods - E.g. leaf in keyhole, hairpin under door - must not be conspicuous. Possibility of leaving trap - E.g. notepaper.

b) As little incriminating material as possible should be kept on **the** premises. Anything no longer needed should be destroyed -E.g. coded writings, carbons. N.B. traces on blotting paper and writing blocks. Quantities of arms and explosives should be put in special caches.

c) Hiding places should be prepared. It may be necessary to have both permanent and emergency hiding places - the latter only to be used if the premises are raided while the incriminating articles are in use.

Fireplaces, and any other places in current fashion with the police, should be avoided. In this connection, information about any successful police searches is most valuable.

Permanent hiding places should be difficult of access rather than subtle - E.g. - burial.

Documents should not be concealed in places where bulky material might be found - in case they are looking for food, for example.

d) Preparations should be made for destroying incriminating evidence which is too dangerous to conceal.

N.B. Quantities of paper burn very slowly, even when petrol-soaked, and ashes may be deciphered unless broken up.

e) Provision should be made for persons to be concealed or make a get-away (alternative exit), and to clear away all traces.

N.B. Danger of Gestapo's entry from all sides simultaneously.

f) If cover permits, someone should always be on guard. It may be very useful (particularly in case of rooms situated in a large block) if someone - E.g. the hall-porter - can be enrolled to act as guard, and a warning system of communications arranged.

g) All-clear and danger signs should be pre-arranged - visual and/or oral - E.g. object of pre-arranged colour, doormat in certain position. Difficulties of black-out. A "normal" sign should preferably be used to denote danger. Possibility of limiting times for calling and only showing sign then.

h) A constant watch should be kept to see whether the premises are under observation; and when any one enters or leaves, a check should be made to see that he is not followed, and, if he is, a warning should be arranged – E.g. stick left behind.

i) It may be wise for frequent visitors to alter their dress slightly and arrive by different methods in order to avoid attracting attention.

j) In case one set of premises comes under suspicion, an alternative set should be ready, with the necessary cover story built up. After change, foster police suspicions of first place.

k) Rents and taxes on premises should be paid promptly to avoid enquiries, unless the "cover owner" has never paid them promptly before.

COMMUNICATIONS AND OPERATIONS

PERSONAL MEETINGS

A. GENERAL

Advantages:

a) More information can be passed.
b) Correct emphasis on information can be made.
c) Immediate replies can be obtained.

Disadvantages:

a) Meeting may be suspicious.
b) Suspicion may be passed on to hitherto unsuspected contact.
c) Meeting may be a trap.

B. METHODS

Three types of personal meetings are discussed with a view to obviating disadvantages:

1. BETWEEN ACQUAINTED AGENTS:

   (a) Cover for meeting

      - By chance. (First arrival mustn't show impatience).
      - On purpose. (NO confusion with chance meeting).

   (b) Choice of meeting-place

      Bad: Railway stations, public-meetings, hotels, brothels, queues (Informers), post-offices. (If you must meet at one of these, use danger signs).

      Better: Small hotels, restaurants, bars, cafes.

      Still better: Street, gardens (exc. France), Catholic churches, cemeteries, Turkish or Swimming-baths, museums, art-galleries, plages, parks, motor-cars, house hired or rented by third party, private houses and offices, "hangabout" places (cf. woods near Oslo on Sunday!); and dance-halls or places

88

of amusement when not controlled (cf. no dancing in Norway).

NOTE: Always have cover for your presence at any meeting place.

(c) <u>Conversation</u>.

Cover conversation. Arrange on arrival.

Don't whisper except e.g. for dirty-joke or love-making.

Smile and laugh as much as possible (Permanent tip for agent.)

(d) <u>Passing messages</u>.

NO tricks, if it is possible to pass message unnoticed. (e.g. in W.C. etc.)

If tricks necessary, take equipment. (Use of identical equipment - swapping brief-cases, matchboxes, newspapers, etc.)

Sign to indicate message passed.

(e) <u>Security Precautions</u>.

- Innocent pre-visits to R.V. as cover.

- Security of pre-arrangements (e.g. time and date given separately and not by same method such as telephone. Communist trick of ADDING one hour to time - therefore, police are always late).

- Safety and danger signs (e.g. NO gloves - danger.)

- Alternative R.V. in case of accidents.

- <u>Be punctual</u> (Synchronise watches or pre-arrange that time be taken from neighbouring public clock.)

- Guard against microphones. (Turn on wireless, bath, gramophone).

- Limit the time you are going to wait.

- Precautions against surveillance. (Meet in black-out where practical).

- Change R.V.'s frequently.

2. <u>BETWEEN UNACQUAINTED AGENTS</u>.

(a) <u>Cover</u>

- Must be chance meeting.

(b) <u>Description</u>

- Proper description (see A.7.) better than combination of signs. (Wearing red rose and drinking green drink). Signs should be used only as check for description.

(c) <u>Passwords</u>

- Never conspicuous - i.e. dramatic, incongruous or compromising.

- Therefore generally banale but marked, esp. in reply. (Use of pause, gesture, special but commonplace word).

- Should be short and spoken verbatim. (Easy to forget passwords in stress).

- Should be introduced naturally. (Some passwords are good 'openers', others have to be introduced gradually.)

- Reply at once.

    (E.G. One agent used a badly chosen password to a M. Viveau staying at a certain hotel. V. looked astonished, and the agent later found that there were three men in the hotel having the same name.)

3. <u>BETWEEN AGENT AND OUTSIDER</u>

<u>Security Precautions.</u>

- If you're suspicious, don't go to R.V.

- Don't accept outsider's suggestions on time, place, date.

- Send cut-out to R.V. to bring him somewhere else.

- Intercept him yourself en route, and take him elsewhere.

- Send man to recce R.V. in advance.

- Have yourself followed.

- Extra search of yourself before meeting.

Appendix
A.18
February 1944

COMMUNICATIONS

L'Organisateur, a Communist clandestine paper in Belgium,
obviously destined for members of the Party only, in its July
1943 issue, gives a solemn warning that many arrests of Party
members have been due solely to negligence, to failure to
observe the precautions necessary to a clandestine movement, and
it therefore sets out briefly the main rules for Security.

1. Arranging a meeting.

No meeting may be entirely arranged in a single letter.
First, a letter should be sent containing the day of the
meeting and the time of the meeting, and, if the two other
members of the Group do not know each other, a sign by which
they may recognize each other. Then a second letter should be
sent, at least one day later, containing the meeting place.
This elementary rule for security must not be neglected under
any circumstances, however acute the urgency. If one of the
Group has something urgent to report, he must verbally summon
the person to whom he wishes to report to some meeting place
which can be mentioned in veiled terms, as for example, "The
place we last saw each other".

Take care that nothing is written in a note book, and that
in no case is anything written down in plain language. Always
sign notes with a number or an initial.

2. Recognition signs for members of a Group.

It has been found in practice that if two comrades do not know
each other, a single recognition sign is not sufficient, and
may lead to trouble. Therefore, two recognition signs should
be given. If one of these signs is some article of clothing,
it must be given in full detail: for example, a 'brown hat'
is not sufficient, but adding 'a breast-pocket kerchief of a
certain colour and design', makes recognition easy.

For passwords, definite replies must be given. For example,
if one comrade asks the way, the other should reply, "It is
a long way", or "It is five kilometres". On no account should
ordinary replies such as "I am going too" be given.

3. <u>Use of Railway Stations and Trains</u>.

Main railway stations or stations in big towns must never be used for boarding or leaving trains. Members of the Party should always use suburban or small town stations, whether they are known or not in the bigger stations.

4. <u>Meeting Places</u>.

No meetings should be arranged in the vicinity of stations or at fixed points. Meetings should be arranged so that one comrade meets another during a walk, one having left point 'X' at a certain time to walk in the direction of 'Y', and the other having left point 'Y' at a certain time to walk in the direction of 'X'. In case they fail to meet each other, each one should walk the full length and back again to allow the other to catch him up, and a final attempt to meet should be made an hour later than the fixed time.

When the two comrades meet, they should greet each other as if it was sheer accident, chat for a moment, watching the while to see they have not been followed, and should then go off together.

5. Members of the Party, and <u>above all, messengers</u>, should cease to arrange meetings one after the other in the same place, or a few steps from the same place. Meeting-places should be at least a quarter of an hour's walking from each other, and during this period, members should take care that they are not followed.

6. <u>When a Party member meets another….</u>

Should one party member meet another by accident, in the street, for example, he should make no attempt to speak to him, or even recognise him. It has become known that one person, who had never taken part in any anti-German activities, has been arrested, and is still in custody, simply for shaking hands with an old friend whom the Gestapo were following. If members have no Party reason for meeting, they should ignore each other, and leave until tomorrow any gossip they may wish to pass on.

7. Each Group Leader is held responsible for seeing that these Security rules are observed.

COMMUNICATIONS - INTERNAL

1. INTRODUCTION.

Organizers must be able to keep in constant touch with colleagues. It will be found that better work is obtained if all subordinates feel that means of communication are assured.

It must be remembered that in communicating an agent endangers himself and friends. Therefore greatest care is essential.

It is necessary to study the wide choice of methods available, adopting the most suitable method to the circumstances.

2. POST.

Much the simplest way for persons at a distance to communicate with one another, but slow, uncertain and fairly easily investigated by police. In occupied territories letters frequently censored, especially in and out of prohibited areas. Letters of suspected persons sure to be opened; thus consider the following measures:

a) Essential to use code (veiled language) or secret inks.

b) If suspected, do not use post for subversive correspondence.

c) Avoid putting precise address at letter-head, except where regulations demand it. If unavoidable, existing address (e.g. real hotel, innocent address, third party, quisling) is preferable to an invented one.

d) Avoid watermarked paper and typewriters of non-standard makes or which have recognizable peculiarities. Only use your typewriter for secret work. Hide it when not in use.

e) Sign with Christian name or nickname.

f) Avoid special classes of mail (air, registered, parcel post). Make use of postcards and business mail, particularly circulars.

g) Post at different post-boxes and at places away from place of residence. Remember sender's letters can be identified if sender is followed (e.g. newspaper thrown into post-box after letter). Therefore take precautions against surveillance.

93

h) When sending instructions by post, allow for delay in delivery owing to war-time conditions.

i) Greater security is afforded by accommodation address, especially if it gives cover for the reception of numerous letters, where organizer has no such cover; conceals your address and identity from your correspondent. Letters must be sent as if to accommodator; no enclosures and passed on by hand or post according to purpose of accommodation address. Special outside markings useful to show that letter contains secret message. Change accommodation address frequently. Only use for two correspondents at most. Avoid post restante – such mail is watched; only use when no other address available.

3. BOITES-AUX-LETTRES.

These are places where persons or their cut-outs can leave and collect messages. A useful means of communicating between principals who do not wish to meet. Very difficult for the police to trace one party by surveillance of the other.

They must afford cover for frequent visits, e.g. tobacconist, cafe, newspaper kiosk, etc.

Remember:

a) Intermediary must be recruited but need not be informed of the nature of the organization.

b) Correspondents should hand in letters clandestinely, or have cover for leaving them openly. Study ways of handing over messages, e.g. in newspaper, in food, with the change, etc.

c) Decoy letter and/or alternative cover (e.g. black market) should be available in case of emergency.

d) There should be danger signs in case of emergency.

e) Clear box regularly.

4. "DEAD" BOITES-AUX-LETTRES.

Same as above, but without living agency, e.g. milestones, lavatories, etc. Here again principals can communicate without meeting.

Note:

a) There is no risk from intermediary.

    b) There would be no warning in the event of discovery, in which case the place would be watched by C.E.

    c) Have cover story for "finding" message, e.g. find by accident.

    d) Police might watch correspondence without principal knowing.

5. COURIERS.

A courier supplies means of circumventing censorship by having messages carried by hand or verbally. Slow but surer than other methods. Message can be destroyed in emergency. On the other hand, if courier should be captured and interrogated, there may be imminent personal danger to several organizers. Precautions:

    a) Courier must have good cover and know route well.

    b) Message is best memorised, but if this is not possible it should be written on paper easy to destroy and/or conceal, e.g. silk paper, rice paper, cigarette paper. In such circumstances

    c) Courier should not know contents or code.

    d) Courier should be instructed in the principles of body searches and snap control. Courier should not have direct contact with principals.

    e) Relay system of short-stage couriers connected through boites-aux-lettres has advantages. Each courier knows stage intimately and should not exceed his stage.

6. "DEAD" COURIERS.

Messages can be concealed on vehicles or in luggage of unknown persons. Same conditions as in case of "dead" boites-aux-lettres.

7. TELEGRAMS.

An easy and quick method of sending short messages between persons at a distance, but very conspicuous and certain to be censored, and of limited use only - to be used sparingly. Sender will almost certainly have to identify himself. Two permanent records of contents. Telegrams a good means of indicating the whereabouts of the sender, arranging rendezvous and answering questions.

Precautions:

    a) Code with good cover must be used.

    b) Use cut-out to transmit wire as his own.

    c) Make sure recipient socially qualified to receive telegrams.

    d) Accommodation address (see Post).

8. <u>TELEPHONE</u>.

Very quick method for those at a distance to communicate, but always assume that telephone conversations are censored.

Conversation of suspected people often recorded automatically.

Therefore use public call-boxes. Trunk callers may have to identify themselves – serious limitations on trunk calls may exist.

Use of foreign languages generally forbidden but careful code must be used, and conventional conversation. Suspicious phraseology likely to be noted.

Telephone can best be used for arranging rendezvous, answering questions, etc.

9. <u>ADVERTISEMENTS</u>.

A means of communicating reasonably quickly with a large number of people simultaneously. Could be used either as a sign or to conceal coded message. Impossible to identify recipients. Best used as general warning or action sign. Remember:

    a) Identity of inserter must usually be established. Possible to use cut-out.

    b) Wording must be normal as it is likely to be carefully scrutinised by C.E.

    c) Good cover for inserting essential. Articles lost preferable to "for sale" or "goods required" notices.

    d) Regular insertions must be made by regular advertisers.

    e) Delay.

10. <u>GENERAL PRECAUTIONS</u>.

a) Messages can often be sent in two parts, either part alone being incomprehensible, e.g. the main message by courier, the key by post.

b) There should always be at least two means of communication between important organizers working together, in case one is "blown".

c) Important messages should be sent in duplicate.

d) May be necessary to arrange for acknowledgement of messages.

e) Avoid numbering of messages.

A.20.
September 1943.

COMMUNICATIONS – EXTERNAL

1. GENERAL.

Communications between agent in field and base are vital and require careful organization. Several alternative routes are advisable in case one is "blown". The following are the principal methods:

a) W/T. Short, urgent messages and/or where immediate reply is required.

b) Courier Service. For long messages, urgent and/or less urgent; maps, material, etc.

c) "Innocent" Letter. Sent to address in neutral country. Short messages for use when agent is out of touch with members of his organization.

Other possible methods are:

d) Telephone or telegram to neutral country.

e) Advertisement in press.

f) Diplomatic bag.

g) Carrier pigeons.

2. W/T.

This is the only method for rapid communication and for obtaining immediate reply. The more it is used the more likely it is to be detected. Operator is highly trained man with special cover. To protect him and/or his activity, the following precautions are required:

a) He should not be used for other work.

b) Other agents should not go to his residence or place of operation. It is even better if they do not contact him direct.

c) A reserve means of communication with him must be maintained if he has to go into hiding.

d) Only messages which cannot be sent conveniently by other routes should go by W/T.

e) Messages must be between 150 and 400 letters.

3. SECURITY DEVICES OF OPERATOR.

    a) Set disguised as suitcase.

    b) Bury set on arrival.

    c) Aerial made of local wire, camouflaged.

    d) Must have cover which allows absence at irregular times. Routine job useless unless employer in organization.

    e) Should live with friends as key-taps audible. Residence must supply hiding place.

    f) Should constantly move set and/or aerial.

    g) Times and length of transmission restricted according to plan.

4. COURIER SERVICE.

A series of linked relays by which messages and/or material are carried. There may be several "termini", each linked with a "branch service" or "main service". It is much slower than W/T, but usually safer. In general, couriers cover each stage.

The following points should be noted:

    a) Each courier should have special knowledge of his relay and good cover for travelling regularly.

    b) Several couriers can be employed on each stage so that there is a frequent service. Often courier will make journey innocently.

    c) Couriers' contact with one another and principals should be through boites-aux-lettres where possible.

5. DIFFICULTIES AT FRONTIER OR SEA.

Special problem arises at a crossing of frontier or sea. The following methods are used:

    a) Smugglers, attendants on trains, lorry drivers, etc. used as couriers.

    b) Trains, cars, other vehicles, used as "dead" couriers.

    c) Material floated down rivers or thrown over frontier line in containers, e.g. "turnips".

    d) Drum taps and puffs of smoke, etc.

    e) Neutral seamen as couriers.

f) Materials smuggled out to submarines, seaplanes, fishing-boats , etc.

g) Material concealed on ships or aeroplanes, etc. by dock or aerodrome workers, etc.

6. <u>LETTER SENT TO ADDRESS IN NEUTRAL COUNTRY</u>.

Safe, but slow method. Letter can contain:

a) Long message in secret writing.

b) Short message in code.

c) Pre-arranged signal, e.g. warning, "all well", etc.

d) Agent's address when he is out of touch with the rest of his organization. This is the commonest use.

<u>Precautions</u>.

i) Addressee does not know purport of letter but believes himself intermediary between innocent person in occupied territory who wishes to write to friends in allied territory and cannot communicate direct. Much innocent correspondence, in fact, passes this way.

ii) Sender must take every precaution against censorship which is stricter for foreign letters than for internal, e.g. choice of address, danger of registered letters, air mail, length of letter, etc.

iii) Not too many letters must be sent to the same neutral address.

iv) It is more important to conceal identity of sender than recipient, who runs little danger.

7. <u>TELEPHONE</u>.

Telephone messages to and from neutral countries are sometimes permitted. Formal application must be made. Use of language restricted. Censorship certain. Therefore good cover essential.

Use of code highly dangerous except between experts. In general only suitable for arranging rendezvous, giving address, etc.

8. <u>TELEGRAMS</u>.

Same considerations apply as to telephones - see previous lecture. Telegrams are useful for indicating address of sender.

9. <u>ADVERTISEMENT IN PRESS</u>.

Enemy papers available in this country within a week. First-class cover required for frequent insertions. See previous lecture.

10. <u>CARRIER PIGEONS</u>.

Rarely used except for notifying safe arrival. Special instruction essential.

a) <u>Advantage</u>. Can take small maps, drawings, etc. quicker than by other methods, except W/T.

b) <u>Limitations</u>.

i) Difficulties of importing and hiding.

ii) Difficulties of feeding and exercising.

iii) Loss of homing instinct after a time.

iv) Limitation to distance and direction which can be flown.

v) Pigeons cannot "home" in darkness or in fog.

THE W/T OPERATOR

1. <u>IMPORTANCE OF THE W/T OPERATOR</u>.

   a) He is the only member of the organization who can maintain quick and reliable communication with your base.

   b) He is a specialist with lengthy training.

   c) The supply of W/T Operators is strictly limited.

   d) A constant objective for enemy C.E.

2. <u>THE W/T OPERATOR AT WORK</u>.

   a) <u>Sets</u>.

   There are several types used.

   Size - Not greater than 2'0" x 1'0" x 6", excluding battery. Weight - Not greater than 40 lbs. Camouflage - Suitcases, gramophones.

   b) <u>Aerials.</u>

   Similar to the ones used for ordinary receiving sets. For transmitting, aerials must be more carefully located than for receiving.

   E.g. - On high ground away from trees, steel structures, overhead power lines and electric power stations.

   c) <u>Power</u>.

   There are two sources of power:

   i) <u>Electric Mains</u>.

   The consumption of electricity will be registered on a meter. The operators will therefore have to tap mains before they enter the meter.

   ii) <u>Batteries</u>.

   Provision must be made for recharging.

   d) <u>Plan</u>.

   Before leaving the operator receives a complete "plan" containing scheds, call signs, etc. This plan is a very secret document, even more important than the set. The operator must work in accordance with the "plan" and any alterations must be sanctioned by the base.

e) <u>Messages</u>.

The operator must be off the air as long as possible and on the air for the shortest time possible. Therefore, messages must be SHORT and CONCISE, eliminating all superfluous words.

f) <u>Codes</u>.

Encoding and decoding should, if possible, be left to organizers and W/T operator should only be required to transmit and receive the messages as they reach him. In some cases he may have to do the encoding and decoding.

3. <u>ENEMY C.E. METHODS FOR DETECTING ILLEGAL TRANSMITTING</u>.

The enemy's organization for detecting illegal wireless transmitting is efficient and scientific. Any or all of the following methods are used.

a) Ban on private transmitters.

b) Informant Service reporting suspicious events and behaviour.

c) Snap controls to detect if sets are being moved from place to place.

d) Search of localities where illegal transmitters are believed to be operating.

e) Interception service which records suspicious messages and attempts to break down the ciphers.

f) Use of the following D.F. (Direction Finding) Equipment:

   i) Fixed D.F. stations to locate the approximate area of the transmitter. These are numerous.

   ii) Numerous mobile D.F. stations to localise the whereabouts of the transmitter.

      - work in pairs or threes.

      - Camouflaged as ordinary vehicles with non-metal bodies.
        E.g. - Delivery vans, ambulances, laundry vans.

   iii) Hand-carried D.F. apparatus for use in places which cannot be reached by car.

     iv) Slow flying aircraft which cruise around over
         suspected area and may fly low over the station.

     v) Electric supply cut off street by street in the
       suspected locality.

       An illegal transmitter is easiest pinpointed in
       country districts, but D.F. apparatus is most numerous
       in the towns. Suburbs are therefore generally agreed
       to be the safest places.

4. W/T OPERATOR PRECAUTIONS.

The operator must continually protect himself against enemy
C.E. and should remember the following points.

a) Cover - for being absent from his work when transmitting
and visiting stations.

b) Alternative Sets - if possible located in different
locations and used at different times on different days.

c) Alternative Places - to which he can move his set whenever
opportunity offers and as often as possible.

d) Friends - to warn him of the approach of mobile D.F.
stations and help him move his set. He should not transport
it himself. Wireless sets are more easily replaced than
operators.

e) Observation Point - from which to observe the approach of
D.F. cars while he is operating.

f) Security - Plan and other suspicious material should be
concealed somewhere apart from the set. Copies of messages
should only be kept if absolutely necessary. Pistol should
be kept with the set.

g) Transmission - Operator must be on the air for as short a
time as possible. Messages must be short and explicit.

h) Power - To counteract cutting off of electricity battery
should be available to enable the transmission to
continue.

5. RELATIONS BETWEEN ORGANIZER AND W/T OPERATOR.

Organizer must do everything possible to protect the W/T
operator and the organization from the consequences of
suspicion falling on him.

The W/T operator must be capable of looking after himself and
not expect the organizer to do everything for him.

The relationship should be governed by the following considerations:

a) Direct contact between the organizer and operator should be cut to a minimum. Communication should be through "Boites-aux-lettres" or "cut-outs" rather than personal meetings.

b) The organizer may have to help the operator find spare parts for his set, arrange repairs, obtain suitable locations, etc.

c) The organizer should tell the operator as little as possible about the organization, only sufficient to enable him to do his job.

d) Only really urgent messages should be given to the W/T operator; the organizer should always have a second line of communication.

e) The organizer can either encode and decode messages himself or give them to the W/T operator to do.

f) The organizer and W/T operator will each number their own personal messages.

g) Usual emergency arrangements must be made for the W/T operator. E.g. – Line of escape, address in neutral country for communication.

6. <u>RELATION BETWEEN W/T OPERATOR AND OTHER MEMBERS OF ORGANIZATION.</u>

a) As few members of the organization should be known to the operator as possible, and of those he should <u>not</u> know their real names or addresses.

b) Communication between him and them should be by "Boites-aux-lettres" or "cut-outs".

c) He should know as little as possible of their activities.

d) The W/T operator should recruit his own assistants. E.g. – To transport his set, warn him against D.F. cars.

7. <u>ARREST OF W/T OPERATORS</u>.

a) If caught a W/T operator may not be executed, but "persuaded" to reveal his secrets so that he can be "played back". The enemy's "persuasion" is difficult to resist. He must therefore arrange "security checks" beforehand, so that recipients will know that messages are being sent under pressure.

b) The organizer must also advise the base at once if he believes the W/T operator has been caught and is being "played back".

PASSIVE RESISTANCE

1. <u>HISTORY</u>.

   a) During the years 1940-41 the Nazis were supreme in Europe.

   b) The people of Europe, ridden by years of propaganda and Fifth Columnism, were apparently powerless.

   c) Britain was holding on by the skin of her teeth, daily expecting invasion, suffering losses at sea, and unable to give assistance to occupied countries.

   The U.S.A. was still neutral.

   d) The people of Europe, deserted and betrayed by their own people, their Allies with their backs to the wall, were disillusioned. In some cases this disillusionment took the form of acting hate of Britain, which was encouraged by the conquering Hun.

   e) There was, however, still a weapon left to fight the Hun, which if co-ordinated and organized could be extremely powerful. This weapon was that of Passive Resistance.

   f) This was recognized by Britain and long-range plans were made to co-ordinate and organize the spasmodic outbursts of Passive Resistance which soon began to appear in occupied countries.

2. <u>DEFINITION OF PASSIVE RESISTANCE</u>.

   Passive Resistance consists of acts which depend for their feasibility and value upon being:

   a) Non-technical - acts which can be done by anyone.

   b) Non-risky - either because they are indetectable or because the resisters have perfect cover.

   c) Unlikely to have unpleasant consequences for the civilian population.

   d) Capable of being carried out by large numbers of people.

   An organized passive resistance campaign can be compared to an attack on a man by hundreds of mosquitoes, each giving him only a tiny sting but all together eventually driving him away.

3. <u>OBJECTIVES</u>.

The main objectives of a Passive Resistance Campaign should be:

a) The obstruction of enemy production.

b) The obstruction of administration.

(For examples – See Appendix "A")

4. <u>TARGETS</u>.

The following weaknesses of the enemy should be borne in mind:

a) Personnel – shortage and bad quality.

b) Home-sickness of enemy personnel and anxiety about their people at home.

c) Character of the enemy – i.e. vanity, self-consciousness and lack of humour.

5. <u>ORGANIZATION OF PASSIVE RESISTANCE</u>.

a) Organization and direction are essential if acts of Passive Resistance are to be effective.

b) Directives may be received from the base from time to time but in their absence organizers should use their own discretion and their own special knowledge. Directives on Passive Resistance are often very effective as coming from outside the country. E.g. – "V" Campaign, "Go slow". This is not the case with directives on sabotage where risks are greater.

c) The propagandist makes the most effective organizer.

d) <u>The cell system</u> can be used for organizing a campaign as close organization is not necessary.

e) Specialization in particular acts of Passive Resistance is sometimes valuable but organizers must be prepared for elaborate checking by the enemy.

f) Incentives should be devised to maintain enthusiasm. E.g. – So many wasted minutes each day represents over a period the sinking of a U-boat.

6. <u>EFFECT OF PASSIVE RESISTANCE ON THE CIVILIAN POPULATION</u>.

A passive resistance campaign organized amongst a civilian population,

a) Gives them something to do – from feeling themselves useless and hopeless they come to the realization that each and every person can, in his own way, fight the enemy.

b) From simple acts of passive resistance they acquire confidence to go one step further, namely towards acts of simple sabotage, and from there to greater sabotage and even guerrilla warfare.

c) The combined effect of a). and b). raises their morale and encourages united efforts against the enemy and prepares them for possible unpleasant reprisals.

COMMUNICATIONS AND OPERATIONS

EXAMPLES:

1. OBSTRUCTION OF PRODUCTION.

   a) Under cover of feigning stupidity, ignorance, over-caution or fear of being suspected of active sabotage, factory workers can obstruct by:

      i) Demanding written orders.
      ii) Asking unnecessary questions.
      iii) Making too frequent checks, in order to avoid being accused of sabotage.
      iv) Rejecting everything not perfect.
      v) Working too well, but slowly.
      vi) Specifying too high quality.
      vii) Obeying rules implicitly regardless of consequences, e.g. - reading all addresses when sorting packages.
      viii) Misunderstanding orders, e.g. - misdirecting trucks.

   b) Under cover of feigning exhaustion by air-raid or under nourishment, they can cause delay by:

      i) Slightly increasing accident rate.
      ii) Ca'Canny.
      iii) Slightly inefficient work.
      iv) Not correcting errors of others.

   c) Under cover of complaints about ersatz they can increase the consumption of materials and general wear and tear.

   d) Further trouble can be caused without serious risk by:

      i) Constantly making "reasonable" complaints.
      ii) Non-cooperation with salvage schemes.
      iii) Not passing on knowledge to unskilled workmen.
      iv) Giving lengthy and incomprehensible explanations when questioned.

2. OBSTRUCTION OF ADMINISTRATION.

   Under cover of feigning stupidity, ignorance, over-caution, over-enthusiasm, over-politeness, the layman can obstruct administration by:

   a) Misunderstanding regulations.

   b) Filling up forms incorrectly.

c) Making unnecessary enquiries.

d) Being verbose and unnecessarily polite.

e) Prolonging correspondence.

f) Denouncing (anonymously) quislings, German Officials, etc. as unreliable.

g) Reporting imaginary spies, suspicious incidents or dangers. This is especially useful at times of invasion. False reports which may cause serious trouble are:

    i) Mines in docks or roads.
   ii) Unexploded bombs.
  iii) German personnel buried in debris of building.
   iv) Allied parachute landings.
    v) Allied personnel in Axis uniforms.
   vi) Guerrilla activity, sniping, etc.
  vii) Suspicious incidents.

N.B. These reports should be:

    - Plausible.
    - Sufficiently detailed to merit investigation.
    - Borne out, if possible, by the corroborative evidence of others - stories should not be suspiciously similar.

They are best reported second-hand, but if not the reporter must have cover explanation for having obtained his information.

SUBVERSION OF TROOPS

1. The essential difference between an Armed Force and a group of civilians is DISCIPLINE. Solvent of discipline is SELF-INTEREST.

2. Influences provoking self-interest among Enemy Occupying Troops are:

   a) Dissatisfaction.
   b) Anxiety.
   c) Terror.
   d) Loneliness.
   e) Deprivation.

   (Note: Terror can be resolved by fight, flight or concealment; anxiety cannot.)

3. Stimuli to provoke these influences are selected by campaign-planners from enemy-troop morale-reports and are disseminated orally and graphically by agents, using:

   a) A hostile approach: Effective, but sometimes unsafe.
   b) A sympathetic approach: Effective and generally safer.

4. Some stimuli known to have provoked above-mentioned influences among German troops in Occupied Europe:

   a) DISSATISFACTION.

      i) Internal feuds between:

         - Officers and Men.
           e.g. Strict discipline in Norway, Poland.
                Racketeering opportunites in France, Belgium.

         - Gestapo and Men.

         - Regional Groups of Axis Forces.
           e.g. Austro-German, Sudeten-Deutsch - Reichsdeutsch.
                Italo-German quarrels in Athens, Bordeaux.

      ii) Irregular Pay.

   b) ANXIETY.

         i) Allied bombing of soldiers' families.
            - Cover for source of news.

111

   ii) Jealously over behaviour of wife or girl-friend at home. On known basis that Germany encourages illegitimacy, two lines of attack are open:

- Sib. that SS-men at home have free and condoned intercourse with German girls.

- Reminder that there are 2,000,000 foreign PW's and 6,000,000 Foreign Workers in Germany - from many of whom German girls are none too safe.

(Note: Sympathetic approach through exchange of snapshots and photos.)

  iii) Departure for Russian Front.

- Especially when disguised as furlough.

  iv) Sib. that heavily-wounded casualties on Russian Front are liquidated.

c) <u>TERROR</u>.

   i) Violent local antagonism.

  ii) Murder, mutilation and castration.

d) <u>LONELINESS.</u>

   i) Geographical isolation from Fatherland.

  ii) Rarity and delay in arrival of mail.

  iii) "Po-Ko" melancholia.

e) <u>DEPRIVATION</u>.

   i) Lack of food - but only when backed by <u>factual</u> intelligence.

  ii) Lack of vitamins.

  iii) Lack of sexual satisfaction.

- Prevent womenfolk from having intercourse with German soldiers <u>except</u> for purposes of spreading venereal disease.

SELECTION AND APPRECIATION OF TARGETS.

1. SELECTION.

a) Two main categories of target:

- Long-term. Attackable at any time or all the time.
  (E.g. enemy morale, railroad-transport.)
- Short-term. Attackable only at a "zero-hour" signal
  (E.g. European second-front targets.)

b) Organizer should compile priority-list of each. Choice
conditioned by:

- Pre-selection of targets by superior H.Q.
- Organizer to use initiative within general directives.

c) We need only be concerned with alternative 2. b). in whose
case selection of targets will be governed by:

- Conformity with general directives.
  Allied Strategy may demand attacks now on transport,
  now on food, now on man-power, not on morale, now on
  industry, etc.
- Importance to enemy.
  Information from H.Q. or own Informant Service on
  bottlenecks, key-personnel, etc.
- Vulnerability.
- Resources available.
  Co-operation of guerrillas, Allied air-forces. State of
  supplies and own man-power.
- Effect on local population.
  - Direct: Lack of food, electricity, etc. as result of
    operations.
- Indirect: Hostages, reprisals.
- Timing.
  Synchronisation with other attacks.

2. INTELLIGENCE.

Prelude to all operations is good information. This can be
acquired by three methods.

a) Regular Intelligence Service.

b) Informant Service.

113

c) Personal Reconnaissance.

It is from your informant service that you will receive information regarding the target to be attacked and the inside knowledge necessary, E.g. industrial information from factory workers, etc.

The Organizer should, himself, recce the target, or detail responsible subordinates, and check information received from other sources, to enable him to draw up detailed plans.

3. <u>INFORMATION REQUIRED</u>.

It is essential when planning an attack to decide what you require to know about the target. Failure to recognize one essential item will mean failure of operation.

Information on most of the following points will be required:

a) Risk to security of organization? Can sabotage look like accident? Line of retreat? Assess worst consequences of detection.

b) Guards - are they alert? Can they be bluffed or bribed? Police or Military - Operation Orders.

c) Walls, fences, etc. - Can they be surmounted by ladders, wire clippers, etc.?

d) Entrances - Are they well protected?

e) Surrounding ground - Does it afford cover?

f) Phases of moon - When will nights be dark?

g) Weather - Will bad weather be helpful?

h) Feast days - Will they reduce efficiency of security measures?

i) Day - When is sabotage likely to be most effective?

j) Time - What time of day is most favourable?

k) Visitors - What sorts of people visit premises?

l) Passes - Can they be forged, stolen or borrowed?

m) Recruitment of employees - Can agents be infiltrated?

n) Reliability of employees - Are they susceptible to subversion?

o) Most normal types of errors and accidents in factory - Can they be reproduced artificially?

p) Bottle-necks - At what point will damage do most harm?

q) Possibilities of fire, flood, etc.?

r) Land-marks, facilities for guiding aircraft – Can such be created or found?

s) Available resources – Can assistance be brought from base? Students can suggest other factors.

4. <u>APPRECIATION OF METHOD OF ATTACK.</u>

From the above information, an appreciation of best method of attack can be drawn up as follows:

a) <u>Object</u>. "To put target out of action."

b) <u>Factors to be considered</u>. These will correspond to the answers to questions asked under Para 2). above, E.g.

   i) Security – attack can look like accident only if in form of fire.

   ii) Guards extremely efficient.

   iii) Walls, fences, impregnable.

   iv) Entrances strongly protected.

   v) No cover in neighbourhood – grounds swept by searchlights.

   vi) Slackness on feast days unlikely.

c) <u>Courses Open</u>.

In attacking a target one of the following alternatives will be used:

   i) Passive resistance, with, or without, outside advice.

   ii) Minor sabotage with, or without, outside advice and supplies.

   iii) Major sabotage, by inside workers, with, or without, outside supplies and/or help.

   iv) Major sabotage by outsiders, with, or without, inside assistance.

   v) Air bombing or sea attack.

Some of these methods can usually be excluded at once. Consider each of the others in relation to factors. Then state course selected, with reasons.

d) <u>Plan</u>.

Here plan for carrying out method selected should be briefly stated. It should be the logical outcome of the previous argument.

EMERGENCY PERIOD

OPERATIONAL ORDERS

1. OPERATIONAL ORDERS.

Vital to issue orders accurately and securely, therefore draw up your plans and orders under definite headings, thus:

>   Information.
>   Intention.
>   Method.
>   Administration.
>   Inter-communication.

Memorise this framework, adherence to this simple form will prevent omissions in passing on orders to subordinates.

Necessary to consider these heading in detail.

a) Information.

   i) Relative to target. All available information obtained, each operator receives that which directly concerns his share in the operation. Sketch plan if necessary, but destroy immediately.

   ii) Relative to own forces. No more than essential for each man to carry out his share in the operation. As an encouragement possible to indicate that substantial forces being used, E.g. if co-operation being received from outside, operators should know.

b) Intention.

Each operator receives concise statement of intention of operation in so far as it concerns his actions and his morale. For security reasons do not give more than minimum information about object of whole operation - may be necessary, however, to indicated this in general terms so that the operator appreciates importance of operation, e.g. total effect of passive resistance when operation,

E.g. total effect of passive resistance when carried out by all employees in a department.

c) Method.

Here detailed instructions must be given to each operator (or party) separately of what he is to do and how he will do it, for the period of operation.

The following points should be considered:

i) Sabotage weapons – fire, water, drought, sand, passive resistance, hammers, mishandling instruments or explosives. Explosives only as last resort.

ii) Sabotage to appear an accident?

iii) Circumvention of security measures at target.

iv) Approach to target.

v) Retreat from target.

vi) Arms, type, method to be used?

vii) Day, time, duration.

d) Administrative Arrangements.

Here deal with general organization, pay particular attention to periods before and after operation - the following will have to be included:

i) Cover story for each operator - either open or clandestine, not a mixture.

ii) Identity of leaders or contacts (if necessary).

iii) Supplies of arms, explosives, money, food and clothes, how and where to be obtained.

iv) Treatment of casualties (if overt operation, casualties may have to be ignored, if clandestine they may have to be concealed).

v) Transport, if any.

vi) Passes.

vii) Clothes search before operation.

viii) Synchronisation of watches.

ix) Dispersal arrangements, after operation complete.

e) <u>Inter-communication</u>.

Before, during and after an operation, inter-communication between operators (or parties) taking part most important. Consider, therefore, the following:

    i) Password(s) or recognition signal.

    ii) Action signal.

   iii) Cancellation signal.

    iv) General warning.

    v) Individual danger signal.

    vi) Other means of communication.

   vii) Location of leader(s) during operation.

2. <u>GENERAL SECURITY</u>.

Necessary to preserve utmost security throughout, therefore organizer and leaders must observe following, and pass on when necessary:

    i) Issue orders as late as possible.

    ii) Avoid writing down orders, etc.

   iii) Give orders to each operator (or party) separately as far as possible.

    iv) Do not tell anyone more than he needs to know for the operation.

    v) Zero hour to be withheld until last minute.

    vi) Warn operators that plans may have to be cancelled at last minute without assigning reason.

   vii) Ask for questions after orders have been given and have verbal orders repeated back.

  viii) Warning not to meet more than necessary after operation, and avoid showing satisfaction at success.

A.25.
September 1943

FINAL ARRANGEMENTS

(Throughout this lecture students will be asked to make
suggestions about important points and articles which might be
useful.)

1. INTRODUCTION.

Throughout the period prior to departure you should go
over the details of your story and your papers to become
thoroughly conversant with each.

Sometime before your departure make sure that you will take
with you everything that you will require and that there will
be nothing which will not accord with your cover story.

It is necessary to carry out checks in the following order:

2. BODY.

Examine your person carefully.

a) Does cut of hair, moustache, beard, conform to cover story?

b) Does condition of hands, nails, feet, conform to cover
story? E.g. manual workers have horny hands; the feet of
people who have walked long distances show it.

c) Remove nicotine stains from fingers.

3. CLOTHES.

Check carefully:

a) Cut and quality - do they conform to cover story?

b) Are they reasonably worn in?

c) Replace unsuitable labels and remove washing marks.

N.B. Tailor's markings to be avoided but clothes of
foreign origin not necessarily suspicious, much foreign
clothing being imported before the war into territories now
occupied.

d) Footwear - particularly trademarks, etc. Do not overlook
repairs, e.g. rubber heels, etc. Remember that shoes worn
by people having walked long distances show it.

119

4. <u>EFFECTS</u>.

Examine all effects which you wish to take with you, e.g.
watch, rings, note-case, brush, comb, fountain pen, pencil,
cigarettes, cigarette case, cigars and cigar case, tobacco,
tobacco pouch, letters, photographs, etc. Leave behind those
which are of unsuitable manufacture or incongruous. It is
conspicuous to have no effects, so replace them in so far as
may be possible with suitable articles, e.g. those purchased
in places where you are supposed to have been - souvenirs,
letters bearing out your story, etc.

5. <u>HABITS</u>.

Check your personal habits and get others to consider them.
Are they conspicuous? Do they accord with your cover story?
E.g. table manners, way of dressing, handwriting, etc.

6. <u>PAPERS</u>.

These will be perfectly forged, if not genuine; you should
make sure that the details are correct, E.g. age, description,
place of birth, visas, etc.

7. <u>EQUIPMENT</u>.

Check over what equipment you will require. Consider the
following:

a) Map - is it of the sort that you might obtain or be able
   to use in the country to which you are going, or should it
   be destroyed once its immediate purpose has been served?

b) Compass and torch - where were they made? Can you retain
   them, and for how long?

c) First-aid kit, water bottle, flask - is it wise to retain
   these after you have landed?

d) Spade and sacking. These must be thrown away immediately
   after the parachute equipment has been buried. Make sure
   that you have material such as sacking on which to place
   the earth when digging the hole.

e) Suit-case. This should be of common appearance for the
   country to which you are going. Outstanding colour or
   pattern would be conspicuous.

f) Money. Make sure that it is of the kind current, E.g.
   silver coins may have been withdrawn from circulation.
   Useful to have sufficiency of small change. Notes of large

denomination may attract attention, and where can they best be changed?

g) Food. If this does not conform to the country of your destination it must be eaten before you leave the 'plane or left in the 'plane.

h) Any necessary accessories, as may be required according to the projected operation or circumstances.

8. WEAPONS.

a) Do you need a gun? It is generally only helpful when you are engaged in activity for which there can be no cover story, E.g. landing by parachute. At other times it is likely to be an embarrassment. If you take one, decide what to do with it after landing.

b) Other weapons are less suspicious or conspicuous but sometimes equally helpful, e.g. knuckle dusters, loaded sticks, truncheons, etc.

9. DRUGS.

Decide whether you will require any of the following:

a) L. Tablets.
b) K.O. Drops.
c) Benzedrine.
d) E. Capsules.
e) Ptomaine Tablets, etc., etc.

10. FINAL CHECK.

Draw up list of all points and requirements so as to be sure that nothing is forgotten at the moment of departure. Carry out second check a few hours before you leave.

a) Body re-check - do not have excessive hair grease.

b) Clothes re-check - brush out pockets, avoid small pieces of tobacco, etc. Be sure shoes are clean.

c) Effects re-check - search clothes carefully so that articles have not been overlooked, E.g. bus tickets, coins, matches, etc. Has anything slipped through the holes in the lining of pockets?

d) Papers, equipment, weapons, drugs - check all over again; be sure that nothing has been overlooked.

ARRIVAL AND FIRST DAYS

1. ARRIVAL.

An agent may proceed to his country of destination either openly or covertly.

a) Openly.

Important part of cover story so don't prejudice it. Perfect papers and reason for journey are implied. Comply with regulations (immigration controls, customs, etc.) and do not attempt to take compromising material through these controls. It can more safely be supplied later.

b) Covertly.

i) By parachute. Carry out drill as instructed.

ii) By sea. Check position. Methods of concealing or destroying boat. Beware of mines, booby traps, patrols. Move inland by night (prohibited area).

iii) By land. Survey frontier beforehand. Memorize landmarks. N.B. danger of recrossing frontier. Discretion in using services of guide (agent provocateur). Proceed at least 20 kilometres beyond the frontier or to a point beyond the nearest town and then turn back into the town thus appearing to come from the interior. Note: Controls for coastal and frontier areas may be some distance into the interior - not necessarily on the coastline or at the frontier.

2. FIRST STEPS.

a) Movement.

May need to cover considerable distances. In general it is better to move by day except in prohibited areas. If stopped by day it is a routine matter; by night it may lead to serious interrogation.

Tips:

i) Don't move in groups of more than two.

ii) At night all cars, motor-cycles and bicycles are potentially dangerous (facilities granted only to

122

Germans or collaborators). Therefore always hide in this emergency.

   iii) Times to move: beware curfew and dusk hour; best to move at rush hours; special care on market days.

   iv) Avoid long-distance trains and try to break up journey. N.B. If cover permits, travel First Class. Small country stations inadvisable as stranger is conspicuous. Care at large termini and junction stations for regular controls. Possibility of alternative exits.

   v) Do something definite during day, particularly when in towns. Don't hang about.

   vi) Lie low if Allied 'plane shot down or any disturbance (escape, shooting, parachute scare) exists in the vicinity.

   vii) Where possible avoid carrying parcels or suitcases except when they are demanded by your cover.

b) Cover Story.

   i) Explanation of present and recent movements and activities essential (especially while moving from landing point to nearest town).

   ii) Necessary to have arrived from somewhere else. Therefore check the details, E.g. train times, contained in your explanation as soon as possible.

   iii) Clothes, state of shoes, etc. must not belie this cover story.

c) Facing Officials.

In early days avoid contact with officials whenever possible. If meeting face to face with an official, better to approach with a question than to "run away".

d) Obtaining Information.

Seek information unobtrusively all the time re regulations and conditions. Watch particularly for signs of an unusual situation, E.g. state of alert, special controls in force due to disturbances, etc.

3. <u>RECEPTION BY FRIENDS</u>.

    a) If met by reception committee, many initial difficulties disappear.

    b) If not met but supplied with a contact address, make this contact as soon as possible (will give cover, information, possible job, etc.).

        i) When contacting a stranger, do not rely only on name and address. Use a description and if possible a password.

       ii) Check to see that information re contact is up-to-date, E.g. still at address, not under surveillance or "blown".

     iii) Prepare cover story for visit. If possible, make it part of your general cover. If you don't know the man, do not pretend you do.

     iv) Choose time for contact carefully – beware of revealing yourself to other members of family, servants or children, except within your cover.

      v) Always beware of contacting your relatives, particularly your parents, except when they are likely recruits.

     vi) Don't take messages in any circumstances.

4. <u>WHERE TO STAY</u>.

Agent may have to take temporary residence. Choice of place is primarily determined by his cover. Following possibilities should be examined:

    a) <u>Hotel</u>.

    Advantages: crowd, moving population, inconspicuous, gives freedom of movement. Disadvantages: usually watched, danger of informers. "International" hotel is not suitable for protracted stay but smaller hotel may be if cover permits.

    b) <u>Pension</u>.

    Less easily watched by the Police. The disadvantage is lack of freedom of movement and curiosity, gossipings, etc. of boarders. If thoroughly reliable pension-keeper is known, this could be used.

c) <u>Lodging</u>.

Difficult to find and stranger is conspicuous. Land-lady may be curious and report to the Police. If lodging is taken, try to win land-lady's sympathies early by some plausible story.

d) <u>Paying Guest</u>.

Difficult to arrange for temporary residence but is possible for permanent purposes provided the family is unsuspected. They may have to be in the know.

e) <u>Villa</u> (e.g. France or Belgium).

Good for permanent residence; independent, away from outsiders. Better not to live alone; best cover is a woman.

f) <u>Charitable Institutions</u>.

For seamen, etc., but considerable danger of mass arrest.

g) <u>Brothels</u>.

Not considered suitable except in real emergency. Danger of informers and police supervision.

h) <u>Prostitute with Flat</u>.

Possible in emergency and certainly better than brothel. Dangerous type, as they can easily be bought and are police informers.

5. <u>EARLY DAYS</u>.

   a) Lie low and undertake no subversive activity.

   b) Build up your cover - job, recent history. Let your actions constantly create cover.

   c) Check up on documents and C.E. controls.

   d) Look for permanent residence.

   e) Check landing grounds if given instructions on this point.

   f) Make arrangements for communication with W/T operator or other member of organization already on the spot.

   g) Begin survey of area.

All the above will involve obtaining information by use of personal reconnaissance and the informant service that must be established from the outset.

SELECTION OF DROPPING POINTS AND RECEPTION ARRANGEMENTS

1. **INTRODUCTION**.

An organisation, or an individual member of one, may have to call for outside assistance for the successful carrying out of an act of sabotage. Personnel or stores, or both, may be called for and in order to ensure the safe arrival of this help, which will be sent by air, the greatest care must be taken in:

    a) The selection of the Dropping Points – that is, the spot where the stores are to be dropped; and

    b) The arrangements made for the reception of this help on the ground.

Dropping operations will be carried out in bright moonlight at approximately 500 feet, with the aircraft flying at 100-120 miles per hour.

2. **DROPPING POINTS**.

First of all the following general principles, relative to the size and selection of a Dropping Point, must be borne in mind:

    a) An open space not less than 600 yards square, unless it is anticipated that several containers and/or men will be dropped, in which case it should be at least 800 yards square.

    By taking this area the ground would be suitable for any wind direction.

    Avoid agricultural ground:

     i) Injury, especially to ankle.

     ii) Evidence in the form of tracks, damaged crops, etc.

    Avoid swamps.

    Grass parkland is ideal for personnel, but for containers most types of ground will be found suitable.

    Cover should be available in the vicinity for the concealment of personnel or equipment, but an area

completely surrounded by tall trees should be avoided
since there is danger of parachute becoming caught in
them.

b) There should be no H.T. or telegraph wires in the
vicinity.

c) There should be no clumps of trees in the middle of
the Dropping Point. Further for an aircraft to be able
to see the light from 500 feet the latter should be at
least 500 yards from 100 foot trees.

d) If possible, there should be at least one "safe house"
within a mile, but not nearer than a mile, for security
reasons.

e) Allowance must be made for "wind drift". It is estimated
that there is a 60 yards' drift for every 5 miles per
hour increase in the velocity of the wind. This is
estimated for a 'plane flying at the height and speed
previously mentioned. No dropping operation should take
place if the wind speed is over 20 miles per hour.

3. SELECTION.

First stage. There are three main considerations:

a) Safety of the aircraft dropping the stores.

b) The D/P's selected must be easy to recognise at night.

c) Arrangements for reception on the ground must be
considered down to the smallest detail.

a) To ensure the Safety of the Carrying Aircraft

The following main principles should be taken into account:

i) The point should not be near a heavily defended area; a
low flying aircraft immediately becomes vulnerable to
light flak.

Direct lines of approach to such areas should also be
avoided to eliminate danger from night fighters.

Vicinity of enemy aerodromes is highly dangerous and
must be avoided for obvious reasons.

ii) Selected areas should be as level as possible and
although high, mountainous and hilly country should be
avoided, since navigation is difficult, a level plateau
giving the dimensions required can be used.

Valleys are unsuitable unless several miles wide.

If a valley is used, it must be very long and wide for big aircraft, as these gather speed slowly. Thus the aircraft would have to go from 100 m.p.h. to 160 m.p.h. to climb, and this would take several miles if the undercarriage is down. Rising ground and hills should be ten miles away for night dropping (i.e. hills more than 1,000 ft. above dropping point).

iii) The dropping operation must be completed and the 'plane clear of enemy occupied territory during the hours of darkness, so consideration must be given to the distance the site is from the base.

b) <u>The Points Selected Must be Easy to Recognise at Night</u>.

Ease of recognition at night is of paramount importance and upon this depends the whole success of the operation. The following aids and indications to quick recognition will be of the greatest assistance to the pilot for guiding him on the D/P for they can be plainly seen in the moonlight from 2,000 feet, at which height he will begin checking up his position.

i) <u>Coast-line</u>. If possible with breaking surf, as this is easily distinguishable. River mouths over 50 yards wide and sharp promontories jutting out into the sea, and inlets are also good guides.

ii) <u>Rivers and Canals</u>. Both give moon reflection which will prove a helpful indication. Wooded banks reduce the reflection very considerably, but generally speaking the width of a river used for indication should be not less than 30 yards wide. Canals need not be so wide as this for they may be easily picked up by their straightness.

Danger of confusion if more than one river. Best to have one solitary river.

Small streams are no good whatsoever.

(The Germans, flying at 6,000 to 7,000 feet, followed the line of the Thames from Oxford on their nightly raids on London.)

iii) <u>Large Lakes</u> - not less than half a mile square. Here, too, light reflection is the indication. Small ponds are quite useless. Care required if two or more lakes of same size.

iv) <u>Forest and Woodland</u>. To be of any use as a guide
these should have clearly defined boundaries or be of
unmistakable shape and at least half a mile square.
Note age of map in case of recent falling.

Irregular patches of woodland are useless.

v) <u>Straight Roads</u>. Stretches of main road, straight
for at least one mile, and especially one or more
intersecting, give quite a good indication; more so
when the road is wet. A series of puddles along the
length of a road have been found to be of considerable
use. Crooked and winding roads and minor roads are
practically useless.

vi) <u>Railways</u>. Of little use except during the winter
months when there is snow on the ground when a main
line cuts out a black ribbon running through the white
landscape.

vii) <u>Towns</u>. If subject to black-out, towns are of little
use unless fairly large, say 20,000 inhabitants. The
possibility of a town larger than this being heavily
defended must not be overlooked.

It is apparent, then, that expanses of water are the
best indication for quick recognition in darkness, and
that small features, such as churches, water-towers,
villages, etc. are of no use whatsoever.

The ideal is to have a combination of features,
and in this case a railway may be quite a valuable
indication.

It is important to remember that the final point of
indication should not be more than three kilometres
from the actual D/P

The D/P itself will be marked by a system of ground
lighting which will be more fully explained. (Here
explain present operational system.)

<u>Second Stage</u>:

It is essential that the air point of view must take
precedence in site selection for it is the pilot who has to
locate the dropping point.

This "bird's eye view" is best given by the study of a map.
It is important that the site be selected first of all
from the map and then checked for suitability by personal

reconnaissance. Several points should be chosen, perhaps as many as twenty or thirty.

A large-scale map will give much of the information desired:

a) Contours, from which can be calculated gradients.

b) Nature of ground, marsh, woodland, heathland, etc.

c) Extent of possible sites.

d) Houses in the vicinity.

e) High tension wire.

f) Expanses of water, rivers, canals, etc.

In fact, it will straight away give you all the important features which can be used as indications for ease of recognition and much information relative to actual suitability.

As soon as it can be foreseen in which area any particular agent will be working, a number of points will be selected from maps/air photographs which appear suitable as D/P's for supplies or/personnel. Agent will then on his arrival recce these points for suitability and report.

These points will be given a code reference consisting of the first three letters of the code name allotted to the agent, followed by a number.

These points will be studied and memorised by the agent before departure.

If all points chosen before departure are unsuitable, the agent will continue his recce until he does find suitable points, and then advise H.Q. of their exact location.

In reporting D/P location, conventional map reference will be used: (27's and 13's only: explain Michelin map reference system).

c) <u>Reception Arrangements</u>.

The operation must be carried out in fairly bright moonlight and the period suitable for dropping is limited to five or six days on either side of the full moon. Certain D/P's, especially if inside 20 miles of the coastline, may be used for longer periods during the month.

The organisation should study on what nights the reception committee can stand by, and in view of uncertainties at least five consecutive nights are advisable, but whichever five nights are chosen the reception committee must be there on all five.

When help is called for, Headquarters should be given approximately fourteen days' grace in which to make their arrangements.

The reception committee is responsible for the disposal of any containers.

Six men may conveniently handle a container, but it is not necessary to provide that number _per_ container if the men understand their job. Each member of the party should be equipped with gloves as carrying becomes painful owing to thinness of handles.

If there is a deep lake or river near the D/P, the container may be conveniently disposed of there.

If it is to be buried a suitable burying point should have been chosen beforehand, and if possible holes dug.

Always remember disposal of outer container must be permanent.

In order to ease carrying of cells, a strap or rope may be used to string them on a man's back. In this way one man can carry one cell without much difficulty or fatigue.

THE NAZI PARTY AND ITS ORGANISATIONS

1. ## GENERAL

A German newspaper account of any official function nearly always includes the phrase "representative of Party, State and Wehrmacht were present", these being the three main bodies in Germany which exercise authority and maintain armed organisations, namely:

> Party - Nazi party and its Organisations.
> State - the German Police Organisation.
> Wehrmacht - the German Armed Forces.

Each of these three bodies is directly responsible to Hitler.

2. ## THE NAZI PARTY

The main principle of Nazi rule is the Fuhrerprinzip or "Leader Principle". On this principle the leader has the right to govern, administer or decree, subject to no control and responsible only to his own conscience. It applies in the first instance to Hitler, Leader of the Party, and in a lesser degree to all other Party Leaders; for them it is modified in so far as a lower leader is responsible to a higher.

The Leader Principle, introduced into Germany and developed there by Hitler and his immediate associates, gives them the right to almost anything. Since, however, so few people cannot administer a state of, at present, 80 million inhabitants, they need a numerous and well-organised Administrative "Followership". This Administrative "Followership" is the Party.

The Party is and will remain a minority of the German people; it consists of between 4 and 6 million members. Membership was closed in 1933, soon after Hitler's advent to power. Since then except for more prominent individuals specially desired, membership is open only to young Germans graduating up from Hitler Youth. (Party Member - Parteigenosse or Pg.)

Function of the Party is to be political soldiers, i.e. to maintain and spread Nazi ideology and Nazi behaviour throughout German population and to see that the activities of the ordinary German, both private and professional, are run

on Nazi lines; furthermore, to control the State organisation
so that it becomes and remains National-Socialist.

The task is carried out by:

(a) The Reichsleitung or Party Cabinet, consisting of 23 members.

(b) The Order of Political Leaders (politischer Fuhrerorden),
which comprises all party members who hold some office in
the Party administration.

(c) The Formations (Gliederungen) - semi-militarised bodies
run by the Party.

(d) Affiliated Organisations (angeschlossene Verbande) -
massed formations whose leaders are supplied by the Party
from suitable Party members. They are intended to cover
all trade and professional associations.

Note: The Party proper, the formations and the affiliated
organisations together are called "Die Bewogung" (The
Movement). The Movement comprises the whole of the
German people.

3. REICHSLEITUNG

The administration of the Party. Shaping and formation of its
policy are carried out by Reichs-leadership (Reichsleitung)
which has numerous departments for the various aspects
of Party's work and interests, e.g. press, schooling,
propaganda, etc.

4. ORDER OF POLITICAL LEADERS.

This covers all Germany geographically and penetrates down
to each German individual. The territorial organisation is as
follows:

a. Gau. Approximates to a province. 42 of them covering whole
of Reich. Chief of each is a Gauleiter who is responsible
for all Party activity in his Gau, excluding the formations.
There is also an administrative board (Gauleitung) similar
to, though smaller than, the Reichsleitung.

b. Kreis. Each Gau is subdivided into districts (Kreise)
each managed by a Kreisleiter and an administrative board
(Kreisleitung). There are over 822 Kreise in Germany.

c. Ortsgruppe. Each Kreis is subdivided into local groups
(Ortsgruppen), each controlling a medium-sized town or
suburb of a large town. Managed by an Ortsgruppenleiter

and an administrative board (Ortsgruppenleitung). There are over 28,000 in Germany (c.f. - v.s. ward).

d. Zelle. Each Ortsgruppe is subdivided into numbers of cells (Zellen), each controlling a parish and managed by a Zellenleiter, who, unlike the officials mentioned above, is not a full-time paid official and has no administrative apparatus apart from three minor officials. There are 93,000 Zellen in Germany (Parish).

e. Block. Each Zelle is divided into Blocks, each controlling approx. 40 households and managed by a Blockwalter who is also a part-time political worker. There are about 482,000 Blocks in Germany.

Blocks are sometimes divided into several house-groups (Hausgruppen), each controlling 8 to 15 households. There is no official title for the Party member in charge of a Hausgruppe.

Functions of the Blockwalter.

i) To act as a sort of "political priest" to the 40 or 50 houses under his charge, ensuring that their thinking and their behaviour are on Nazi lines.

ii) Seeing that they all vote at elections.

iii) Reporting any misdemeanour of a political nature.

iv) Reporting monthly on anything he thinks important in the attitude of the population, e.g. grumbling at new regulations, injustices in the social order, waxing and waning of enthusiasm for the regime, etc, etc. These monthly reports are sent in by all Blockwalter throughout the Reich to their Zellen where they are consolidated and go upwards to the Ortsgruppen etc., until the Party leadership has a complete picture of the sentiments of the population.

Thus the Party leadership:

a. Keeps its fingers on the pulse of the German people.

b. Has a most useful spy network to ensure its fidelity.

c. Gives work to a great number of bureaucrats, so that a considerable and influential section of the population has a direct personal interest in the maintenance of the regime.

<u>Uniform</u> of Political Leaders is brown tunic and riding-breeches worn over brown shirt with black riding-boots. It differentiates from the S.A. uniform by:

a. Black tie instead of brown.

b. Flat military-style cap with a brown velvet band round it as opposed to the S.A. kepi.

c. Ortsgruppenleiter upwards wear golden belts.

<u>Occupied Territories</u>. This organisation has only been introduced into occupied territories which have been incorporated into the Reich proper. In districts which the Nazis intend to keep permanently without incorporating them into the Reich proper, a slightly modified Party organisation for Germans is being built up. Quisling governments of occupied countries are trying to copy the German system in their own countries - e.g. Norway.

5. <u>FORMATIONS OF THE PARTY</u>.

The formations have been developed by the Party for particular purposes - mostly military or semi-military ones. Their leadership and finances are closely connected with those of the Party. Apart from a large proportion of Party members, they contain a few million other Germans.

a. Sturmabteilung. (S.A. or Brown-shirts)

The highest leader of the S.A. is Hitler himself. His deputy for the S.A. is Chief of Staff of the S.A. It is organised into groups (Gruppen). As a rule each party covers a Gau. The groups are divided into Brigades (Brigaden), these into Regiments (Standarten), these into Battalions (Sturmbann), these into companies (Sturm) etc. Origin of this body was a number of young ruffians whom Rohm organised for Hitler in the early days of the movement to protect Party meetings from Communist interruptions and to break up Communist meetings, etc.

After Party-Army crisis of June, 1934, S.A. only supplied the background on all Party occasions, but since January, 1939, it has been entrusted with the task of giving pre and post-military training.

Membership in the S.A. can be obtained quite easily. Except for highest ranks, staffs and one or two administrative N.C.O's in every unit down to Sturmbann, service is part-time; members earn their living during the day and wear uniforms and do training in spare time. Down to the rank of Standartenfuhrer, S.A. leaders are employed on a full-time basis and a minority of junior S.A. officers earmarked for further promotion are also serving in the same way. Membership amounts to about 3 million.

Since outbreak of war, majority of S.A. have been called up for military service. Those who remain guard P/W camps, etc.

<u>Uniform</u>. Brown breeches; brown tie; black or brown riding boots; brown kepi-type hat with coloured band indicating district of origin; sometimes a brown tunic. They carry a decorative dagger usually no other weapons.

<u>Occupied Territories</u>. S.A units of ordinary pattern have been formed in all territories which now officially form part of Germany proper. In those territories which are now getting the amended special form of Party organisation (Poland, etc.) S.A. units are also set up. Nothing has been reported up to now about the formation of S.A. units in countries the occupation of which is only supposed to have been temporary. On the other hand, Hirdmen in Norway and N.S.B. men in Holland are local equivalent of the S.A. in Germany.

b. <u>N.S.K.K. (National-Sozialistisches Kraftfahrer-Korps)</u>.

This formation has been entrusted with the "motorisation" of the German people; also with the pre- and post-military training of Germans who desire to service or have served in the motorised branches of the Army. The only difference in organisation between the N.S.K.K. and S.A. is that the Sturmbann of the N.S.K.K. is called Staffel and the supreme leader Korpsfuhrer.

<u>Uniform</u>. Same as S.A., except that black breeches are worn instead of brown; black F.S. caps with N.S.K.K. eagle on side; brown tunic with N.S.K.K. badges. Sometimes a brown kepi-type hat like that of the S.A. is worn instead of the F.S. cap. The N.S.K.K. kepi always has a black band and, instead of the ordinary eagle, the special N.S.K.K. eagle is worn on it.

Note: N.S.K.K. have been seen in:

i) Tunics of army pattern with brown N.S.K.K. collars and black F.S. caps with N.S.K.K. eagle on side of cap as well as on the upper left sleeve.

ii) Blue Luftwaffe uniforms but with N.S.K.K. badges.

Occupied Territories. Since war, N.S.K.K. have been taken over in bulk, together with their leaders (not individually as in the case of the S.A.) and are used very widely wherever the German army makes its appearance. Besides doing technical transport work, they are partly used as messengers, dispatch riders, and sometimes even as traffic policemen.

Belgium and Holland appear to be the only occupied countries in which non-German people have been recruited into the N.S.K.K.

c. **N.S.F.K. National-Sezsolistisches Flieger Korps)**.

Was formed from the D.L.S. Verbande in 1939. Is controlled by German Air Ministry but organised like the other formations. It gives pre- and post-aviation training. Close co-operation between the N.S.F.K. and air units of the H.J.

Uniform. Same cut as S.A. with brown shirt, but breeches, tunic and cap (beret) are air-force blue.

Occupied Territories. Not employed.

d. **SS (Schutzstaffel or Black Guards)**.

Originally formed as the elite of S.A., i.e. higher standards for height and physical fitness; also for "political reliability". Since Hitler's advent to power, have been split into professional and part-time sections. Have great prestige and authority as elite of Nazi movement.

Head of SS is Heinrich Himmler - Reichfuhrer SS.

i) **Allgemeine SS** (ordinary SS)

Part-time organisation. Number approx. 250,000. Reservoir for armed SS, SD and ordinary police forces. Organised in:

Oberabschnitt - corresponds to Wehrkreis.
Abschnitt - division.
Standarte - Regiment
Sturmbann - Battalion.
Sturm - Company.

ii) **SS Verfugungstruppe** (SS auxiliary troops).

Full-time organisation serving for 4 years but belonging neither to police nor army; in fact a sort of private army whose primary function is to ensure internal security. Young Germans due for military service can, if desired and if physically and politically suitable, volunteer for the SS. Serve for 4 years instead of 2. They are organised into 4 regiments.

SS Leibstandarte Adolf Hitler (Hitler's Bodyguard)
SS Standarte Deutschland.
SS Standarte Der Fuhrer.
SS Standarte Germania.

They have their own artillery, recce units, transport and supporting arms. They undergo full military training and are equipped as motorised forces. Besides being used in peace-time as a "show" guard on high state occasions, they were garrisoned so that in the event of civil dissensions they could act quickly.

iii) <u>Totenkopfverbande</u> (Death's Head Units).

Formed as concentration camp guards; completely militarised; service is for 12 years.

Since outbreak of war, special SS Divisions have been formed from the Verfugungstruppe and the Totenkopfverbande. These divisions, which are all motorised, are known as the "Waffen SS". They are:

  i. SS Division Adolf Hitler (motorised).
 ii. SS Division Das Reich (motorised).
iii. SS Totenkopf Division (motorised).
 iv. SS Ritter Brigade (cavalry).
  v. SS Viking Division (motorised; Norwegian, Danish, Finnish, Belgian, Dutch volunteers with German strengthening).
 vi. SS Polizei Division (not motorised; recruited from the Schutzpolizei and the Allgemeine SS).

Since the outbreak of war, many new specialist units including

A.A., Alpine troops etc. have been set up within the framework of the Armed SS. In all, there appear to be 9 divisions of SS.

<u>Uniform - Peace</u>. Black uniform (breeches, tunic and military cap) over brown shirt; this is today worn by

non-militarised SS. Death's head is worn on centre of the
cap. On right collar patch the SS sign is worn and on left
collar patch the wearer's rank. A band worn round left cuff
will give number of company or name of regiment.

Uniform - War. On active service the SS Divisions wear the
field-grey uniform of the German army except:

   i. The Hohheitsabzeichen is not worn on right breast but
     on upper left sleeve.

  ii. Collar patches are black with SS insignia.

 iii. Shoulder straps carry ordinary army badges of rank.

Occupied Territories

   i. Besides fighting as elite front-line troops, the SS
     are called upon if troubles arise or are met with
     in occupied territories. They co-operate with the
     Verfugungspolizei.

  ii. German SS men in black uniforms will be seen here and
     there in occupied territories. They will probably be
     high SS officers attached to German administrative
     services or high police officials in their peace-time
     uniform. Waffen SS have been known to wear their black
     uniform off duty.

 iii. SS organisations have been set up in some occupied
     territories. Among them are both Allgemeine and Waffen
     SS. Among the latter are the Norwegian Regiment
     "Nordland", the Dutch Regiment "Westland" and the
     Danish, Dutch and Flemish Kreikorps as well as some
     Finnish units. Among the former are the Allgemeine
     SS in Norway, the Netherlands and the Schut Scharen
     Vlaanderens. The German press now uses frequently the
     term "Germanische SS" **to** indicate that these SS units
     do not serve their respective quisling governments
     but in the first place Germany - a fact which is also
     stressed by the oath of allegiance which they swear to
     Hitler.

e. Hitler Juaend (H.J.)

Every German child, male or female, must join the Hitler
Youth at the age of 10. The official organisation for boys
is called the Deutsches Jungvolk and that for girls the
Deutsches Jungmadel.

At the age of 14 the children are transferred to the H.J. proper or the B.D.M. (Bund Deutscher Madchen). The H.J. is organised on a regional basis within the Reich. A Gebiet (usually covering one Gau) is divided into Banne (usually one or two to every Kreis). The Banne are divided into about ten Stamme (450 boys per Stamm). These are divided into lower formations, the lowest being a Rotte (3-5 boys). They do semi-military training and learn National-Socialist doctrine.

Through this organisation the Germans control the juvenile labour in Germany.

Bannfuhrer upwards (H.J. leaders) are employed full-time.

Hitler Youth is divided into H.J. ordinary, naval, motorised, cavalry and flying.

The girls stay in the B.D.M. up to the age of 21.

At 18 the boys leave the H.J. and go into the Labour Service.

f. Reichsarbeitsdienst (R.A.D).

Consists of 6 months' training prior to military service, military discipline and weapon training; largely engaged on land reclamation etc. Since the war they are found in occupied countries building aerodromes etc. R.A.D. building battalions are also used in close connection with the fighting units of the Army and Air Force.

Uniform - Working. Light grey overalls.

Uniform - Walking-Out. Dark khaki uniform with jacket cut similar to officer's tunic.

Red armlet carrying a swastika worn on left arm.

The building battalions wear steel helmets with the Army or Air force eagle.

6. AFFILIATED ORGANISATIONS

They are intended to represent all public and private activities, thus replacing all organisations, political or non-political, which existed before 1933. All the important and most of the unimportant jobs in them are held by Party members. Each affiliated organisation is controlled by a department of the Party organisation. E.g. all teachers are organised in the N.S. Lehrerbund, all workers in the Deutsche

Arbeitsfront etc, etc. Membership is not compulsory but a
man would not find work unless he was a member of one of the
organisations.

7. <u>THE GERMAN'S PROGRESS</u>

The progression of a German from his childhood is therefore
through the following bodies which govern his activity and
shape his thinking:

a) <u>Jungvolk</u> from 10-14 years.

b) <u>Hitler Jugend</u> from 14-18 years.

c) <u>Arbeitsdienst</u> from six months before military service.

d) <u>Military Service</u> for 2 years (or 4 years in the SS).

e) <u>Professional Organisation</u> during his working hours.

f) <u>S.A., SS. N.S.K.K. or N.S.F.K</u>. during his spare time.

Much care is being taken about schooling Germany's future Nazi
leaders. Specially selected boys are sent to schools where
they are given the ordinary education with a good deal of
raciology, politics and military training added to it. (Adolf
Hitler-Schulen and Nationalpolitische Erziehung-sanstalten;
the latter always and the former more recently supervised
by a high SS officer.) If a boy has shown great promise up
to the time of leaving school, labour service and military
service, he will, after a short time in the lower spheres of
the Party organisation, be sent to a "Schulungsburg" of the
Party to be trained to become a higher leader.

In this way, the Nazis control the German population and,
through the Hitler Schools, hope that they have laid the
foundation of the continuance of Nazi rule in Germany.

That the Nazi system is not only rather new but also rather
unnatural, and is certainly not the result of anything innate
in the German people, is shown by the safeguards that the
Party leaders have had to devise for it. For example, they
have founded the most powerful and all-embracing police and
spy organisation the world has ever known. This organisation
could not, of course, be kept outside politics; it could not
function as a detached (and professional) State authority.
It has, as we shall see in our study of the German police
organisation, to be brought into the closest contact with the
organisations of the Party.

GERMAN POLICE SERVICE AND ITS ORGANISATIONS

INTRODUCTION.

There are four Police and Security Services which are dangerous
to our agents:

1. German Civil Police.
2. National Police of student's own country.
3. German Intelligence Service.
4. German Military Police.

GENERAL

It is clear from our study of the Nazi Party that the conception
of the Nazi-controlled state is based on a very simple principle
– i.e. the maintenance of the authority of a dictator who has
supreme power and is responsible to no one but himself by:

1. ruthless elimination of all political opponents.
2. ensuring that all actions and thoughts of citizens
        both in their professional and private lives accord
        with Nazi doctrine.

With the police force of the traditional democratic set-up,
competence and outlook, this cannot be achieved.

HISTORICAL SUMMARY.

Under the Weimar Republic each State had its own uniformed
police force. In addition, there existed everywhere a special
police force called the "Politische Polizei", a branch of the
Kriminalpolizei, for dealing with foreigners and with those
political forces inside Germany which were openly or in secret
aiming at the overthrow of the Constitution. It had a very
restricted scope and was not very efficient.

The Nazi plans included, therefore, the unifying and nazifying
of the uniformed police and the formation of a nucleus for a
future super State police force.

There already existed inside the Nazi party a few spying and
information services. One of these was formed from the ranks of
the SS and developed rapidly after Heydrich had been appointed
its leader in 1932. He later admitted officially that already in
those days the Sicherheitsdienst (S.D. - Security Service), as

this SS branch was called, prepared itself for the future tasks of staffing the coming super police force.

When Hitler came into power in <u>1933</u> the careful preparatory work done by Heydrich and his colleagues was put into practice. The Nazis knew everything about their opponents; and, with comprehensive black-lists and executive power on their side, they were able to reduce their political opponents to utter ruin.

This state of affairs, however, could only be maintained and extended if the work, so far done by a small faction of SS - namely, the S.D. - was perpetuated and officialised - in a word, if the super police force planned for such a long time was organised. This was started without delay.

In Spring, 1933, Himmler was made head of the Munich Police and, under him, Heydrich head of the Political Police Section in that town. Within a few weeks he had restaffed his forces from the S.D. and wholly reorganised their work and procedure.

Also in 1933 a secret State Police Force, the "Gestapo", with extensive powers, was formed by Goering in Prussia. After a year of intrigue, Himmler persuaded Goering to appoint him Deputy Chief of the Prussian Gestapo and, soon afterwards, in all the provinces of Germany he extended his activities to the control of the old political police by the process of "infiltration". S.D. members and the Nazi aristocracy took the place of any but the most co-operative officials. By this process of "infiltration" the influence on the police of the party and central executive was increased, and that of federal authorities weakened. A decree of Jan. 1934 finally subordinated the federal authorities and with them the federal police to the Reich Government.

In 1936 Hitler created by decree a new post of "Chief of the German Police in the Reich Ministry of the Interior", to which Himmler, the chief of the SS, was appointed. He is thus the chief of Polizei in Reichsministerium der Innern; and thus combines State and Party functions.

The description which follows of the detailed organisation of the various branches of police will reveal even more clearly than a historical account the extent of the control which is exercised by the small inner circle of the "chosen" over the millions of ordinary German citizens. It will also prepare the student for the spirit in which the German police has played and is playing its part in the Nazification of Europe.

Himmler divided the police functions into those of:

A. <u>CONSTABULARY</u> (Ordnungspolizei - Orpo) under Generaloberst der Polizei Daluge.

    1. Town Constabulary (Schutzpolizei - Schupo).
    2. Barrack Police (Kasernierte Polizei).
    3. Rural Police (Gendarmerie).
    4. Motorised Gendarmerie (Motorisierte Gendarmerie).
    5. Railway Police (Bahnschutzpolizei).
    6. Water Police (Wasserschutzpolizei).
    7. Technical Emergency Corps (Technische Nothilfe - Teno).
    8. Auxiliary Police (Hilfspolizei).

B. <u>SECURITY POLICE</u> (Sicherheitspolizei - Sipo) under Ernst Kaltenbrunner.

    1. Criminal Police (Kriminalpolizei - Kripo).
    2. Secret State Police (Geheime Staatspolizei - Gestapo).
    3. Security Service (Sicherheitsdienst - SD).

A. <u>CONSTABULARY</u>

1. <u>Town Constabulary</u> (Schutzpolizei).

    a. <u>Duties</u>. Employed generally in Germany. Performs ordinary patrol and traffic duties and is generally responsible for law and order. Semi-military body.

    b. <u>Organisation</u>. In large towns Schupo are organised into Groups, Districts and Sections. Groups exist only in Berlin, Hamburg and Vienna; and a small town may only have a section.

    c. <u>Uniform</u>. <u>Greenish field-grey</u> uniform with brown cuffs and collar and a shako. Black riding boots or leggings. Black equipment. The official police emblem (the eagle and swastika, enclosed in and resting on a wreath of oak leaves) is worn on left sleeve and on centre of shako (or field cap and steel helmet, when worn).

    <u>Note</u>: The old dark blue tunic and black breeches are still worn, especially by reservists posted to the Town Police to replace the serving police who have been sent to occupied territory. Reservists in blue uniform have occasionally been seen in occupied territory.

2. <u>Barrack Police</u> (Kasernierte Polizei).

    a. <u>Duties in Occupied Territory</u>. Barrack Police to date are only working in <u>Norway. Holland and Poland</u>. There are none in France and Belgium. Besides their main function of dealing with civil disorder, they are used for a variety of tasks – e.g. suppression of guerrilla bands, searches for illegal arms, transfer of population, escorting prisoners or others going to compulsory work, protection of German L. of C. etc. Much of their work demands close co-operation with G.F.P., F.G., Gestapo and S.D.

b. <u>Organisation</u>. Are really a section of the Town Constabulary. They are organised into Battalions and live in barracks. These battalions are generally organised into Regiments – three bns. per regt.; one regt. per district. In the case of Poland, these regiments are given the name of their district – e.g. Polizeiregiment Warsaw. The regiments are either stationed in the chief town of the district or scattered in the larger towns – e.g. Polizeiregiment Lublin: the Regt. H.Q. is at Lublin, and the battalions are in Lublin, Chelm and Zamosc.

Apart from these regiments, there is usually a certain number of independent battalions. The organisation and equipment of the police regiments and battalions are similar to those of equivalent units of motorised infantry. The strength of a battalion is 500-700 men. In every regiment and independent battalion there have been created so-called Polizei-Jagdzuge, composed of 40-50 men, specially trained and equipped, with lorries and motor-cycles. These platoons are always in a state of immediate readiness.

c. <u>Uniform</u>. Greenish field-grey uniform of Germany Army pattern but with dark brown collar and cuffs with two silver buttons on each cuff. The national emblem is not worn at all, but the police badge (a large laurel wreath enclosing an eagle with outstretched wings) is worn on the upper left sleeve and on front of field service cap. Rank badges on shoulder straps are same as for the army.

d. <u>Training</u>. Recruits receive political, as well as intensive military and police training – especially in street fighting and guerrilla warfare.

3. <u>Rural Constabulary</u> (Gendarmerie)

a. <u>Duties</u>. Their duties are those of a rural constabulary.

b. <u>Organisation</u>. The Gendarmerie operate in areas where there are no Schupo.

c. <u>Uniform</u>. Is same as for the Town Constabulary, but their boots, leggings and equipment are brown instead of black.

4. <u>Motorised Police</u>. (Motorisierte Gendarmerie).

   a. <u>Duties</u>. They control traffic on ordinary roads and on Autobahnen. They have in this war been employed occasionally in occupied territory on traffic control and prevention of sabotage in rear areas.

   b. <u>Organisation</u>. Really a branch of the Gendarmerie. They are a semi-military body and fully motorised.

   c. <u>Uniform</u>. Uniform is same as for Schupo, but in addition they wear a narrow armband on left arm with the words "Motorisierte Gendarmerie".

5. <u>Railway Police</u>. (Bahnschutzpolizei).

   a. <u>Duties</u>. Protection of stations and railway junctions, railway workshops, transport – whether stationary or on the move – railway bridges; suppression of illegal transport of food etc.; control of passengers.

   b. <u>Organisation</u>. Organised into Bahnschutzwachen, which operate at railway stations.

   c. <u>Uniform</u>. The position is not at all clear. Recent information suggests three different uniforms:

      i. Old blue railway police uniform.
      ii. Same but in field grey.
      iii. Waffen SS uniform with an armband – "SS Bahnschutz".

   d. <u>Method</u>. In carrying out these tasks the Bahnschutzwachen are aided by guarding units of the Army, SS or police battalions; though, in Western Europe, the National Police of the particular country is responsible for Railway Police work.

6. <u>Water Police.</u> (Wasserschutzpolizei.)

   a. <u>Duties</u>. It performs invaluable and multifarious duties, both as normal harbour police and as port security and control police, in conjunction with the Security Services.

   b. <u>Organisation</u>. The Water Police are organised on inland waterways and at ports throughout the Reich. They also provide personnel for coast-guard service (Marine-Kustenpolizei – MKP) which is stationed along the whole coastline of occupied Europe, on the Danube and elsewhere.

   c. <u>Uniform</u>. Water Police wear a dark blue uniform with a reefer jacket and blue peaked cap. The coastguards wear same uniform but in addition a yellow armband (Wehrmachtsband).

7. <u>Technical Emergency Corps</u> (Technische Nothilfe).

   a. <u>Duties</u>. Restore vital communications, fit lighting installations, repair broken-down machinery, etc.

   b. <u>Organisation</u>. Formed as auxiliary corps of technical experts to deal with break-down of public services. Teno commandos have been sent to occupied territories to work with Armed Forces. They are under the orders of the Police Commander.

   c. <u>Uniform</u>. In Germany, dark blue uniform; abroad, army pattern uniform with narrow armband eight inches from the bottom of the left sleeve, bearing in white on a dark background the words "Techische Nothilfe".

8. <u>Auxiliary Police</u> (Hilfspolizei)

   a. <u>Duties</u>. To help the uniformed police.

   b. <u>Organisation</u>. In the early part of the war, auxiliary Police were enrolled in Berlin in Battalions. Since then German nationals living in conquered countries have been enrolled for part-time duties with Police. In addition, in Holland and Poland, for example, Dutch and Poles have been recruited for the same purpose.

   c. <u>Uniform</u>. Generally the same as ordinary Schupo uniform; but this varies in different countries.

B. <u>SECURITY POLICE</u>

1. <u>Criminal Police</u> (Kriminalpolizei - Kripo)

   a. <u>Duties</u>. The specific task of the Kripo is the detection and prevention of crime so long as it has no political motive. Is not employed in Western Europe, but is working in Poland.

   b. <u>Organisation</u>. Criminal Police stations (Kripostellen) exist in all main towns and districts. In rural districts or small towns the nearest Kripostelle directs the work through the Gendarmerie.

   c. <u>Uniform</u>. Its members are plain-clothes men.

2. <u>Secret State Police</u> (Geheime Staatspolizei - Gestapo).

   a. <u>Duties</u>. These vary in individual countries, but in the main are:

     i. Discovering and destroying all forces, either organised or not, which are acting or may act to the detriment of the National Socialist Party, the State or the German nation.

   ii. Keeping a check on and selecting the directing personnel in all spheres of state and national life.

 iii. Enforcing rules and orders regulating the flow of economic and political life.

b. <u>Organisation</u>. H.Q. are in Berlin, in Colombia House, Prinz Albrechtstrasse. The Gestapo has three main departments which work in close co-operation yet possess an individual authority.

<u>Abteilung I</u>. Organisation and administration of the Gestapo. Security of Government offices. Central card index and supervision of concentration camps.

<u>Abteilung II</u>. Handles political matters connected with the security of the Party and State. It watches the activities of all opposition movements (e.g. Communists and Social Democrats, Freemasons, Churches, etc.)

<u>Abteilung III</u>. Contre-espionage. Subdivided into three main departments: East, West and South; each of which has subsections specialising in one or more countries. In occupied territory it regulates and controls political life and all social activities; combats all symptoms of national political life – secret organisations, underground press etc. – and sees to the loyalty of all Germans living in the country. It also watches people in key positions.

c. <u>Territorial Organisation in Germany</u>. Gestapo Officers are organised under the following terms, shown in order of importance:

   i. Staatspolizeileitstelle (Stapolste) – provincial office.
  ii. Staatspolizeistelle (Staposte) – larger towns.
 iii. Aussenstelle – works under Staposte.
  iv. Grenzdienstelle – frontier posts.

In villages where police are represented by one single constable, he has to look after Gestapo as well. Gestapo officials may interfere or take over if they wish to do so.

d. <u>Occupied Territory</u>. The organisation of the Gestapo is not rigid but will be adapted to suit local conditions. The important bureaux or Stellen work openly, but they direct and control other posts which are secret. These secret posts will vary in number according to the density of the population, the importance of the area and the amount of underground activity.

e. <u>How the Gestapo Works</u>.

    i. It works through a network of agents recruited from all sections of the population. National minorities are widely used.

    ii. It collates their reports and the results of their observations. (Black lists.)

    iii. It card-indexes and watches all outstanding individuals from all spheres of activity (police, mayors, industrialists etc).

    iv. Provocation (creation of secret pro-allied organisations).

    v. Penetration.

    vi. Mass arrests - from black lists, special lists of professions etc.

    vii. Terror - torture, reprisals.

f. The Gestapo is above the law. Its activities cannot be challenged or investigated. They are summarily covered by the authority or the State - e.g. protective custody without trial.

g. <u>Personnel</u>. All Gestapo officials were at one time highly trained, but since the occupation of such large hostile areas considerable expansion has been necessary. The newcomers to the force are of poorer quality and untrained. It is believed that non-Germans have been recruited into the Gestapo (France).

h. <u>Conclusion</u>. The Gestapo has had to rely more and more on the use of traitors and methods of terrorism, corruption and bribery. Without traitors it would be practically ineffective. Corruption is spreading to the Gestapo itself.

i. <u>Uniform</u>.

<u>Peace-time</u>. Plain clothes or black SS uniform.

<u>War-time</u>. Field-grey uniform with an open collar worn with brown shirt and tie; collar patches like the Waffen SS and the SS rank badges, while the shoulder straps carry the ordinary military rank indications. As for the Waffen SS, the Hoheitsabzeichen is worn on the left sleeve, and on the left sleeve just above the cuff there is the same black band with white lettering as on the black uniform.

3. Frontier Police (Grenzpolizei).

   a. Duties. Checking the infiltration of dangerous influences, in the form of news, persons and clandestine supplies etc. Censorship of written material coming from abroad other than by post. Frontier guards are assisted by Orpo for control of passes and patrol service.

   b. Organisation. The control of the Frontier Police which is part of the Sipo, is in fact the responsibility of the Gestapo. They are organised in motor-cycle and pedal-cycle squads (Staffeln). Control is exercised from the local Gestapo station, via the Frontier Police Commissariats, to Frontier Police Posts. Frontier guards who man Frontier Police Commissariats etc. are mainly SS men.

   c. Uniform. SS uniform with narrow armlet bearing the word "Grenzpolizei", and are armed with revolvers, carbines, tommy-guns and light machine-guns.

4. Security Service (Sicherheitsdienst - SD)

   a. Duties. It appears that its work is divided into three main branches:

      i. Study and penetration of all political movements which may prove useful or hostile to National Socialism.

      ii. Contre-espionage, contre-sabotage and contre-propaganda work of all kinds, and in particular the prevention and detection of corruption among German officials.

      iii. Espionage in neutral allied countries not completely under German control - e.g. Hungary and Vichy France.

      It would appear that the S.D. does same work as the Gestapo, but on a higher level. It may be that it actually directs the Gestapo work. It is certain that it is even more dangerous, as its personnel is composed of specially selected members of the S.S.

   b. Organisation. Although we know little enough of the activities of the S.D., an efficient organisation is known to exist in each of the occupied countries.

      When Himmler took over the whole of the German Police in 1936, he restaffed it with men from the S.D.; but the S.D. itself still continued. It was co-ordinated in its work and administration with the Gestapo. Both were incorporated in the Sicherheitspolizei, whose chief was Heydrich.

c. <u>Uniform in War-time</u>. As for the Gestapo, but, in addition, a diamond-shaped black tab with the letters S.D. in white is worn on the bottom of the left sleeve.

NATIONAL POLICE OF STUDENT'S OWN COUNTRY.

All available information on the national police of the Student's particular country will be given.

GERMAN CIVIL POLICE CONTROL IN OCCUPIED TERRITORIES

A. <u>Eastern Europe</u>.

In Eastern Europe, where administration is entirely German, police control is in the hands of an H.SS.PF (Higher Police and SS Chief) who is in fact a Himmler in miniature and commands all police and SS in the particular country. Although natives do many police duties, they only do so either in the ranks of the German police organisations or under direct German control.

B. <u>Western Europe</u>.

In Western Europe control is of a different and less obvious kind. Civil administration in general is either under different varieties of direct German control (in Norway, Belgium, France) or remains in the hands of the native governments (in Denmark, France).

Whether or not an H.SS.PF is appointed for an individual country, the police of that country carry out most of the duties of the uniformed, and in some cases plain clothes, branches under German supervision and in accordance with German directives. The odium for repression is therefore placed in the first instance on the national police.

C. <u>Conclusion</u>.

German police control thus varies in different countries, and the student will be given the latest information on his own country.

GERMAN MILITARY POLICE AND INTELLIGENCE SERVICE

1. MILITARY POLICE (FELDGENDARMERIE)

a. Duties.

They are of two categories:

i) Ordinary military police duties, such as traffic control (their most usual task), collection of stragglers, burial of the dead, control of fire-fighting, prisoner-of-war cages, etc.

ii) Enforcement of general security measures; supervision of national police of occupied countries; minor investigations and controls, carried out either on their own initiative or, more usually, on directives issued by the Secret Field Police. If acting on their own initiative, they must at all times inform the Secret Police, who will decide on any further action which may be necessary.

All members of the armed forces are bound to help the F.G. if called upon to do so.

b. Organization.

The F.G. is a corps of military police under army orders. It is composed of battalions, companies, platoons and sections. In general practice, an army disposes of at least one battalion, a corps and division of one company each; Feld and Ortskommandantur dispose of one section each.

c. Uniform.

The F.G. wear army uniform with the addition of:

i) Police badge (the eagle and swastika in an oval of oak leaves) on the upper left arm.

ii) A narrow brown arm-band stitched to the lower part of the left arm with the word "Feldgendarmerie" in aluminum-coloured gothic script. The Waffenfarben piping is yellow.

When on duty the F.G. personnel carry a white metal chain round their necks from which is suspended a semi-lunar brass plate with "Feldgendarmerie" inscribed on it.

d. _Personnel_.

The personnel, both officers and men, of the F.G. is primarily drawn from the civil uniformed police, but members of the armed forces may, if suitable, be drafted into the F.G. They must also be of the N.C.O. type.

2. SECRET FIELD POLICE (GEHEIME FELDPOLIZEI)

The principal executive security organization in military areas is the G.F.P.

a. _Duties_.

i) To discover and destroy enemy espionage, sabotage and para-military organizations.

ii) To see to the execution of all security measures.

iii) To act as security advisers, principally to the Ic/AO (Security Officer at Army H.Q.) but also to all other security officers.

b. _Organization_.

i) It is purely a military organization. Normally allocated on the basis of one G.F.P. Truppe per army.

ii) Occupied Territory. Information suggests that there is a G.F.P. Truppe in most important towns in areas under military control. These sections are subdivided into sub-sections, each sub-section specializing in certain work -e.g. contra-sabotage, contra-para-military organizations, etc.

c. _Uniform_.

i) Mostly in plain clothes.

ii) When in uniform, army uniform of the army official (Wehrmachtsbeamte) is worn, with on the shoulder-straps the letters G.F.P. in brass (yellow metal).

d. _Rights and Privileges_.

i) By virtue of their light blue pass, G.F.P. officials are:

- Authorized in urgent cases to call upon the immediate services of the Feld Gendarmerie or any other member of the armed forces in so far as their duties permit;

- Authorized to enter any military office or building, pass through any military barrier, and make use of all means of communication.

ii) By an order of Hitler, dated 15th August, 1941, they have the power of command over all N.C.O.'s and O.R.'s in the German Army.

iii) They are empowered to make provisional arrests of members of the armed forces and of the civilian population.

e. How the G.F.P. Work.

They have working for them a great number of agents, and they rely chiefly on penetration, provocation, informers, etc. Agents working for them are never received at the H.Q. but in residences which are specially taken for this purpose.

In security matters generally, they use the Feldgendarmerie and the national police for minor investigations and controls.

f. Personnel.

They are not usually professional policemen, but civilians in uniform - e.g. barristers, professors, accountants, actors, etc.

3. INTELLIGENCE SERVICE.

a) General.

The Intelligence Service is the senior German Intelligence authority in and outside Germany taking precedence over the Gestapo and all other security, police and frontier authorities. It is important, therefore, in making a full study of German C.E., to understand its organization and duties.

b) History.

i) The German Intelligence in the last war, under Col. Nickolai, was responsible for the censorship of the Press and the maintenance of morale at home as well as the main aspects of intelligence work.

In the present war most of that work has been taken over by the Nazi Party.

ii) Under the terms of the Treaty of Versailles, Germany was allowed to maintain a contra-espionage service

but not an offensive intelligence service. This was
known as the "Abwehrdienst" (Defence Service), or
Abwehr for short. It was not long before this so-called
contra-espionage service became an offensive secret
service under various guises such as the Oberseedienst
(Overseas Service) which was ostensibly commercial.
Prominent industrialists also began to employ ex-secret
service officers in positions where they could work
undercover. The head of the "Abwehr" is or was until
recently Admiral Canaris.

c) Organization.

  i) The Abwehr is an inter-service organization working for
the Army, Navy, Airforce and War Economics Directorate.
It is part of the Wehrmachtsamt under the German High
Command (O.K.W.), for whom it discharges all intelligence
functions - espionage, sabotage, contra-espionage and a
certain amount of propaganda work. (See chart)

  ii) The Headquarters of the Abwehr, known as the Abwehramt,
is in Berlin and controls directly or indirectly
all stations of the Abwehr organization throughout
the world. It is divided into three main departments
(Abteilung).

    Abteilung I - Intelligence
    Abteilung II - Sabotage
    Abteilung III - Contra-Espionage

    It is also divided laterally into Army, Navy, Airforce
and Economics. (See following diagram)

	Army	Navy	Airforce	Economics
	Heer	Marine	Luft	Wirtschaft
Abteilung I	E S P I O N A G E			
Abteilung II	S A B O T A G E			
Abteilung III	C O U N T E R - E S P I O N A G E			

Thus,

Abteilung I-H = Intelligence of interest to the Army.

Abteilung III-M = Contra-Espionage (Navy)

Abteilung III-Wi = Protection of Industry.

Abteilung I-Luft = Espionage of interest to the Airforce.

ORGANIZATION

CHART SHOWING CONNECTION WITH O.K.W.

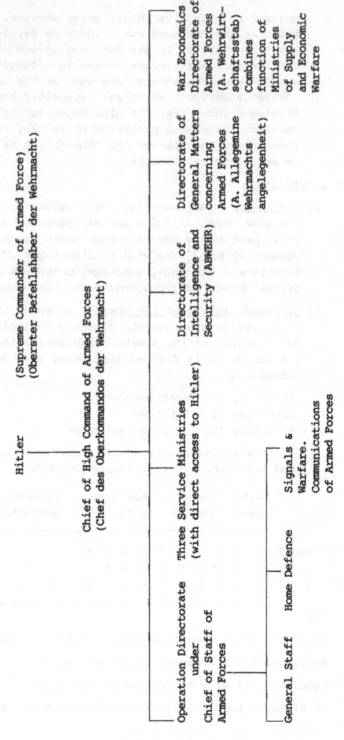

Hitler
(Supreme Commander of Armed Force)
(Oberster Befehlshaber der Wehrmacht)

Chief of High Command of Armed Forces
(Chef des Oberkommandos der Wehrmacht)

Operation Directorate under Chief of Staff of Armed Forces

General Staff · Home Defence

Three Service Ministries (with direct access to Hitler)

Signals & Warfare. Communications of Armed Forces

Directorate of Intelligence and Security (ABWEHR)

Directorate of General Matters concerning Armed Forces (A. Allegemine Wehrmachts angelegenheit)

War Economics Directorate of Armed Forces (A. Wehrwirtschaftsstab) Combines function of Ministries of Supply and Economic Warfare

Abteilung I is further subdivided into areas, i.e. I-H (west)

Abteilung III is further subdivided into numbered departments, i.e. III-H-4

Abteilung II seems to be organized rather differently from the others and is divided as follows:

(Eastern Europe & the East)	(W. Europe & W. Hemisphere)
II East	II West

II O/N	II O/S	II W/N	II W/S
(East-North)	(East-South)	(West-North)	(West-South)

iii) <u>Organization in occupied territory</u>.

- <u>Abwehrstellen.</u>
  Within the territory under German control, branches of head office called Abwehrstellen (Asts) are opened in the more important towns. They carry out in their prescribed areas the same functions as Headquarters and are subdivided vertically and laterally in the same way.

  In Germany itself there are eighteen main Asts in all but three of the twenty-one Army Commands (Wehrkreis). Five of these Asts control groups of stations abroad:

Berlin:	The Iberian Peninsula, Italy, Scandinavia, Russia and others.
Hambourg:	The British Empire, North and South America, Turkey and others.
Vienna:	The Balkans and the Near East.
Wiesbaden:	France and the French Colonies.
Studgart:	Switzerland and others.

  The chief of an Abwehrstellen is known as a Leiter, and if the station is large enough there will be a Leiter for each of its three groups.

- <u>Nebenstellen</u>. (Nests)
  These are subordinate to the Abwehrstellen. The organization is the same. The division of duties between the three departments is recognized, though it may mean that one man acts in three different capacities. The function of a Nest will depend largely on local conditions; i.e. a Nest on the

coast of Norway will probably be largely concerned with naval matters.

- Abwehrort (A.O.)
Subordinate to the Nests, with a staff of approximately one officer and five men.

- Meldekopf.
Usually a kind of postbox where agents can receive and send their reports. It is used in order to conceal from agents the location of the more important offices.

It can be safely said that there is no major town in German occupied territory, and few in neutral Europe, which does not have a local Abwehr station. E.g. Oslo controls Bergen, Aalesund, Trondheim, etc. Paris controls Cherbourg, Le Havre, Brest, etc.

Each Abwehr station is a replica of Headquarters, even though it may have a very small staff. It represents all three departments for all four services, though it will probably specialize in certain types of work.

iv) Organization Abroad.

- Aussenstellen.
In foreign countries not under German control Abwehr stations have been established, usually equipped with W.T. sets and taking their orders from the appropriate Ast in Germany; i.e. a station in Turkey would probably take orders from Hambourg.

- Embassies and Consulates.
The Abwehr also work through these channels and are at present using Japanese, Spanish, Swiss, etc. embassies and consulates where they cannot use their own.

- Abwehrkommandos.
These are mobile units sent in with invasion troops. They were usually recruited, shortly before operations were due to begin, from the nearest Ast to the theatre of the proposed operations, and were disbanded when the operations were over.

Their functions consisted, among other things, of
- Spreading short term propaganda.
- Preventing destruction of materials and buildings vital to the Germans.

- Rounding up nationals of the country on the
  Abwehr black list.

4. MAIN FUNCTIONS OF THE ABTEILUNG.

a) Abteilung I.

The main function of this department is to obtain
information **for** all four services over a very wide field by
means of secret agents.

Examples of Activities:

i) Detailed information of the allies' war potential
before the outbreak of war.

ii) Comprehensive shipping information.

iii) Meteorological information by means of stations in
Greenland and other parts of the north.

iv) Detailed military information from agents on the
Turkish General Staff.

b) Abteilung II.

i) This department is concerned with sabotage of the
enemy war machine which includes the spreading of
rumours and propaganda.

ii) It works in close co-ordination with the services, and
it is a fundamental principle that acts of sabotage
should be carried out in accordance with a general
plan and not on isolated occasions.

iii) The object of these combined operations is to destroy
communications and supplies of the enemy and damage
their morale.

iv) Detailed preparation beforehand is the general rule.

Examples of Activities:

- Fifth Column Activities immediately prior to and
  during invasions and creation of spy psychosis.

- Sabotage campaign in Spain against British shipping.

c) Abteilung III.

This department is responsible for Counter-Espionage,
Counter-Sabotage and Counter-Propaganda within the
Wehrmacht, i.e. C.E. in the widest sense, and makes great
use of penetration.

5. <u>METHODS</u>.

a) In order to acquire information the Abwher employs a large number of informers, local police, quislings, rewards and particularly blackmail.

b) Their <u>penetration system</u> is very highly developed. E.g. Founding escape organizations, recruiting nationals of a country ostensibly on behalf of a pro-ally organization and allowing them to build up their own ring and even indulge in minor acts of sabotage.

   - Sooner or later such a ring will be bound to find itself in touch with a genuine allied organization.

   - They are prepared to let one of their agents who has penetrated an organization run for a considerable time before they take action on his reports.

   - They frequently arrest their own agents for purposes of cover.

c) D.F.-ing, although under a separate military organization is closely controlled by the Abwehr.

d) Censorship is probably controlled by the Abwehr.

e) They are as much interested in building up an order of battle of enemy organizations as in actually catching a single enemy agent, in order that they may uncover a complete organization.

f) The principle executive arm of the Abwehr in occupied territory is the G.F.P. They also frequently call in the services of the Gestapo.

g) Where subversive activity is wide-spread in a military area the G.F.P., the F.G., the Gestapo, the S.D. and the local police will probably act in unison under the directions of Abteilung III.

6. <u>RELATIONS WITH THE S.D. AND GESTAPO</u>.

The three departments work closely together. The difference between them is as follows:

a) The S.D. deals entirely with political matters. E.g. They sent agents to work with Ribbentrop, when he was ambassador in London to investigate pacifist elements in England, and many of their agents were responsible for the corruption of French politicians and industrialists some time prior to the invasion of France.

b) The Abwehr is responsible for espionage, sabotage and contra-espionage in connection with the Armed Forces (Wehrmacht).

c) The Gestapo performs executive functions for the S.D. and Abwher.

It is inevitable that the functions of these three organizations should overlap and as a result a certain amount of dissension between them occur. This is known to have happened, as between the Abwehr and the Gestapo who made a point of poaching on the Abwehr's preserves in order to enhance their own prestige.

7. RECRUITING AND PERSONNEL.

The Abwehr recruit by the following methods:

a) The Party, particularly through the Auslands Organization. This organization is in close touch with Germans and German sympathizers abroad and runs a recruiting organization in order to put people in touch with the Abwehr.

b) Concentration Camps. People are released from concentration camps on condition that they work as German agents. The fear of returning is so great that it has the desired effect. E.g. "K.R", who was caught in May 1941 in England had been sent back to a concentration camp after training and before going over to England in order to impress upon him what would happen should he fail.

c) Labour Exchanges, particularly at seaports.

d) By threats of violence against themselves and relatives.

e) By blackmail.

PERSONNEL.

The majority of agents in the field, at any rate those who have been caught, have been non-Germans of low quality and low character, motivated by the desire for money and by fear.

The Abwehr officers are usually German and drawn from the Armed Forces.

During 1940-41, evidence connected with agents landed in the U.K. shows that they were badly treated, badly organized, ignorant of conditions in the U.K., and dissatisfied with their pay and treatment by the Abwehr Officers. The explanation of this probably is that they were sent in large numbers regardless of quality in the hopes that some would get through, since the invasion was considered so imminent.

It must be presumed, however, that a large number of extremely efficient Abwehr agents are still at work as there is no doubt that the enemy frequently receive first-rate information of allied activities. E.g. Submarine warfare.

8. <u>TRAINING</u>.

A number of training establishments for the Abwehr are located in Germany proper and in occupied territories.

Abteilung II frequently draws upon the <u>Lehr Regiment. Brandenburg</u> for saboteurs and pre-invasion troops.

This Regiment was formed in January 1940 to take care of Auslandsdeutche arriving from abroad, and has grown into three separate Battalions. It is administratively self-contained and elastic and has no insignia.

Its main purpose is to train men to work in advance of the Army in small parties, and for special undertakings in connection with military operations. I.e. The attack on the railway at Daba, North Africa prior to Rommel's advance into Eygpt.

9. <u>CONCLUSION</u>.

The Abwehr is directed by the O.K.W. and acts in close co-operation with the general staff; their activities often give a clue to moves by the O.K.W.; for example:

a) Their activity prior to 1940 was mainly directed against France.

b) After the fall of France their activities were concentrated on the U.K. with a view to invasion. E.g. Between September and November 1940 over twenty-five agents were known to have arrived in the U.K.

c) Information concerning the Ast in Vienna and its connections with the Middle East in 1942, suggested immediate plans of the O.K.W. concerning moves in Egypt and the Caucasus.

d) Recruiting and mobilising of Abwehrkommandos often gives a clue to the military situation. E.g. Preparation of these bodies was begun in Vienna six weeks before the Yugoslav Campaign.

NOTES ON ACTIVITIES OF THE ABWEHR

1. Concentration at the Centre of Operational Zone.

   a) From 1933 - 1939 Abwehr was active against Britain and France. About 30 agents were discovered, all controlled by Hamburg. (Mrs. Jessie Jordan, Mrs. Brandy)

   11 of these reported themselves.
   6 reported by suspicious private persons.
   9 caught through using the post to write to cover addresses.
   3 by official action.
   1 as a result of letter being found.

   Development of Auslands Organization in Britain suggested possibility of members being used for sabotage; large number arrested on outbreak of war.

   Greatest effort concentrated in France, by corruption of politicians like Laval, and undermining morale.

   b) After fall of France activities of Abwehr became more concentrated on the U.K. with invasion in view, working up to a peak in the Fall of 1940, and falling away again after the defeat of the Luftwaffe by the R.A.F. in the Battle of Britain.

   Six agents caught in Eire between May and July 1940 (Herman Goertz), may have had a far reaching effect on German strategical plans, which certainly included the invasion of Eire.

   September - November 1940, over 25 agents are known to have arrived in U.K. by parachute or small boat. Short term agents connected with invasion plans. (Druker, Walti and Eriksen, **Ter** Braak)

   Between March and September 1941 a number of agents were landed by small boats from Norway. Objects varied from naval espionage to penetration by escapees on behalf of counter-espionage (M.V. Hernie).

   All this time during 1940 and 1941 a number of long term agents were despatched for various purposes (Gerth van Wijk), and quite a few seamen were sent via the Iberian Peninsula to report on shipping movements, coastal defences, etc. (Timmerman)

Between September 1941 and March 1942, so far as is known, Abwehr activity against the U.K. practically ceased. The "Battle of Britain" had been won, the "Battle of the Atlantic" now occupied the thoughts of the O.K.W.

2. <u>Extension of Activities to the Periphery of Operational Zone</u>.

After the occupation of the Atlantic Coasts of Europe in summer of 1940 the "Battle of the Atlantic" assumed a more dangerous form, and simultaneously the Abwehr began developing its organizations in <u>Norway</u>, the <u>Iberian Peninsula</u>, and the <u>Western Hemisphere</u>. <u>The Balkans</u> also assumed importance as a base for the threat to the <u>Suez Canal Zone</u>, and <u>Middle East</u>.

At the same time the Abwehr were also entrusted with the obtaining of Meteorological Reports and for this purpose made special arrangements in <u>Greenland</u> and <u>Janmayen Island</u>. Many of their other agents were also required to make meteorological reports as a matter of routine.

<u>Norway</u>.

Headquarters is the Abwehrstelle Oslo, which controls five major districts with branches at Bergen, Trondheim, Tromsoe and Kirkenes.

Main functions were:

i) C.E. or III-F activities against Norwegian and Allied Intelligence in Norway.

ii) I.M. undertakings - small boats to Britain.

iii) Espionage against Russia.

<u>Bergen</u>.

Main energies directed to C.E. work owing to activities of patriots in that area.

Very active in organizing double-cross work with "refugees" to the U.K. (M-14-N.L & M.V. "Hernie")

Organized patrols of fishing smacks along Norwegian coast to keep watch on "escapees" and penetrated their organizations.

<u>Trondheim, Tromsoe and Kirkenes.</u>

I.M. activities.

<u>Iberian Peninsula</u>.

As a result of German help during the Spanish Civil War and subsequent Spanish - German relations, the Abwehr have enjoyed many advantages, example:

a) Use of Spanish agents with diplomatic cover. Spanish Embassy in London riddled with them. (Suñer)

b) Diplomatic reports, many of them with very detailed accounts of times of air-raid alerts, morale, bomb damage, etc.

Organization.

Two parent stations Madrid and Lisbon.

a) <u>Madrid.</u>

    i) H.Q. Staff of 20 full time German I.O.'s and about 30 others in out stations. H.Q. housed in German Embassy.

    ii) San Sebastian, Bilboa, Vigo, Huelva, Cadiz, Algeciras, La Linea, Cartagena, and Barcelona, Morocco (Tetuan), Canary Islands, Spanish Guinea and Fernande Po. with sub-stations.

    iii) San Sebastian deals with the transit of agents. Barcelona responsible for IM & IW work and supposed to have a training school.

    iv) Abteilung III also represented.

b) <u>Lisbon.</u>

    i) Similar organization to Madrid though not so big; all officers work in German Legation.

    ii) Permanent out stations all overseas - Azores, Cape Verde, Bissau and Lourenco Marques, and mostly manned by Portuguese who are not very satisfactory.

    iii) Bissau works into Gambia and Sierre Leone, Lourenço Marques works into South Africa.

    iv) Abteilung III also represented.

Activities.

    i) <u>Despatch of agents</u> from Occupied Europe through Iberian Peninsula to South America or Allied Territory.

    ii) <u>Communications</u> by outside agents to cover addresses in Spain or Portugal by secret writing, or courier. One German agent on every Spanish ship - usually acting as courier.

    iii) <u>Penetration</u> by Abteilung III into Allied Intelligence Services.

    iv) <u>Sabotage</u> - more here than anywhere else, chiefly directed against Allied Shipping and military objectives in Gibraltar.

Equipment manufactured in Spain, delay mechanism in Germany. Diplomatic bag used for conveying it. Spaniards used to do the work, most unreliable (drunk agent at Huelva). Abwehr II encourages Spanish Police to arrest any of doubtful loyalty, rather than be penetrated by the Allies.

Not much sabotage has been done in Lisbon.

v) An elaborate <u>Watching Organization</u> is in existence, on both sides of the Straits, observing Gibraltar - well equipped with technical apparatus.

Western Hemisphere.

U.S.A.

Very important base for shipping and production information until Fall of 1941 when F.B.I. broke spy ring. Regular flow of information between New York and Berlin. Intended for U-Boat warfare and the Luftwaffe.

Good example of penetration by F.B.I., who in fact controlled the communications until they were ready to pounce.

Thereafter information had to go via South America.

Not much evidence of sabotage.

South America.

Large scale, chiefly directed towards shipping information.

Quality of agents good; mostly recruited from local German population, who have long been educated by the Auslands Organization.

Main centres have been Rio and Valparaiso.

Sabotage.

Some possibility of sabotage especially in the realm of political strife, but no evidence of any concerted plan.

Conclusion.

Every network of information very powerful and efficient as evidenced by reputation amongst captured U-Boat crews.

Balkans and Turkey.

Yugoslavia.

Abteilung II played an important part in the attack on Yugoslavia.

H.Q. in Vienna controlled sub-branches in the other Balkan capitals.

By April 1941 sabotage agents were grouped around the main centres, Split, Zagareb, Belgrade and Skoplye, housed in the German consulate and working directly under M.A. Belgrade.

Agents were recruited from Volkdeutchen, and received assistance from local German firms - Lehr. Regt. Brandenburg also used.

Unlimited funds were available but strict instructions were given against any premature action.

Alarmist rumours and propaganda directed at disuniting the population were widely used.

Greece.

Abteilung II were thoroughly prepared by the time the Italians invaded Greece.

After the occupation sub-stations of Abteilung I were established around the Aegean at places like Chios and Lemnas to obtain detailed information on the military dispositions of Turkey.

Schools were set up in Athens and Salonika for the purpose of training Arabs.

H.Q. of Abteilung II at Athens was in close touch with Rommel, controlled agents in Syria, Iraq, Armenia, etc., and penetrated the Greek Army in Egypt and the French Army in Syria for the purpose of undermining morale.

Turkey.

Hamburg opened a sub-branch in Ankara, but Berlin also controlled the Lietstelle Naher-Orient there. The two chiefs quarrelled - the situation had to be adjusted by Canaris in person.

Ankara was the chief source of information until 1941, when Athens, Salonika, and Istanbul took over.

End of 1940 considerable number of saboteurs known to be in Turkey with plans for destroying plants and power houses. Used as jumping-off ground for saboteurs for the East and even India, also as a recruiting ground for pro German Arabs.

Lot of information obtained from Turkish officials in Ankara until 1942 when the Government took a stiffer attitude towards Germany.

Pera Palace explosion was the work of Abteilung II.

Middle East.

Preparatory Moves.

In 1938 Alfred Rosenberg became interested in the Middle East.

Arab residents in Berlin were approached and a "Permanent Defence Committee" was set up to contact the Arab world. But the Arabs used the Germans as much as the Germans sought to use the Arabs.

Syria.

Abwehr did not make much headway until the collapse of France. Then set up H.Q. in Beirut with the intention of making it the centre of activities in the M.E. - in autumn of 1941 had 400 -500 agents.

British invasion of Syria drove the Abwehr back to Turkey.

Iraq.

Activities centred around the German Legation in Bagdad, where Dr. Grobba, the Minister, an Arab expert, was fairly successful. He had been there some years. The removal of the Mufti of Jerusalem to Bagdad in 1939 also helped to make that city the centre of intrigue.

Iran.

Centre of Abwehr activity was German Legation in Teheran. Irwin Ettel, the Minister, controlled three classes of agents:

a) His own service, local and German.

b) A group of officers under the Military Attache.

c) An organization set up by the Mufti.

Egypt.

The German colony was organized in the usual hierarchy by the Auslands Organization, and evidence shows that the latter were closely connected with the Abwehr.

On the outbreak of war the arrest of the suspect Germans made it necessary for the Abwehr to fall back on the Italian Secret Service. The Germans, no doubt had acquired considerable influence then in Rome.

On the entry of Italy into the war both nations fell back upon Japan, and when the latter entered the Spanish Legation seems to have been the purveyor of information to the Axis.

The activities of the Abwehr became extremely complicated and difficult to unravel,

a) Because no one AST controlled Egypt, many had a finger in the pie.

b) The importance of these ASTS, such as Ankara, fluctuated.

c) The Italians played an important role.

Arabia.

Germans left Transjordan, Saudi Arabia and the Yemen to the Italians, who were also interested in Palestine. Mussolini regarded this part of the world as his zone of influence and subsidized the Syrian Nationalist Leader.

Ibn Saud refused to have anything to do with the Germans and the Italian Legation at Jedda, the centre of Italian Secret Service work, was closed in February 1942.

The Italians were more successful in the Yemen, where intelligence work was carried out by means of medical stations in the various towns giving free treatment, but the Imam refused to be drawn in against the British.

Italians also had a station at Aden established in 1934.

It is known that the Asts in Hamburg, Ankara, Cyrenaica, Lisbon and Sofia (Luft) all had agents in Arabia.

Palestine.

Activity of Abwehr increased in March 1941.

Apart from trained Germans sent into the country, the local German Colony, established 1880 and very pro-Nazi, were used, as well as Jews who had fled from Jewish persecution but were still pro-German; but mostly Arabs, Syrians and Armenians were used. Some German agents were sent in as volunteers for the British forces.

3. Extension of Activities beyond Operational Zone.

West Africa.

Indication of a network of agents among old German Colonists.

South Africa.

Abteilung II fairly active amongst dissident population. Portugese East Africa used as a jumping-off ground.

January 1942 there were widespread acts of sabotage connected with Robey Leibrandt, who had been trained in

politics and Nazi propaganda, and admitted being sent to
South Africa in 1941 to start a rebellion, but the Ossewa
Brandwag, a South African subversive organization, refused
to co-operate with him

Instructions were issued to Abwehr agents to avoid isolated
acts of sabotage and work to a pre-arranged plan: it is not
clear whether this outbreak of sabotage was premature or
timed to influence the Battle of Libya by drawing off South
African troops.

India.

Branches of the Auslands Organization existed before
the war, which may have served as a base for the usual
preparatory activity.

The usual German-Italian intrigues in Afghanistan were
probably controlled from India.

Abteilung II organized training for Indians in Kassel, the
idea being to drop them on the Russo-Indian border to raise
a revolt.

China.

There was an organization in Shanghai used for obtaining
naval information until 1941.

In 1939 there was a Hamburg agent in Dutch East Indies to
obtain intelligence on Singapore and naval and shipping
movements.

Australia.

A very small German community in Australia and New
Zealand, each with the usual Auslands Organization, but no
indication of subversive activity.

GERMAN ARMY

General Organization

A. THE WEHRMACHT.

To know something of the history of the German Army is essential for a proper understanding of its position and character today.

1. Pre-1918.

Until the Treaty of Versailles the German Army was composed of contingents of troops from the Federal States - Prussia, Saxony, Bavaria and Wurtemburg. Each had its own War Minister and its own Army, and each king commissioned his own officers, but armaments and training were uniform.

It was a conscript army of 850,000 men. At the time of the Armistice the German Army was 240 divisions - approximately 5,000,000 men.

2. Treaty of Versailles.

Object was to make aggression impossible for Germany. Means taken were:

a) The German army was reduced to 100,000 men, including maximum of 4,000 officers, organized in 7 Infantry Divisions and 3 Cavalry Divisions.

Conscription forbidden. Voluntary enlistment was for 12 years for N.C.O.'s and O.R.'s, and 25 consecutive years for officers, to make it impossible to build up a trained reserve.

b) Weapons were also restricted. There were no aircraft, A.F.V.'s, guns or hows of more than 10.5 c.m. calibre, A.A. or A.Tk. artillery. Fortresses were dismantled, Rhineland demilitarised. No general staff or military missions were allowed.

c) Other weapons and ammunition were limited in quantity.

3. The Reichswehr.

The name of this limited army, together with the limited navy, was the Reichswehr. The Supreme Commander was the President of the Republic, who delegated his powers to the

Reichswehr Minister, under whom were both Services (no Air Force). The Reichswehr Minister appointed the C.-in-C. of each Service.

The first C.-in-C. of the Army (Chef der Heeresleitung) under the Reichswehr Minister was General von Seeckt, an officer of old Imperial Army; such were also the other Reichswehr officers. It was an incongruous situation, bound to cause trouble, in that a republican, socialist and pacifist state had an army officered exclusively by a class which was monarchist, reactionary and militarist in character.

Ostensibly non-political but actually anti-republican, the Reichswehr concentrated on building up first-class "cadre" army - "the army of N.C.O.'s".

Von Seeckt was dismissed in 1926. The best-known of his successors was von Fritsch, 1934-1938.

4. <u>Evasion of Treaty of Versailles</u>.

The Reichswehr early began to evade disarmament clauses and the government connived - partly through fear of alienating the sympathy of so powerful a body, and partly through the love of militarism common to all Germans, even socialists.

a) Weapons were hidden, not surrendered to Inter-Allied Disarmament Commission.

b) Staff Officers were secretly trained and a skeleton general staff was formed.

c) The number of trained men was increased by premature discharges and militarisation of police.

d) Secret training with gas, aircraft and tanks was carried out in Russia after the Treaty of Rapallo, 1922.

e) Civil aircraft were made convertible to bombers - e.g. Junkers 52.

f) Weapons were made in secret factories and abroad - e.g. story of the workman who stole parts from a perambulator factory when his wife had a baby but found that when assembled they made a machine gun (!)

All this began long before advent of Hitler.

5. <u>Hitler - Accelerated Expansion</u>.

In January, 1933, Hitler became chancellor, and expansion of the services was accelerated and secrecy was gradually abandoned.

October, 1933:	Germany withdrew from the League of Nations and Disarmament Conference.
June, 1934:	Party-Army crisis owing to ambition of Roehm and Brown-shirts to form basis of new army. Murder of Roehm and 1,182 others. Decided for the moment that Party's work was political, and military matters were province of the Services. Hitler was biding his time.
August, 1934:	Death of Hindenburg; oath of allegiance to Hitler.
March, 1935:	Existence of Air Force admitted and conscription introduced.
March, 1936:	Demilitarized zone of Rhineland occupied.
July, 1936:	Compulsory service raised to 2 years.
1936 - 38:	Spanish Civil War - testing ground for weapons.
February, 1938:	Blomberg marriage. Reichswehr Minister Blomberg and C.-in-C. Fritsch dismissed, with 12 generals. With Fritsch disappeared the last restraining influence on Nazi aggressive designs.
March, 1938:	Austria invaded and Austrian Army incorporated in German Army.
September, 1938:	Sudetenland Crisis. Wehrmacht now ready for war.

6. Re-Organization of the Services.

In February, 1938, when the clean sweep of the Higher Command was made, opportunity was taken for a re-organization.

a) Title of Reichswehr, associated with 100,000-man Army of the Republic, was replaced by Wehrmacht (Defence Forces) including all three Services.

b) The post of Reichswehr Minister was abolished and Hitler became Supreme Commander (Oberster Befehlshaber) of the Wehrmacht. His staff, under his orders, is the High Command of the Defence Forces (Oberkommando der Wehrmacht or OKW) whose chief is Field Marshal von Keitel (Chef des Oberkommandos der Wehrmacht).

c) The heads of the three services responsible to the Oberkommando were:

Army: Generalfeldmarschall von Brauchitsch.
Navy: Gross Admiral Raeder.
Air Force: Reichsmarschall Goering.

7. New Organization of the Higher Command.

System instituted in February, 1938, still stands, but Hitler has taken over the Army personally, and Dönitz has replaced Admiral Raeder.

The dismissal of von Brauchitsch in the winter of 1941, and the taking over by Hitler himself of the command of the Army, was largely a propaganda move. Hitler had been built up as the supreme military genius of all time, and consequently a scapegoat had to take responsibility for the disasters in Russia. Von Brauchitsch was that scapegoat.

B. COMPOSITION OF GERMAN ARMY TODAY.

Hitler
(Oberster Befehlshaber der Werhrmacht)
(Oberkommando der Wehrmacht (OKW)

| Adjutantur (Personnel) | Wehrtnachtsamt (various, including SS and CE) | Reichs-kriegs-Ministerium (Hitler) | Marine-Ministerium (Dönitz) | Luftfahrt-Ministerium (Goering) |

The German Army today is composed of the following types of Divisions, grouped in Corps, Armies and Army Groups:

Infantry Divisions - Offensive:	163
- Defensive:	55
- Administrative:	43
Panzer:	27
Motorised:	11
S.S.:	9
Light:	8
Mountain:	7
	323

Note:

i) S.S. Divs. include two now rated as panzers, one in process of conversion to a panzer, two motorised, two Mountain, one Infantry and one Cavalry.

ii) Defensive Divs. are L. of C., training and frontier Divs. (Nos. 701-720). Not suitable for mobile operations unless reinforced.

iii) Training Divs. inside Germany and Z.B.V. Divs. are rated as administrative.

This force of 323 Divisions is scattered over Europe. Many of these divisions are locked up in police duties, and by no means all can be deployed for one operation. The number has in any case to be seriously reduced by the disasters in Russia.

C. **THE ARMY UNDER HITLER**.

Three main aims have been pursued by Hitler during the years when the German Forces were being developed:

1. **To Remove the Memory of Defeat in 1918**.

Intensive propaganda and the easy victories during the early years of war led to a considerable measure of success in this aim.

Now the tide has turned and the possibility of defeat is present in the mind of every German soldier. He fears the revenge which will be taken by the population of occupied countries. He fears the prospect of being sent to the Russian front. He fears the growing material power of the Allies which will soon overwhelm him. Although the pay and living conditions of the German soldier in the West are good, his morale is low. It should not be inferred, however, that he will not fight. Certain sections of the armed forces - in particular, the SS and the Air Force - will fight to the last, but, generally speaking, there seems some prospect that resistance may crumble after stern initial fighting.

2. **To Make the German Forces Independent of Foreign Raw Materials and Superior in Equipment to any Enemy**.

In their attempts to achieve self-sufficiency the Germans have had considerable success. Although they have many difficulties, their shortages have not so far seriously affected the quality of equipment.

3. <u>To Assert the Influence of the Party in all Matters of Policy and Confine the Armed Forces to Purely Executive Duties.</u>

Friction between the Army and the Party is of long standing, as can be seen from events since Hitler assumed power. Slowly but surely resistance by the army has been broken. Officers not loyal to the Party have been retired or even assassinated. They have been replaced by men, like von Zeitzler, who are thoroughly Nazi in outlook and will do as they are told.

The Party's private army, the Waffen SS, has been developed in size with the object of creating a powerful and reasonably reliable body under command of the Party. This has, of course, led to jealousy between the Army and the SS.

D. <u>CONCLUSION</u>.

The German Forces are strained to the utmost. Organizations in occupied territory can, by subversion of German troops now and by armed intervention later, render invaluable help to the Allied cause by supplying just that extra pressure which will cause a break.

PROPAGANDA

PROPAGANDA - INTRODUCTORY

1. WHAT IS PROPAGANDA?

There are two kinds of propaganda.

a) Preparational.

"The art of persuasion with a view to producing, merely, a frame of mind."

E.g. Goebbels persuaded German people to adopt a mental attitude vis-a-vis the concept "Lebensraum" before he called on them to do anything about it.

b) Operational.

"The art of persuasion with a view to producing action."

E.g. Today it is useless for our propaganda merely to persuade Frenchmen that the Boche is a swine. It must also instruct Frenchmen how to kick the Boche out of France.

Our propaganda to enemy and occupied countries is now mainly operational; and, as such, should always contain the joint elements of persuasion and action.

2. WHAT CAN PROPAGANDA DO?

These lectures deal only with underground operational propaganda - i.e. with propaganda as one weapon in the whole armoury of underground warfare. Passive resistance, sabotage, guerrilla warfare and internal revolution are other weapons which, with propaganda, must be knitted into a whole.

Thus propaganda, calling in its action element for passive resistance, may lead to passive resistance; passive resistance plus propaganda may lead to sabotage; passive resistance and sabotage plus propaganda to guerrilla warfare etc. (Cf. oil in a machine.)

Therefore propaganda, though an important weapon, is never an independent one. It must be co-ordinated with the other weapons at our disposal. (Cf. Goebbels' "Fourth Arm".)

3. WHY DO YOU NEED TO KNOW ABOUT PROPAGANDA?

If ever you are called on to become an organiser, propaganda
will be one of the weapons at your disposal. It is therefore
right that you should know its scope, its power and its
relation to the conduct of underground warfare.

We shall best perceive these things if we follow, in some
detail, the career of a propaganda-agent from the moment when,
in this country, he is told to undertake propaganda work to
the moment when, in his own country, he has distributed his
first leaflet among his people.

4. STARTING-POINT.

The propagandist finds his raw material in the facts of
the political situation. A thorough knowledge of such facts
as they affect his field of operations is essential for
successful work.

5. POLITICS.

The propagandist's approach to politics should be governed by
two main considerations:

a) Politics, which in our grandfathers' day were relatively
   static, have now become fluid. (Cf. British Right and Left
   Wing rapprochement since Russia's entry into the war.)

   The clear picture of the political scene, which an agent
   should initially work out in his area, should not be like
   a chart, map or photograph with its details fixed and
   rigid, but like a moving film at a cinema - where the frame
   remains fixed but contents are mobile.

b) Politics, to the propagandist, are not merely Party
   Politics; but a detailed examination of every factor
   affecting the self-interest of each group, class and
   organisation that exists within his field of operation.

6. GROUPINGS.

It is one of the early duties of a propagandist, even before
leaving this country, to ascertain what groups exist in his
area. This gives rise to two questions:

a) Why?

   Having ascertained a particular political fact that affects
   his area, the propagandist may easily find that each group

of people has a different attitude to the same political fact.

Therefore it follows that our propaganda relative to that one fact must differ vis-a-vis each group.

E.g. Propaganda against agricultural plunder by the Boche will have to be distinct, if addressed to country-folk who see the plunder happening, from that addressed to townsfolk who, perhaps, only know that their bellies are empty.

By addressing our propaganda to a relatively small specific group rather than to a large amorphous mass, we ensure that we shall appeal more directly to the self-interest of that group and therefore incite it the more easily to the action required.

This is, in fact, one of the main reasons why we send a propaganda-agent to work inside a country since his leaflets, alone of all our propaganda media, can be addressed to and distributed among a specific group. B.B.C. broadcasts and R.A.F. leaflets cannot be thus addressed and distributed with certainty of success.

b) How?

It is possible to group any given population under eight main headings:

- Party Political. (Conservative, Liberal, Socialist etc.)

- Vocational. (Miner, lawyer, journalist etc.)

- Regional. (Town, country, coast etc.)

- Religious. (Catholic, Prostestant, agnostic etc.)

- Age. (Students, Youth Movements, Sports Clubs, Pension ex-Servicemen etc.)

- Sex. (Workers' wives, feminist movements etc.)

- Economic. (Employers, workers, Trades Unions etc.)

— National. (Racial minorities.)

7. CHOICE OF TARGET.

From the many groups at this disposal, our propagandist must choose the few groups that he can most profitably attack.

E.g. One might ignore extreme loyalists (already sufficiently active) and extreme pro-Nazis (already beyond conversion) in order to concentrate more effectively on the "attentiste" element of a population.

Once a specific group is chosen, the propagandist must determine (very broadly) which of the eight factors listed above is that particular group's predominant factor.

E.g. Socialists: predominantly a Party Political group. Students: predominantly an age group.

He must now ascertain whether the impact of the other seven factors on his chosen group is of sufficient importance to warrant splitting that group into smaller sub-groups.

E.g. Q. "Does the fact that there are old, young and middle-aged socialists warrant my further splitting the main group?"

A. "Probably no."

Q. "Does the fact that there are rich socialists (Theoreticians) and poor socialists (practicians) warrant my further splitting the main group?"

A. "Probably yes."

8. CONCLUSION.

With his population grouped and a specific group chosen as target, the first preparational stage of our propagandist's work is complete.

Two further preparational steps remain to be taken:

a) The ascertainment of the chosen group's opinion on a given political fact or facts.

b) The receipt from a superior authority of a propaganda line or policy.

These two steps form the subjects of ensuing lectures.

OPINION SAMPLING

(NOTE: This lecture deals with an activity which can only be
engaged-in on definite orders and in relation to the
specific security arrangements made in connection with
each individual student. The lecturer must make it
perfectly clear that he is not directing enquiries to be
undertaken by students on arrival. The general principles
which emerge from the talk are, however, of importance in
all work of appraising a milieu.)

1. PROPAGANDA DEPENDS ON FACTS.

The propaganda worker must know the facts of the political
situation. (Cf. C.1). The propagandistic treatment of those
facts is influenced by the opinions of the public to which
propaganda is addressed. Methods of investigating opinions
quickly and accurately form the subject of this talk.

2. DANGERS OF INADEQUATE INFORMATION.

Reports are constantly reaching us, often at the cost of
agents' lives, to the effect that "German propaganda is being
successful"; that "The population of region X is 80% pro-
British". These reports are valueless, because:

     a) they do not yield facts precise enough to form a
        basis for work, and

     b) they are guesses.

What we need are reports of observed fact, the accuracy of
which is above suspicion.

3. INVESTIGATION AS A SCIENCE.

The science of investigating opinion has made great strides
in recent years, and the movement of large sums of money
in commercial advertising and market research is actually
determined by its findings. Cf. Fortune and Gallup Surveys;
Literary Digest Straw Votes; Mass Observation.

Concrete cases of political and commercial propaganda based
on good or bad interpretations of public opinion. (E.g.
Petain and Lux soap.)

4. Investigation methods in their normal peacetime thoroughness are obviously not applicable to our work. But the principles that govern it must also govern us, just as the propaganda principles which govern the vast output of the B.B.C. must also govern the small town printer working in a basement by candlelight.

5. "THE RANDOM SAMPLING METHOD".

This is the most accurate method of investigating opinion. Broadly it may be described as follows:

If a large group (Group "A") is under investigation, a sample (Sample "a") is taken. If this is accurately done, i.e. if Sample "a" is completely representative of Group "A" the trends opinion found in the sample will be found in the group, and in the same proportions. Similarly for a complicated group (ABCD) when sample abed will be required with "a" proportionate to "A" and "b" to "B", etc.

To achieve accuracy, rigid adherence to certain rules is required:

a) <u>A sample need not be large</u>.

E.g. the Gallup forecast of Roosevelt's second election was based on only 2,000 views out of 130,000,000, yet it came within one percent of accuracy. For small town, local or craft reconnaissance, a much smaller number is sufficient.

N.B. Whereas Gallup and other nation-wide surveys organized on a commercial profit-making basis require a high degree of accuracy, accuracy within 10 or 20% is valuable for propaganda guidance.

NOTE: The introduction to Section 5 and also Para. i) can be omitted when students are lacking either command of English or minimal grasp of mathematics.

b) The sample must be chosen at random.

Never let any arbitrary factor influence your choice. E.g. If we are investigating opinion in a coalmine, do <u>not</u> choose the foremen, the first ten men to reach the pithead, the secretaries of the local union, your brother-in-law, or anybody distinguished by unrepresentative characteristics.

c) <u>Check fact rather than opinion</u>.

People are not reliable guides to their own opinions. In fact, on matters not violently affecting personal advantage, most people tend to give either the answer they think you want or an answer that does them credit. People's actions are a more reliable guide to their opinions than their words. E.g. Don't ask people their opinion of R.A.F. leaflets. Find out whether they pass them on.

d) <u>Use of observation rather than questioning</u>.

What papers do people read? Where do they shop? Do they talk to Germans? Do they watch German newsreels? Do they listen to the B.B.C.?

e) <u>Avoid all hypothetical questions</u>.

Instead of asking "What would you have done if you had not joined the army?", ask "What work were you doing or applying for when you were called up?"

f) <u>Avoid all words of vague meaning</u>.

Words like "often", "much", "occasionally" tend to obscure facts rather than reveal them. They open the door to all kinds of wishful thinking and guesswork.

g) <u>Never try to prompt people</u>.

When it is difficult to get an opinion, there is a temptation to suggest one. This is a frequent source of error. No answer is better than a prompted answer; no information better than misleading information.

6. <u>FOR REPORTS, NEVER CONFUSE FACT WITH INTERPRETATION</u>.

Interpretation may be useful on occasion, but, when reporting, always distinguish clearly between fact and interpretation. Reports should read something like this:

"<u>Fact</u>: X miners and Y railwaymen in Blanktown have volunteered for work in Germany within the last Z days. Miners give reasons A, B and C; railwaymen give reasons B, C and D.

<u>Interpretation</u>:

On the basis of the above facts, my opinion is that Germany's attack on Russia has produced a marked swing towards collaboration among working-class circles in Blanktown."

(Students are asked to criticize this report for errors or omissions.)

On the basis of sound information, collected in the manner described above, the formulation of effective operational propaganda is facilitated.

7. <u>SECURITY PRECAUTIONS</u>.

   a) <u>Formulation of Questions</u>.

   Ideally all questions addressed to a group vis-a-vis an identical political fact should themselves be identical.

   With the principles enunciated above in mind, they should therefore be carefully phrased in such a manner that they can be slipped innocently into any conversation.

   If this is impossible for security reasons, take care to phrase all your questions so that the answers "add up".

   E.g. the answer "Yes" to one question would be useless when juxtaposed with the answer "On a Wednesday" to another question on the same subject.

   b) <u>Behaviour.</u>

   Apply methods of information-gathering listed under A.3. Sec. 3) b).

   Do not frequent too obviously certain areas or cultivate too obviously the members of a particular trade.

   It is possible to elicit information without appearing to ask for it, to overhear gossip in cafes and queues, to observe behaviour in the group affected. This is proved by the fact that people have done it.

LEAFLET WRITING

1. Fundamental Principles

INTRODUCTION:

Good advertising is based on set principles; good writing on deep feeling. Good propaganda needs both; and the good propagandist will use the latter to mask the former.

The principles must never be allowed to "show through." We are not sending men back to Occupied Europe to sell soap.

Nevertheless propaganda presentation must always conform to the following fundamental principles:

1. Simplicity of:

a) General Idea.

Let each leaflet present but one General Idea - from which there should be no digression.

b) Argument.

In support of the General Idea one may produce Particular Ideas. These should be logically linked and linked so closely that the reader is unable to escape from climbing the rigid "mental stairway" that leads from an existing attitude to a required attitude.

Such linking is most effective when it binds sentence to sentence (for examples, see Appendix A); but, where this is impossible, one should always link Particular Idea to Particular Idea.

c) Language.

Be simple, but never patronising. Do not speak as a scholar writing down to fishermen. Lower you mentality to that of a fishermen and write up. (For example, see Appendix B.)

2. Concreteness.

a) Avoid abstract words like the plague, because:

i) Such words as "democracy", "patriotism", "freedom", have become platitudes without significance.

185

ii) Even where abstracts are not yet platitudinous, they can never affect a reader's self-interest so powerfully as concrete words. E.g.:-

- For "patriotism" say "Love of France."

- For "hunger" say "empty bellies."

- For "The Peace Loving Dutch nation are now resisting German oppression" say "The Dutch people, who once grew tulips and made cheese, are now stabbing Germans in the back."

- For "Germany's death-rate is rising in Russia" say "German corpse is piled upon German corpse among the blood, the bone, the twisted tripes and scattered bowels of the Russian battlefield."

b) In thus appealing to a reader's self-interest, recall that such self-interest is normally two-fold:

(i) Selfish: "The Germans have taken away your cattle."

(ii) Unselfish: "The Germans have enslaved France."

The most powerful possible appeal is one directed towards a combination of selfish and unselfish elements, i.e. "Your cattle have been taken away because France is enslaved."

3. Repetition.

a) By this is meant the choice of one urgent, compelling General Idea, and the repetition of that idea from many different points of view and/or by many different methods - leaflet, broadcast, rumour, etc.

b) By constant repetition we can be certain of securing:

(i) A larger audience.

(ii) If not a conviction, at least an effect on the mentality of the audience. Cf. Goebbels' anti-Semitic and anti-Czech. propaganda. This effect can often be strengthened into conviction by:

4. Action.

Action must always be recommended because:

a) Action is the aim of all propaganda.

b) Action drives home the persuasive lessons of repetitive propaganda - i.e. people will remember a propagandist's line of talk if they can associate it with an action in which they themselves have taken part, E.g.

(i) Germans will remember Goebbels' anti-Semitic propaganda because they have seen, read of or taken part in Jewish persecutions.

(ii) They will remember his anti-Czech propaganda because Germany won a "bloodless" victory over the Czechs.

(iii) They do NOT remember Goebbels' anti-Italian propaganda in July 1934, because nothing was done about it.

LEAFLET WRITING

2. Mechanics

INTRODUCTION:

The "hit-or-miss" author, who writes primarily to please himself and only incidentally to please his readers, is a vile propagandist.

The propagandist writes solely with the intention of appealing to his readers' interest. He aims to hit, because he cannot afford to miss.

Accordingly his work is based on the formulae of modern advertising, to whose task his own runs broadly parallel.

It differs only in that the propagandist is at greater pains that the copywriter to disguise his medium. The reader of an advertisement should never be provoked into feeling: "This is only an advertisement." The reader of propaganda should, if possible, never be allowed even to suspect that he is reading propaganda.

Before actually writing a leaflet, the propagandist must:

A. Ask and answer the seven basic questions listed below. As a matter of self-discipline they should be asked and answered on paper.

   1. <u>What</u> General Idea am I trying to sell?

        Cf. C.3. No digression from single choice.
        Cf. Goebbels' brilliant choice of isolationism to U.S.A.

   2. <u>To whom</u> am I trying to sell it?

        Remember "groupings" in C.1.
        Cut out each word, phrase and sentence that does not
            appeal to your "target's" interest.

   3. <u>Where</u> am I sending my message?

        Depends on answer to 2.
        Knowledge of "social geography" showing where and
        therefore in what conditions a given group live.

4. <u>When</u> must my message be delivered?

> News value.
> Seasonal factors.
> Anniversaries.

5. <u>Against what</u> opposition?

> Where possible, anticipate enemy propaganda.
> Where impossible, counter evidence with better
> evidence - never with a flat denial, to which complete
> silence is preferable.

6. <u>From whom</u> does my message come?

> In covert propaganda, preferably from nationals of the
> country concerned and from an organisation rather than
> an individual.

7. <u>How</u> can my argument coming from (6) best convey the
General Idea (1) in terms appealing to the self-interest
of my audience (2) at (3) place, at (4) time and against
(5) opposition?

B. Determine that the message will do three things:

1. Convince group that they <u>should</u> undertake required action.

2. Convince group that they <u>can</u> undertake required action

3. Convince group that required action justifies personal
   risks involved.

To fulfil these three requirements, most appeals may be based
on the following three elements:

1. Statement of grievance. ("We are in a mess.")

2. Message of hope. ("But not too deeply.")

3. Call to action. ("How to get out".)

(See specimen leaflet - Appendix to this Lecture.)

<u>Note</u>: More intelligent Students are now asked to write
a leaflet on a set subject. On its completion they
are provided with the following check list of
questions:

<u>Content</u>.

1. Have I digressed from my General Idea?

2. Does my "story" fit the facts, as I know them?

3. Are the subdivisions of my "story"

    a) logical?
    b) in order?
    c) linked up?

4. Have I made the most of:

    a) absolute news value?
    b) propaganda news value? (Propaganda news value – a new way of looking at an already known fact.)

5. Have I related this news to the point I wish to make?

6. Have I used, <u>wherever possible</u>, proof, evidence and examples?

7. Have I made contact with the reader's personal self-interest? i.e. is it concrete?

<u>Style</u>.

1. Is my message

    a) clear?
    b) simple?
    c) unmistakable (no possible double meanings)?
    d) free of contradictions?
    e) concrete?

2. Have I used

    a) short sentences?
    b) short paragraphs?
    c) liaison between paragraphs?
    d) enough sub-heads?

<u>Objective</u>.

Have I remembered that propaganda is designed to produce BEHAVIOUR (i.e. a state of mind or a line of action)? In other words, does my reader <u>know clearly</u> WHAT IS WANTED OF HIM?

APPENDIX

Specimen Outline Leaflet

Assumed Basis:	Compulsory labour-conscription in German-occupied Ruritania.
1. What Idea?	Go to Germany and do damage.
2. To Whom?	Workers of Blankville, Ruritania.
3. Where?	Note degree of local compulsion in Blankville.
4. When?	Early morning, 2 days before next departure for Germany.
5. Against What?	Enemy C.E. and security-measures in Ruritania and Cermany.
6. From Whom?	Ruritanian workers already in Germany.
7. How?	By establishment of fact that Nazi demand for labour is a weakness that should and can be attacked in reasonable safety.

HOW TO BECOME A SPY

	<u>HOW YOU CAN INVADE GERMANY</u>----- <u>Conscription, now our shame can become our pride.</u>	HEADLINE must get attention, provoke further reading. Sure to do so if it appeals to self-interest and offers new information. Trick often useful (and sound) is to start with "How", "Why", etc.
1. Grievance	(Elaborate degree of compulsion in Blankville. "We were cattle without pasture – and they had the whips!")	
2. Hope	<u>But now we can gain the whip-hand.</u> (The mere fact that the Nazis thus conscript us, their bitterest enemies, shows them weak. We can attack that weakness.)	Subhead not essential, often useful to amplify headline. But should not give away whole story.
3. Action	<u>How we can butcher the butchers.</u> (Assume reader's agreement that this is his duty, and tell him cleary how to attack Nazi production and Nazi morale in Germany without undue risk. Hold out certainty of success if all co-operate.)	Subheads in text help to break it up, make it more readable. Should also mark stages in the argument.
	You are the advanced Invasion Front! -----	Footline sometimes useful to crystallise the appeal.
	League of Ruritanian Workers in Germany. -----	Signature or symbol if required.

PROPAGANDA

The following extract, taken from an article issued by the British Army Bureau of Current Affairs, illustrates how much more profitable than contradiction by "flat denial" is contradiction by "better evidence":

1. "The Jews run the British Press", says Hitler.

   ONLY 1 OUT OF 116 DAILY AND 17 SUNDAY PAPERS HAS A JEW IN ANY "CONTROLLING" POSITION ON IT.

2. "The Jews control finance", says Hitler.

   THERE IS NOT A SINGLE JEW ON THE BOARD OF THE BANK OF ENGLAND, ONLY ONE JEW AMONG THE MANAGERS OF THE LONDON STOCK EXCHANGE, AND ONLY THREE JEWS OUT OF ABOUT ONE HUNDRED AND FIFTY PERSONS ON THE BOARD OF THE "BIG 5" BANKS.

3. "The Jews are responsible for the Black Market", says Goebbels.

   IN HITLER'S GERMANY, WHERE NO JEWS ARE ALLOWED TO TRADE AT ALL, THE BLACK MARKET FLOURISHES.

4. "The Jews encourage the war, but they do not fight in it", says Goebbels.

   50,000 JEWS OUT OF A TOTAL JEWISH POPULATION OF ABOUT 400,000 (INCLUDING WOMEN, CHILDREN AND REFUGEES) ARE IN THE SERVICES AND OVER 8,000 OF THESE ARE IN THE R.A.F. ALONE. IN THE LIST OF AWARDS FOR DISTINGUISHED CONDUCT AT DUNKIRK THERE WERE THE NAMES OF MORE THAN 30 JEWS WHO RECEIVED DECORATIONS OR WERE COMMENDED.

REPRODUCTION AND DISTRIBUTION - 1

REPRODUCTION.

A. Printing.

> Note: (i) It takes seven years to make a master-printer.
> Our aim has been to instruct propaganda-agents
> sufficiently in such basic knowledge of printing as
> will enable them to recruit an expert, appreciate
> his problems and even, to some extent, instruct
> him in clandestine printing to which he may be
> unaccustomed.
>
> (ii) In Occupied Countries our best work has been done
> by friendly printers working inside the print-shops
> of German controlled newspapers - often under the
> very noses of the Nazis. This because:
>
> - The Nazis have sacked all anti-collaborationist
> writers, but could not afford to sack printers.
>
> - Lack of metal, ink and paper supply is least felt
> in German-controlled newspapers.
>
> - Jobbing-printers are always more suspect and
> therefore under closer surveillance than
> newspaper printers.
>
> (iii) Our instruction therefore outlines the principal
> methods of overt newspaper-printing and adds
> advantages and/or disadvantages of each method from
> a covert point of view.

1. Definition.

"The application of paper to an inked metal surface on which
the message (reversed) stands in relief."

Of the three elements - metal, ink and paper - that go to
make any printing operation, it is proposed to discuss only
the metal and the paper.

2. Metal.

a) Type.

(i) MONOTYPE, cast in single letters; assembled by machine
or by hand in "stick"; completed message

> locked in framework consisting of metal "chase" and held in position by "furniture" and "quoins" - whole called the "form".

- Can "accidentally" be dropped or "pied" to avoid detection.

- Is difficult to transport covertly from one department to another or out of the printshop.

(ii) LINOTYPE, cast in single lines; each line produced mechanically and assembled by hand as for monotype.

- Can "accidentally" be dropped, to avoid detection, into molten-lead container that is part of every linotype machine.

- Can easily be transported from one department to another or outside the print-shop, distributed in the pockets or on the person of a courier, the lines being arranged in the correct order either by friendly compositor inside the print-shop or by safe jobbing printer or propaganda-agent with own plant outside.

- Can be "run-in" secretly alongside innocent work. E.g. a linotype-operator could easily set, say, seven lines of "Gringoire" under surveillance and then, when head printer's back was turned, one line of a subversive leaflet.

(Examples of Monotype and Linotype are shown.)

b) Blocks.

A picture transferred by a photographic process on to a single sensitized metal plate so that the image (reversed) stands in relief.

The picture, known as the "original", may have been drawn, painted, typewritten or printed.

Two main types of block:

(i) Line-Block: Made of zinc, reproduces plain black and white.

(ii) Half-tone: Made of copper, reproduces with tone - gradations like a photograph.

Line-block is easier to produce covertly and more suited to leaflet reproduction than half-tone.

Specimens of line-block ("zinco") in the making are exhibited:

- Original

- Negative

- Print

- Print half-etched

- Print fully-etched

- "Finished" print

- Cut zinco ready for mounting

- Matrix or mould (to facilitate covert distribution)

- Mounted stereo

- Proofs

Remember two security advantages:

    (i) Blockmakers work in separate department less surveyed by head printer.

    (ii) They can diminish an "original" to a size that makes it easy to distribute, easy to hide and still easy to read.

3. Paper.

  a) "Wove" - dried, after manufacture, on felt.

  b) "Laid" - dried, after manufacture, on ribbed screen.

"Wove" is difficult to track back to source; "Laid" easy, owing to individual dimensions of screen. Make for national newsprint, where possible, and avoid watermarks.

B. Commercial Duplicator.

1. Safer and more accessible but less authoritative than printing.

2. Impossible to trace back duplicated tract to individual duplicating machine. Other security factors permitting, one may therefore "borrow" someone else's machine.

3. Use Gestetner or Roneo machines where possible.

4. Use only absorbent or semi-absorbent paper.

5. If inexpert and unable to enrol aid of expert, practise on innocent occasions. Unskilled work liable to make one conspicuously dirty.

6. Remember noise-factor.

7. Care in choice of typewriter. (see below.)

C. <u>Typewriter</u>.

Duplicated work cannot be traced back to a duplicator, but can be traced to an individual typewriter. Therefore consider the following security precautions:

1. Only use your typewriter for secret work. Never "borrow" anyone else's. Hide it when not in use. This a golden rule. The rest are subsidiary precautions.

2. To avoid detection through damaged letters, use newish machine and consider possibility of alternately cleaning and dirtying keys for alternate leaflets.

3. Never use new ribbon for secret work.

4. When making line-block from typewritten "original", use carbon-copy for "original". This blurs the outline of damaged letters and makes detection more difficult.

REPRODUCTION AND DISTRIBUTION — II

METHODS COMBINING REPRODUCTION AND DISTRIBUTION

A. Chain Letter

1. Difficulty of addressing specific group; therefore stick to straight news.

2. Overcome recipient's laziness by keeping letters short (5 or 6 censored news-items sufficient) and legible.

3. If mechanically reproduced, add handwritten personal message and signature.

4. Evidence of effectiveness from German counter-measures.

B. "Toys"

1. Chalk

   Should always be carried, provided owner has good cover. E.g. tailor, shopkeeper, teacher, pupil.

2. Stickers.

   Notch, if regular shape, to ensure applying it right way up in dark. Observe "sticker drill". (demonstrated.)

3. Stencils.

   Notch, as for stickers.

All above should be employed in black-out, and are especially valuable for:

a) Defacing enemy propaganda.

b) Bitter, purposive ridicule (cf. "Gringoire" & Salengro.)

c) Decoy propaganda. (Meaningless signs, etc.)

C. Rumour

Specialist method on no account to be lightly used owing to risks of confusion and (propaganda's most heinous sin) contradiction. Essentials are:

1. GOOD ORGANISATION

   (a) Authorative source obeyed with discipline.

198

(b) Source must not be known to actual "whisperers".

(c) "Whisperers" must not be known to each other.

2. GOOD DIRECTIVES

(a) Rumours must have specific objectives.

(b) Rumours must be easy to believe and difficult to dismiss.

(c) Rumours must be concrete and precise, never abstract or vague.

(d) Curious exception of religious and superstitious rumours.

3. GOOD DISSEMINATION

(a) Try never to talk more than once yourself. Make others talk. Arrange for innocent interception of your "sib" on fertile ground e.g. garrulous barber, gossipy barmaid, Spanish Ambassador.

(b) "Jetsam" method of dropping provocative letters or parts of letters, which contain libels, calumnies and rumours, in places where recipients will find them when they are alone - e.g. railway-carriage at beginning of a journey, telephone-boxes, public lavatories.

DISTRIBUTION

A. BY HAND

1. Indirect:

(a) Through boites-aux-lettres and accommodation addresses.

(b) Through insertion of leaflets between leaves of books and newspapers in public libraries.

2. Direct:

(a) Never appear to be carrying more than one leaflet. You came on it by chance or it was passed to you by someone you don't know - i.e. never be recognizable as "a distributor."

(b) Fold leaflet, before distributing, so that recipient (if subsequently interrogated) may say he received it through the post. (See B.1. below)

B. BY POST

1. Safe method for recipient of leaflet who can only be penalised for retention or distribution - not for actual reception.

2. Safe method for sender, provided he takes following precautions:

a) Check whether you are being followed to mail-box (see A.8).

b) If you always use the same mail-box, there is no need to follow you. Therefore post in various boxes at varying times.

c) In large town, best time is commercial mailing-time. (cover for carrying large number of identical envelopes and little fear of talk from postman).

d) In small locality, break up appearance of mail by never having more than two or three letters in the same handwriting, in the same envelope or bearing the same arrangement of stamps, etc. in the same box.

BASIC PLAN OF ALLIED PROPAGANDA TO OCCUPIED COUNTRIES

I. <u>INTRODUCTORY.</u>

    A. <u>Allied Objectives.</u>

        1. To unite Ruritanians in a common hatred of the Hun.

        2. To encourage non-cooperation.

        3. To encourage passive resistance.

        4. To encourage undetectable sabotage.

        5. To prepare every Ruritanian for D-day.

    B. <u>Allied Platforms.</u>

    In order to attain these objectives, Allied propaganda falls under five main headings:

        1. The certainty of Allied victory.

        2. Hatred of the German.

        3. Ruritania's future assured by Allied victory.

        4. Ruritania fights on.

        5. How Ruritania can help hasten victory.

    These headings remain constant; but the emphasis on each may change, as must also the themes and evidence grouped under each heading.

II. <u>THE PLAN.</u>

    A. <u>Certainty of Allied Victory</u>.

    Emphasis on this heading, strong until 1942, decreases daily as certainty of Allied victory grows more axiomatic.

        1. <u>Comparison of Potential</u>.

        Object of such comparison in two-fold:

        - By showing Allied Superiority, to strengthen belief in certainty of Allied Victory. (But only link "potential" talk to actual Allied successes.)

        - By showing specific Axis inferiority, to encourage attack by friendly elements of enemy in occupied territory.

    a) War-industrial potential.

    b) Man-power potential.

    c) Food Potential. (Emphasis at present off comparison. See "Ruritania's Future".

    d) Transport Potential.

2. <u>Strategy.</u>

We are concerned with three broad strategic themes:

    a) <u>"Germany is the main enemy."</u>

    Once Germany is defeated we can concentrate on Japan. Cf. Roosevelt-Churchill discussions.

    b) <u>"Unconditional Surrender."</u> Cf. Casablanca communique.

    c) <u>"The Last Lap."</u>

    Emphasis on "last" and off length of "Lap".

B. <u>Hatred of the German.</u>

Today primarily a "unifying" theme. (See objectives: I. A. 1.)

1. Expose German "Divide and Rule" policy.

2. Expose Germany's present tendency to conciliate Ruritania. Despite isolated acts and frequent promises of kindness due to:

    a) Germany's pre-occupation with Russian war and defence of "Festung Europa";
    b) Germany's need for Ruritanian economic collaboration;
    c) German's fear of Ruritanian hostility.

Nazidom's real aims are:

    a) De-education.
    b) De-industrialisation.
    c) De-population.

      - Recruitment of Ruritanian workers.

      - Colonization schemes to shift and split population.

      - Retention of prisoners-of-war.

C. <u>Ruritania's Future Assured by Allied Victory.</u>

1. Written commitments.
2. Oral commitments.
3. Safe-guard through Emigre Governments.

4. Allied interests.
   - "Allies need a stronger Ruritania to help keep Germany in check."
5. Food relief.
   - See P.W.E. and O.W.I. presentation of UNRRA Directives.

D. <u>Ruritania Fights On</u>.

1. News of internal resistance.
2. News of external resistance.

E. <u>How Ruritania Can Help Hasten Victory</u>.

Through action against:

1. <u>German Potential</u>.

   a) Against <u>war-industrial</u> potential by:
      - Passive resistance and undetectable sabotage in Ruritania <u>and</u> Germany.

   b) Against <u>man-power</u> potential by:
      - Non-cooperation and passive resistance against administrative personnel.
      - Subversion of German troop morale.
      - Subversion of German civilian morale.

   c) Against <u>transport</u> potential by:
      - Passive resistance and undetectable sabotage to rail, road and marine transport.

   d) Against <u>food</u> situation by:
      - Beginning to hoard.

2. <u>German Strategy</u>.

   - By assistance to secret armies.
   - By collation of military intelligence before D-day.

3. <u>German News</u>.

   - By spreading Allied news and gospel everywhere.

4. <u>Aims of German Occupation</u>.

   - <u>De-education</u>.   Boycotting Nazi or quisling clergy, teachers and propaganda services.

   - <u>De-industrialization</u>. See "War Industrial Potential" (II. A. I. a)

   - <u>De-population</u>.   Refusal (if possible) to work in Germany; entr 'aide; exposure of colonisation schemes; agitation for return of P.W.'s.

203

PROPAGANDA is the Art of PERSUASION With a View to Producing ACTION

PROPAGANDA

FACT FINDING

Knowledge of facts of political situation

Grouping of Population

Ascertainment of given groups' Opinion on given political fact(s)

Established facts provide foundation for

POLICY

OBJECTIVES
1. Unification
2. Non-collaboration
3. Passive Resistance
4. Undetected Sabotage
5. D.Day action

PLATFORMS
1. Certainty of Allied Victory
2. Hatred of Hun
3. Future Assured
4. Ruritania fights on
5. Action

"Fact-Finding" and "Policy" pave way for

COMPOSITION

PRINCIPLES
1. Simplicity
   a. General Idea
   b. Argument
   c. Language
2. Concreteness
3. Repetition
4. Action

PRELIMINARY QUESTIONS
1. What general Idea?
2. To Whom?
3. Where?
4. When?
5. Against what?
6. From Whom?
7. How.

FRAMEWORK
1. Grievance
2. Hope
3. Action

Once composed your message is ready for

REPRODUCTION

A. TYPESETTING
1. Machine setting
   a. Monotype
   b. Linotype
2. Handsetting
B. BLOCKS

MIMEOGRAPH

TYPEWRITING

Reproduced, message is ready for

DISTRIBUTION

1. By Hand.
2. By post.

METHODS COMBINING REPRODUCTION AND DISTRIBUTION

1. Chain Letter
2. Toys
   a. Chalk
   b. Stickers
   c. Lino-Stencil
3. Rumour

D.1.
September 1943.

CODES AND CIPHERS

CODES AND CIPHERS—INTRODUCTORY

1. <u>PURPOSE</u>.

   a) That a message should be capable of being understood
      by the addressee, and not by the enemy.

   b) That the enemy should not realize that a secret
      communication is being passed. As suspicious to send
      a wire containing the group "BXGCT" as one saying
      "BLOW UP THE BRIDGE".

   <u>Note:</u> In all countries there exists a censorship which
   is very thorough for messages leaving the country, and
   more haphazard for messages passing within the country.
   To beat the censorship would be a fair summary of the
   object of most secret writings.

2. <u>WHEN USED</u>.

   Codes and Ciphers may be necessary whenever it is desired to
   communicate in writing, e.g.:

   - By post, internally or externally.
   - By courier carrying a message or plan.
   - By carrier pigeon.
   - By telegraph.
   - By advertisements in the press.

3. <u>ESSENTIAL REQUIREMENTS</u>.

   a) <u>The Need for Security</u>.

      - Discovery of coded documents or secret ink
        preparations place possessor in a very suspicious
        position. Code systems and inks taught have been
        deliberately selected in order to reduce this risk
        to a minimum.
      - Essential to destroy all paper used in enciphering
        or deciphering messages, and all materials used in
        writing or reading a message in secret ink.
      - Do not keep a written note of any code arrangements
        unless absolutely unavoidable.

b) <u>The Need for Secrecy.</u>

- No one except the actual correspondents should know the system, keywords or ink used.
- An organizer could make different arrangements with each member of his organization. He would know all the systems, but each member should know no other than his own.

c) <u>The Need for Care</u>.

- One error may result in the message being indecipherable.
- General carelessness may arouse suspicion in the mind of the censor.

d) <u>The Need for Concealment</u>.

- As stated above, the fact that a secret message is passing must be concealed from the enemy. This will usually be done by the code system itself. But special papers may help a person carrying a message to conceal it. (Exhibits.) Practise writing on thin paper.

4. <u>CODES AND CIPHERS</u>.

For the purposes of our work, codes and ciphers may be distinguished as follows:

<u>A code</u> is a method of concealing a message in such a way as to make it appear innocent.

<u>A cipher</u> is a method of converting a message into symbols which do not appear innocent, and which have no meaning to a person not possessing the key.

The following varieties of codes and ciphers will be explained:

- Simple code words.
- Innocent letter codes.
- Playfair substitution cipher.
- Double transposition cipher.

5. <u>SIMPLE WORD CODES.</u>

a) <u>General</u>.

A simple word code is the arrangement by conventions of certain words or phrases to mean other words or phrases. Only a limited variety of messages can be sent by such a code as this.

b) <u>When used.</u>

- Telegraph.
- Telephone.
- Personal advertisements.

c) <u>Examples</u>.

- <u>In a Telegram</u>.

NO NEWS RECEIVED FOR AGES ARE YOU WELL
might be agreed upon to mean
CARRY ON WITH THE SCHEME AS ARRANGED.

- <u>On the Telephone</u>.

Heavily veiled and guarded language would usually
be sufficient, such as "usual time and place"; but
code names can also be used, e.g. the word "cat"
can be a word of warning that a third person has
just entered the room.

- <u>In a Personal Advertisement</u>.

"Gold ring lost in Cafe de la Paiz, night of
24 Sept; if found, please return to 6 Rue de
la Croix." might be a general warning to all
members not to visit the organizer until further
notice.

6. <u>INNOCENT LETTER CODES</u>.

a) <u>General</u>.

A code which is concealed within a communication
which looks completely innocent.

b) <u>When used</u>.

To send a message through the post within the country
and from the field to headquarters.

c) <u>Particular Method</u>.

See D.3.

7. <u>PLAYFAIR CIPHER</u>.

a) <u>General.</u>

A substitution cipher in itself easily susceptible of
solution.

b) <u>When used</u>.

To conceal a message in clear which is itself to
be concealed in an innocent letter. The combination
intensely difficult to break.

c) <u>Particular method</u>.

See D.2.

8. <u>DOUBLE TRANSPOSITION CIPHER</u>.

    a) <u>General</u>.

      - A "straight" cipher, i.e. a cipher that looks like
a cipher.

      - Very secure if proper precautions taken.

    b) <u>When used</u>.

      - Transmission by W/T.

      - Message carried by courier.

      - Used in conjunction with invisible ink, e.g.
through post.

      - As a military cipher in the event of an armed
rising.

    c) <u>Particular method</u>.

      - See D.4.

PLAYFAIR CIPHER

This cipher, first used during the 1914-1918 war, combines
comparative security with great simplicity. It is based on a
square grille, containing 25 cells.

A key word or phrase containing at least eight different letters
is memorized. This key word is then written into the square. Any
letters which recur are omitted.

Example: Key work - BALKAN SOBRANIE

B	A	L	K	N
S	O	R	I	E

The remaining letters of the alphabet are then written in to
complete the cage.

As we have only 25 squares, one letter has either to be
suppressed or combined with another.

B	A	L	K	N
S	O	R	IJ	E
C	D	F	G	H
M	P	Q	T	U
V	W	X	Y	Z

209

<u>To Encipher</u>.

Divide the message to be enciphered into groups of two letters,

    E.g.   ARRIVE CHARING CROSS AT FIVE.
            AR RI VE CH AR IN GC RO SS AT FI VE.

When the same letter occurs twice in a group as above, 'SS', the two letters must be separated by a null or dud letter, which has previously been selected for this purpose. When one letter is left over at the end of the message, the group is made up by adding a further dud letter.

    <u>Example</u>: AR RI VE CH AR IN GC RO SX SA TF IV EX

There are now three possible ways in which a pair of letters may occur in the square - on the same horizontal line, in the same vertical column, as opposite corners of a rectangle.

1. <u>Letters on the same horizontal line</u>.

    Substitute the letter immediately on the right:

      <u>Example</u>:   C G - D H
                P Q - Q T

When the last letter of a line is to be changed, return to the beginning of the line (cyclic order).

      <u>Example</u>:   N - B
                E - S
                Z - V
      and   U - P M
                K N - N B

2. <u>Letters in the same vertical column</u>.

    Substitute the letter immediately below:

      <u>Example</u>:   A D - O P
                I G - G T

When the bottom letter of a column is to be changed, return to the head of the column:

      <u>Example</u>:   X - L
                V - B
                Z - N
      and   C V - M B
                U Z - Z N

3. <u>Pairs of letters forming opposite corners of a rectangle</u>.

Take the other diagonal as they appear in the grille:

Example: (i)   (ii)   (iii)

B	A
S	O
C	D

S	O	R	H	E
C	D	F	G	H
M	P	Q	T	U

T	U
Y	Z

     (i) B D – A C
    (ii) M E – U S
   (iii) Z T – Y U

NOTE: Always start from the same level as the <u>first</u> letter of the group.

4. EnCiphered message reads: LOESZSDCLOEKHDIR . . . etc.

NOTE: i) Figures should be replaced by letters on an agreed system.

Example: A – 1
               B – 2

A B C D E F G H I O
1 2 3 4 5 6 7 8 9 0

It may be necessary at times to preface these letters by "FIG" or some such sign to indicate figures are enCiphered.

   ii) Punctuation should be used to make the sense of the message clear. STOP is the only point necessary and should be spelt in full.

  iii) In order to mix the letters round in the square a keyword including two of the letters "U V W X Y Z" would be suitable:

Example: EVIDENTLY.

E	V	I	D	N
T	L	Y	.	.
.	.	.	.	.
.	.	.	.	.
.	.	.	.	.

5. <u>To deCipher</u>.

   a) Take the Keyword and complete the square, omitting the agreed letter.

   b) Divide the cipher message into pairs.

   c) Substitute the pairs into the square, performing the <u>reverse</u> movements to encipherment, i.e.:

i) <u>Horizontal Line</u>.	Move to LEFT.
ii) <u>Vertical Line</u>.	Move UP.
iii) <u>Opposite Corners of Rectangle</u>.	Take the OTHER diagonal.

6. <u>Conclusion</u>.

   This cipher should only be used for short messages.

   When combined with the Rimmer System in an 'Innocent Letter' code it is of high security.

INNOCENT TEXT LETTER

1. <u>DESCRIPTION</u>.

   A method of concealing an enCiphered message (e.g. Playfair) in a letter whose appearance is entirely innocent.

2. <u>METHOD</u>.

   a) Plot a skeleton of the proposed letter including, at the appropriate interval, the letters of the enCiphered message, thus:

L		O		E		S etc.

   b) Using the letters of the enCiphered message as the initial letters of your innocent text letter, write in a letter with an innocent meaning, thus:

Let's	all	go	Qut	together	on	Easter	Sunday	as	Soon	as etc.

3. <u>CONVENTIONS</u>.

   The following conventions must be previously arranged:

   a) Indicator to show letter conceals a secret message – e.g. date, address, signature, courtesy form.

   b) Position of beginning of message – e.g. at beginning of 2nd para., 3rd word in 3rd line. ("Numerical" convention recommended.)

   c) Interval at which "pregnant" words occur.

   d) Treatment of hyphenated and apostrophized words as one or two words.

   e) Treatment (if necessary) of X's – e.g. use "pregnant" words beginning with "ex".

   f) Position of end of message – e.g. at a special word, phrase, point of punctuation. ("Numerical" convention NOT recommended.)

   NOTE: Where possible, simplify conventions for easy memorization. E.g. word interval of 2; message begins at 2nd line of 2nd para., hyphenated and apostrophised words are two words.

4. <u>CONTENT. SUBJECT MATTER AND STYLE</u>.

In the light of recent information obtained from our censorship the following points should be noted in connection with the preparation of a letter containing an enCiphered message:

a) <u>CONTENT</u>.

   i) <u>Sender's Address</u>.

Often it will not be necessary to put your full address at the top of the letter - e.g. in France, when writing from one town to another, it is sufficient to put the name of the town together with the date. When writing abroad it is usually necessary to put the address at the top of the letter and on the flap of the envelope outside.

The address should never be your own (unless this is unavoidable) and either a fictitious address, or that of a quisling, should be used.

Business letters should always be sent on paper headed with a printed letter-head.

   ii) <u>Courtesy Form</u>.

Our censorship informs us that letters beginning with expressions such as "Dear Friend" are usually regarded with some suspicion. Consequently a vague opening phrase of this type should be avoided, as the same practice will probably be observed by the enemy censorship.

b) <u>SUBJECT MATTER</u>.

   i) <u>Theme</u>.

It is difficult to lay down definite rules as to what should be included. Certainly one should avoid harping on the same theme throughout the whole letter. A happy medium of length should be sought. Letters which are too short will attract attention on this account. The actual facts and names mentioned in the letter should all be ones which can be substantiated fairly easily. If the writer of the letter actually gives his name and address, he should be in the possession of good reasons for and proofs of everything he states. It would be advisable to avoid vague hintings and generally woolly references to things "understood between us".

ii) <u>Consistency</u>.

In order that letters may be produced which have some
semblance of reality, it is as well for the student
to write a cover address always in the same manner.
One is not always in the position to tell whether the
correspondence is being watched by the censorship or
not, and consistency in style and subject-matter will
carry more conviction to the reader. It is suggested
that the student selects a person whom he actually
knows in real life and addresses his letters to him
- talking about the things which they have in common
and in the style he actually would use in real life.
If all the letters are dealt with in this way, there
should be no reason for suspicion to be aroused. (What
actually happens in practice is that one time a student
sends to his cover address a business letter, the next
time a love letter, and the next time an appointment
for a visit in the holidays. If the censorship were
watching such correspondence, the hand-writing would be
recognized and suspicion definitely aroused.)

c) <u>STYLE</u>.

i) <u>Consistency</u>.

The style throughout the letter must remain
consistent. It is no use having a flowing style at the
beginning, a staccato style throughout the part where
the secret message is hidden, and once more a flowing
style at the end.

ii) <u>Cover</u>.

The tone must fit in with the general cover, the
addresses, etc.

iii) <u>Punctuation</u>.

It is as well to avoid exaggerated punctuation.
Censors are always on the look-out for semaphore
and morse symbols in the punctuation of letters,
and, consequently, if punctuation is used to denote
the beginning or ending of a message, it should be
recorded as delicately as possible.

iv) <u>Capital letters</u>.

Capital letters - proper names can be used, but not
excessively, and not only at the beginning of pregnant
words.

v) <u>Difficult letters</u>.

Often the message to be sent in the text will be
enCiphered on a system such as Playfair, Multi-
Alphabet, Switch, etc. and certain difficult letters
from the point of view of camouflage will have to be
dealt with. If the cipher message contains too many
of these, the text will be much influenced by the
difficulty of inserting them in an innocent manner.
Should such a difficulty arise, it would be far better
to re-cast the message in a fresh form to avoid the
occurrence of these letters.

DOUBLE TRANSPOSITION

This method is suitable for long messages but not more than 200 letters should be sent at a time. If a message of greater length has to be sent it should be divided into several parts and it is advisable to have means of numbering these, either internally or in the preamble of your messages, to differentiate among them.

1. KEY WORDS.

These should be from 8-20 letters in length and it should be arranged that there is no identity of idea between the first and second key word, i.e. fish and chips, Tottenham Hotspur, etc.

The key words are of no value in themselves but act as a mnemonic. Any series of letters would serve, as the key is derived from the jumbled order they would give alphabetically, i.e.:

E L E M E N T A R Y
2 5 3 6 4 7 9 1 8 10

C R Y P T A N A L Y S I S
3 8 12 7 11 1 6 2 5 13 9 4 10

Take the first key word (Elementary). Vertical columns are dropped for each letter and the message is then written across the columns:

E	L	E	M	E	N	T	A	R	Y
2	5	3	6	4	7	9	1	8	10
F	O	U	R	E	N	E	M	Y	A
I	R	C	R	A	F	T	S	H	O
T	D	O	W	N	O	V	E	R	B
E	N	G	H	A	Z	I			

217

Care should be taken to leave the cage irregular. Count the number of letters.

NOTE:
  i) It may be necessary to use punctuation in order to make the sense clear. Only "stop" (or "comma") are used and these should be spelt in full.

  ii) It would be insecure to use figures in the transposition as they would give clues to sequence of letters. A simple letter substitution should be adopted, e.g.:

    A B C D E F G H I J
    1 2 3 4 5 6 7 8 9 0

  iii) If the message gives a regular cage, extra letters that have no meaning can be added to make an additional partial line. Pick the letters vertically from the columns in the order indicated by the figures indicated at the head of the columns:

    MSE/FITE/UCOG/EANA/ORDN/RRWH/NFOZ/YHR/ETVI/AOB

The resulting series is known as a "single" or "simple" transposition cipher.

The security of the system depends, however, on a further transposition.

Take the <u>second key word</u>, number it alphabetically and drop perpendiculars. Write the letter of the simple transposition across the columns as if they were a clear message:

C	R	Y	P	T	A	N	A	L	Y	S	I	S
3	8	12	7	11	1	6	2	5	13	9	4	10
M	S	E	F	I	T	E	U	C	O	G	E	A
N	A	O	R	D	N	R	R	W	H	N	F	O
Z	Y	H	R	E	T	V	I	A	O	B		

Once more pick the number of letters <u>vertically</u> from the columns in the order indicated by the numbers at the head of the columns. Check to see that no letters have been lost or added en route.

The resulting <u>double transposition</u> is the message to be transmitted. It is usual to divide the letters into groups of five, e.g.:

TNTUR IMNZE FCWAE RVFRR SAYGN BAOID EEOHO HO

The security of double transposition messages is in direct proportion to their length, thus it is not suitable to transmit or even hide in an innocent letter short messages enciphered on this system. They are a prey for anagramming.

NOTE: If several messages are being enciphered on the same pair of keys and sent on the same day or soon after, it is a safety precaution to confine messages to within 10 letters either way of each other, i.e. a message of 80 letters long should not be sent with one from 70-90 letters in length.

2. TO DECIPHER.

If one remembers that this process is merely the reverse of the encipherment, no difficulties should be encountered. At each stage one has to do the opposite to the encipherment, thus:

i) Take the second key word (the one last used) and number it.

ii) It will be necessary to reconstruct the complete cage, as the depth of the columns cannot be determined otherwise. Divide the number of letters in the message by the number of columns given by the key word. This will give the number of columns deep, and any remainder will be an extra column on the left hand side of the cage, i.e. 37 divided by 13 = 2 and 11 over:

3	8	12	7	11	1	6	2	5	13	9	4	10
M	S		F		T	E	U	C			E	
N	A		R		N	R	R	W			F	
Z	Y		R		T	V	I	A				

Replace the letters vertically into the columns in the order indicated by the key.

The cage when completely filled will correspond to the first transposition written as a message on the grille formed by the second key word. Calculate in the same manner the correct cage on the key given by the first key word. Reading off the letters <u>horizontally</u>, replace them <u>vertically</u> into the cage, e.g.

2	5	3	6	4	7	9		8	10
F		U						M	
✗		C						S	
T							✗		
E									

The result will give the message.

This cipher can easily be varied in a number of ways, the most popular of which would be blocked grilles, e.g.:

2	5	3	6	4	7	9	1	8	10
		▓				▓			▓
				▓					
		▓							
▓							▓		
				▓					▓

3. <u>CHANGING THE KEY WORD</u>.

In order that key lengths and column order may vary as much as possible, a precaution against the cryptographer, a system can be employed of using several sequences, e.g.:

    i) Memorization of a poem or a given piece of text from which certain passages are chosen. An <u>indicator</u>

group would be necessary to show what the keys were.

ii) The correspondents make their keys from two identical copies of a book, e.g. page 149, omit first 5 words, line 20.

Let us assume the constant is the five words per line omitted. The rest of the words on the line would give keys of varying length. In this particular instance the indicator group would be 14920. This can be disguised by adding a personal number, for example:

$$
\begin{array}{ll}
14920 & \text{- Actual Key} \\
\underline{52135} & \text{- Personal No.} \\
67055 & \text{- Group transmitted}
\end{array}
$$

FGOEE - In letter

This group, 67055, is the indicator which can be transmitted in the normal manner.

SECRET INKS

The serious use of secret inks is generally confined to war or preparations for war and bound up with the inevitable accompaniment of intrigue and espionage. Such inks are also used by criminal gangs and secret organizations for personal correspondence, but the inks and methods are generally primitive, because the object is rather to correspond while eluding curiosity than to get information or messages through an active and watchful censorship. The criminal or seditionist is rarely a chemist and relies on well tried inks, the secrecy of the mails and general avoidance of suspicion rather than on elaborate formulas.

In war the mails cease to be secret, but an agent can still get away with the use of primitive inks, if he uses them carefully and is careful to avoid arousing suspicion as to the letter or its address.

Secret inks of the simple order such as lemon juice have long been known, but the modern high grade ink is almost entirely a product of the interest caused by the World War. From the time of the development of chemistry and especially organic chemistry (say 1860-80) to 1914 the wars fought were all short, none much over a year's duration, or between powers not possessing high technical skill, e.g. the Boers. In these cases the old inks continued to be used, which depended on simple well known colour reactions such as:-

Iron Alum $\rightleftharpoons$. potassium ferrocyanide or thiocyante (reversible) Lead acedate - ammonium sulphide - starch - iodine, or on the application of heat to natural liquids such as milk, fruit juice or wine.

Early in the World War these methods were still used, both sides expecting an early victory and enemy agents were caught in England using lemon juice and potassium ferrocyanide.

As a stalemate set in and a long war became probable such things were no longer good enough and both sides set out to improve upon them. The Germans, it must be admitted, with their dominance in the fine chemical trade and superiority in skilled men set the pace until near the end of the War, with the Allies striving to catch up.

The Germans concentrated first on simple drugs, which could be carried without incurring suspicion. Antipyrin, aminpyrine and phenacetine, the bases of many headache and anti-fever powders, served them well. However, developers were soon found as the Allies gained experience and the best of simple medicinal or household articles available as secret inks became exhausted. Substances which had no common use, and which were thus ipso facto incriminating, then came into use and were supplied to agents concealed in hollow soap cakes, dentifrice tubes, hollowed places in hair brushes, shaving sticks and so on. Later, with the increasing concentration on the subject the Germans succeeded in giving their agents impregnated articles of clothing, socks, ties, etc. with instructions to soak the article in water for a given time, to obtain ink. The agents were usually quite ignorant of the nature of the inks even of their development. Similar methods of concealing inks are still used. The Germans later used colloidal silver, carried as pin head tablets easily hidden. This had to be developed like a photograph. Silver protein, sold as an antiseptic under various names, was a similar ink.

Both sides worked to find a universal developer, which would reveal all secret writing, whatever the ink. In 1917 the Allies hit on iodine, as a vapour or a special solution, in a wooden, glass fronted box, filled with iodine vapour by warming a few crystals in the base, the iodine attached itself to the writing which became clearly visible, brown in colour. When the message had been read or photographed, exposure to sunlight or sulphur dioxide gas, bleached it. The solution brushed on and later bleached with "hypo" solution behaved similarly. Thus messages could be tapped and sent on which is usually necessary to avoid alarming the enemy and shutting down on a line of communications.

Soon after Allied chemists made this discovery, it was found no longer to work on some documents where secret ink was known to exist; the enemy had devised a counter. The iodine test depended on no chemical reaction but on the disturbance to the sizing and fibres of paper always caused by water, and which is unavoidable with any ink. It could and did develop writing made with pure distilled water. The obvious counter was to disturb the paper structure equally all over, by damping. This was done by steaming, or swabbing with water. (This of course would not avail where the ink reacted chemically with iodine, such as tin chloride or reducing agents in general).

With the war development, highly secret and elaborate inks were introduced and as with codes and Ciphers each side had to learn to read its enemy's inks and devise new ones which would baffle the enemy. The former especially was technically most difficult; a new ink had to be analized, which was a job requiring great skill and patience, considering the minute quantities of chemical available, and a developer predicted from the analysis, where possible, and worked out as to conditions or else discovered by trial and error.

Shortly after the war ultra violet rays were discovered as an aid in detecting falsifications, such as note and bond forgeries, and the mercury vapour lamp used for such purposes proved a valuable aid in the secret ink field.

Other than sound waves, the most important waves known are the electromagnetic waves. These are independent of air, and can be transmitted through a vacuum which sound cannot. These waves vary widely in their properties and their impact on the life of mankind, and apparently the sole factor determining the various kinds of electromagnetic waves is the <u>wave length</u>

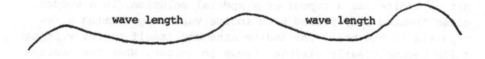

which may vary from a foot to a mile or more for the Herzian or wireless waves, down to distances comparable to the size of an atom or about one hundred-millionth of an inch (the finest X rays and radium rays).

The light rays are a tiny band on this huge range of variation, from the violet rays (wavelength about .00002 inch, to the red rays (about .00004 inch). Rays longer than this are the infra red or heat rays and waves a little shorter are the violet rays, both of which are invisible, but so resembling light in other rays so as to give to ultra-violet rays the popular name "Black Light".

Many substances have the power of absorbing such rays and emitting the energy as longer wave length, light or visible light. This property is called "Luminescence". If the substance can "store up" the rays, and emit when the stimulation has ceased, it is "phosphorescence". If emission takes place only while the stimulating rays are being received it is "fluorescence". The luminous paint on watches is phosphorescence. Fluorescence is seldom seen in ordinary life, since it is caused by sun or arc light, but at the same time masked.

Examples of fluorescence are shown by motor oil, olive oil, quinine and many dyes. The fluorescence colour bears no relation to the ordinary colour and in fact is rarely exactly the same, e.g. motor oil (blue-green), rhodamine a crimson dye (salmon pink), leaves (crimson).

Many secret inks are easily detectable under the mercury lamp, which contains a filter absorbing nearly all visible light which might mask the effect and passing only a faint purple glow, as well as black light. Paper usually has a mauve fluorescence. Gums on envelopes appear blush white. Human skin and teeth fluorescence.

A secret writing might appear either fluorescent, or by absorbing the black light which makes the paper fluorescent, it appears darker. Yellowish compounds especially do this. Damping is no precaution against this test, which leaves no traces on the paper. A record can be kept by photographing the writing under the rays. Often the lamp will show that writing exists without showing it legibly. Other means must be found to read the writing.

After the foregoing summary it is necessary to consider secret inks in more detail:-

The essential properties for a secret ink, apart from the fact that it must be invisible and capable of being developed, are:-

1. It must be sufficiently soluble in water.

2. It must be non-volatile, with no pronounced smell (obviously menthol or camphor would not do).

3. It must deposit no crystals on the paper, and be invisible in glancing light.

4. It should not be visible under ultra-violet light.

5. It must not decompose or rot or colour the paper (silver nitrate slowly turns black on paper or cloth and is used in marking ink).

6. It should not react chemically with iodine or any other of the usual developers.

7. The developers for it should be as few as possible.

8. It should not develop under heat.

9. If possible it should be obtainable by laymen without
   difficulty and should therefore have at least one innocent use.

An ink complying with all these conditions would be a valuable
acquisition. In practice (6) is nearly always incompatible with
(9), since nearly all common chemicals usable as inks have known
developers. Mixed chemicals are rare as inks since this increases
the number of developers, but mixtures having properties absent
in the various constituents are useful.

Secret inks fall into two classes. Dealing first with class B:-

B. Animal secretions, natural or semi-natural liquids – saliva,
   urine, seminal fluid, lemon or any fruit juice, wine,
   dissolved gum or mucilage, milk, diluted white of egg, soap
   suds, porridge fluid, diluted blood or blood serum.

These are the oldest, simplest and most easily detected secret
inks known. None of them would pass a competent testing station.
Urine, saliva (usually), seminal fluid, wine, gum, all show in
ultra violet rays; fruit juices, milk, egg-white, wine, saliva,
urine, porridge fluid and soap suds are revealed by heat.

Diluted blood requires a special test and is certainly the best
of the group (blood clots on standing, leave a clear straw
coloured serum, dilute this about one in ten).

In spite of the insecurity of these inks they were valuable for
their ready availability, for use within a country. The human
secretions are much used by prisoners. Even water can be used if
the message is not damped. But where any censorship has to be
passed, they should only be used if nothing else is available
and the risk of detection has to be taken, and obviously not for
close secrets.

A. The inks in Class A consist of chemicals (in the usual
   sense) of all kinds, from simple (and unsafe) inks like alum
   and potassium ferrocyanide, ferric alum, gallic acid, lead
   acetate, etc. to the most modern and secret high-grade inks.

A further sub-classification is necessary.

A "high-grade" ink may be defined as one which no foreign power
can read. It is always a closely guarded secret. When a foreign
power discovers the secret, the ink ceases to be high grade, but
it may be used for work in technically more backward countries,

or for less important work. Thus we arrive at a natural classification:-

1. High grade inks as defined above.

2. Inks of secret composition, no longer high grade.

3. Other chemical inks, of which the composition and the developer are known generally to those concerned, in all nations. These like class B, are unsafe where vigilant censorship is to be feared, and the considerations mentioned in Class B, generally apply.

It is now useful to consider the question from the censor's point of view.

A document is received for testing with the possibility of secret ink being present. The chemist examines the surface in glancing light for any unevenness in the surface or any grease or wax marks. Then it is examined in strong light with a lens, for any irregularities. The visible ink writing is examined for any blurring or streaking, for any hints as to treatment (e.g. the word "heat" or any marks which would inform the receiver of the presence of a hidden message. Any wrinkling or cockling of the paper due to careless damping would arouse instant suspicion.

The paper is next examined in filtered ultra-violet light, and with iodine vapour, and any other means, which can be used without altering the appearance of the document such as ammonia fumes for phenolphthalein (commonly sold as a laxative, turns magenta when exposed to alkali).

Obviously for the censor, it is seven-eighths of the battle to know that a secret message is there. He will then do everything in his power to read it, taking days if necessary and using every known means and resource. Otherwise, if the writing and damping are well done, an ink which is at least safe against the foregoing tests is used and there are no outside grounds for suspicion, it is probable that the examination will be carried no farther and the letter allowed to pass. Heating to the charring point is left till last, as a rule, but heating below 175°C (350°F) may be tried without leaving traces.

For invisible ink writing clearly the ink is important but hardly less important is the writing surface, usually paper. The use of cloth, garments etc. for secret writing must never be overlooked, as it avoids some of the troubles of paper, but such use for regular messages through the mails is difficult without

227

arousing suspicion. Where the clothes are worn, or carried in luggage over a frontier, this is useful for long messages, which could not be memorized without great difficulty. Invisible ink has been used on a person's skin and developed by sitting before a fire, but such methods are not generally possible. A resourceful agent can profitably devise new variants of them, if he understands the new conditions involved, but for secret ink the medium in 90% of cases is paper.

This must never be a glazed paper, far less any kind of coated art paper with heavy sizing, which reveals at once when viewed in glancing light, the presence of a message. Also it should not be ruled since the rulings often reveal where the secret ink pen has passed over them.

The duller the surface the better; newsprint, being poorly sized is best of all, and letters or words can be picked out with dots of invisible ink. Censors know this, of course and are vigilant in cases where bundles of newspapers are regularly sent to a given address, unless direct from the papers' offices. Then, of course there is the old trick of writing (or dotting on newspaper) an apparently secret but less important message in an ink fairly easily (but not too easily) detected, and the real message in a really safe ink. Many censors have fallen for this, but the times when it can be used are limited, as the message is usually sent on with instructions to watch the person collecting it. If the first message is well done, to appear to be about innocent but private (e.g. family) affairs, such a message may be allowed into neutral territory or ignored.

An agent should always experiment with his proposed ink and paper and satisfy himself as to the best ink strength, and conditions of steaming, or damping and ironing.

As in the case of codes and Ciphers whenever a simple ink is used a sample should be developed to ensure that the correct strength is being used.

A secret ink should always be used at the maximum dilution capable of being detected by the best developer, and this dilution ascertained before hand. It is useful to memorize that -

A 1% solution is made by dissolving - 1 gramme (gm) in 100 cubic centimeters (ccs) or Millimetres (ml).

The British apothecaries amounts equal to the above are 15 grains (gr) and 3½ fluid ounces (fl.oz). Other dilutions can be calculated from this.

Spoons and cups are not reliable units of volume, but a medicine bottle is usually marked with its volume in fluid ounces.

A grade of paper technically called "onion skin" which is thin and strong with marked "rattle" is often favourable for secret ink work since it has a natural wrinkle or cockle like that produced by secret inks. Censors know this also however, and since such papers are not normally used for writing (except sometimes for air mail), they are perhaps best avoided. The writer has seen a letter to a German prisoner of war tested for no other apparent reason than the use of this paper.

Ball pointed nibs were formerly used but their possession is enough to hang a man in war time. A turned up nib such as the universally known "Waverley" is as good. The pen should be held level, at the smallest angle to the paper possible and used with a light touch, so long as liquid is actually being deposited.

A clean nib should always be used, preferably a brass one.

Secret inks have this advantage over Ciphers and codes, except the well known "innocent letter" code, that Ciphers and codes are suspect at once and can always be broken if enough time and material is available. The "innocent letter" if well done, is probably the best means of all, but it requires a definite standard of intelligence and education. If these are lacking, or there was no possibility of compiling a code, secret inks, well managed, are the next best. In any case secret writing is really only a variation of the "innocent letter", since it is never sent on a bare sheet, but always accompanied by an innocent letter, typed or written.

REFERENCE TABLE

SYMPATHETIC INK	FLUORESCENCE (Visibility to Naked Eye under Ultra-Violet Light)	BEST DEVELOPERS
Acetic Acid	Yes - very faint	Heat Ultra-Violet Light
Alum (Potassium Aluminum Sulphate)	Yes - faint	Heat Ultra-Violet Light
Ammonium Chloride	Yes - very faint	Silver Nitrate and light Heat
Anthracene	Yes	Ultra-Violet Light
Aspirin (Acetysalicylic Acid)	Yes	Ultra-Violet Light Heat
Benzoic Acid	Yes	Ferric Chloride Solution Ultra-Violet Light
Berberine	Yes	Ultra-Violet Light
Blood	Yes - very faint	Benzidine and Hydrogen peroxide Eosine in Alcohol Ultra-Violet Light
Borax	No	Heat
Calcium Sulphide (Phosphorescent)	Phosphorescent	Darkness
Chrysaniline	Yes	Ultra-Violet Light
Citric Acid	No	Heat
Cobaltous Chloride	Yes	Heat Ultra-Violet Light Hydrogen or Ammonium Sulphide
Cobaltous Chloride with a Nickel Salt	Yes	Heat Ultra-Violet Light
Cobaltous Nitrate	Yes	Heat Ultra-Violet Light
Copper Chloride	Yes	Ultra-Violet Light Heat

Copper Sulphate	Yes	Heat Hydrogen or Ammonium Sulphide Iodine Fumes Ultra-Violet Light
Damp sheet pressure writing	No	Iodine Fumes
Eosine	Yes - Orange Yellow	Ultra-Violet Light
Esculin	Yes - Blue	Ultra-Violet Light
Ferrous Chloride	Yes	Potassium Ferricyanide Ultra-Violet Light
Ferrous Sulphate	Yes	Potassium Ferricyanide Ultra-Violet Light
Ferric Chloride	Yes	Potassium Ferrocyanide Potassium Thiocyanate Tannic Acid Hydrogen or Ammonium Sulphide Ultra-Violet Light
Galls		Ferric Chloride
Gold Chloride	Yes	Heat Ultra-Violet Light
Gum Arabic (Acadia Powder)	Yes - very faint	Dust and Powders Ultra-Violet Light
Hydrochloric Acid	Yes	Silver Nitrate & Light Heat Ultra-Violet Light
Invisible Laundry Marking Inks	Yes	Ultra-Violet Light
Lactic Acid	Yes - Faint	Heat Ultra-Violet Light
Lead Acetate	Yes - Faint orange inge	Hydrogen or Ammonium Sulphide

		Heat
		Iodine Fumes
		Ultra-Violet Light
Lemon Juice	Yes - Faint	Iodine Fumes
		Heat
		Ultra-Violet Light
Manganous Chloride	Yes	Silver Nitrate and
		Light Hydrogen or
		Ammonium Sulphide
		Ultra-Violet Light
Manganous Sulphate	Yes	Hydrogen or
		Ammonium Sulphide
		Ultra-Violet Light
Mercuric Chloride	Yes - Faint	Heat
		Silver Nitrate and
		Light Iodine Fumes
		Hydrogen or
		Ammonium Sulphide
		Ultra-Violet Light
Mercuric Nitrate	Yes	Heat
		Ultra-Violet Light
		Hydrogen or
		Ammonium Sulphide
Milk	Yes	Iodine Fumes
		Ultra-Violet Light
		Heat
Mucilage (dilute)	Yes	Heat
		Ultra-Violet Light
Murine	Yes - Yellow	Ultra-Violet Light
Nickelous Chloride	Yes	Heat
		Hydrogen or
		Ammonium Sulphide
		Ultra-Violet Light
Oil of Lemon	Yes	Ultra-Violet Light
		Ink
Onion Juice	Yes	Ultra-Violet Light
		Iodine Fumes Heat
Onion Juice & Saliva	Yes	Iodine Fumes
		Ultra-Violet Light
		Heat

Oxalic Acid	Yes	Heat Ultra-Violet Light
Petrolatum	Yes	Ultra-Violet Light
Phenolphthalein	Yes	An Alkali Ultra-Violet Light
Potassium Ferricyanide	Yes	Ferrous Chloride Ultra-Violet Light
Potassium Ferrocyanide	Yes	Ferric Chloride Ultra-Violet Light
Potassium Hydroxide	Yes - Faint	Heat Ultra-Violet Light
Potassium Thiocyanate	Yes	Ferric Chloride Solution Ultra-Violet Light
Pyrogallol	Yes - Dark Violet	An Alkali Ultra-Violet Light
Quinine Bisulphate	Yes	Ultra-Violet Light
Quinine Sulphate	Yes	Ultra-Violet Light
Reduced Fuchsin	Yes	Air and Sunlight Ultra-Violet Light
Salicylic Acid	Yes	Ultra-Violet Light Ferric Chloride Solution
Saliva	Yes - Very faint	Iodine Fumes Heat Ultra-Violet Light
Silver Nitrate	Yes	Any soluble Chloride and Light
Soda (Baking)	Yes - Faint	Iodine Fumes Heat Ultra-Violet Light
Soda (Washing)	Yes	Iodine Fumes Heat Ultra-Violet Light
Soap Solution	No	Iodine Fumes Heat
Sodium Chloride	No	Silver Nitrate and Light

Sodium Napthionate	Yes	Ultra-Violet Light
Starch Solution	Yes - Very Faint	Iodine Heat
Stearic Acid	Yes	Ultra-Violet Light
Storage Battery Acid (Dilute Sulphuric Acid)	Yes Yes - Faint	Heat Ultra-Violet Light
Sugar Solution	Yes - Faint	Heat Ultra-Violet Light
Tannin (Tannic Acid)	Yes - Faint	Ferric Chloride Solution Ultra-Violet Light
Tin Chloride	Yes	Ultra-Violet Light Hydrogen or Ammonium Sulphide
Titanium Oxide	Yes - Pale Blue	Ultra-Violet Light
Uranium Nitrate	Yes - Yellow	Ultra-Violet Light
Uric Acid	Yes	Ultra-Violet Light
Urine	Yes	Iodine Ultra-Violet Light Heat
Whites of eggs	Yes - Faint	Iodine Fumes Ultra-Violet Light
Wine	Sometimes	Heat
Zinc Sulphide	Yes (also Phosphorescent)	Ultra-Violet Light

LIST OF INKS

U.V. - Detectable by Ultra-violet rays

INK	DEVELOPER	COMMENTS
Salt 5%	Silver nitrate 5% (For warts & light)	Fair
Milk Aqueous solution	By graphite	Very bad.
Alum 1%	Heat.	Good. Easily obtainable.
Anti-pyrene .75% (For headache)	Ferric Chloride 10%	Good. "High grade" ink.
Phenolphthalein .-1 (For laxative) In Ammonia and water (about 1 pt. Amm. to 3 pts. water)	Saturated solution sodium carbonate (Soda)	-do-
Lead acetate 1%	Ammonium sulphide 5%	Good. Ammonium sulphide hard to obtain
Sulphuric Acid. Very dilute.	Heat	Poor.
Chalk Few grains dissolved in acetic acid (White vinegar).	Iron until paper begins to turn yellow. Bathe in .5% silver nitrate. Iron again.	Very good but difficult development.
Sugar 1%	Heat.	Bad.
Urine. U.V. Dilute.	Heat	Bad.
Sulphates (Magnesium)1% Epsom Salts.))	) Wash paper in 1% lead acetate. Wash in running water.	)) Good but) difficult to) obtain ammonium

Zinc sulphate)	Immerse in 5%	) sulphide.
Calcium Sulphate)	ammonium sulphide.	)
(Plaster of Paris))		)
Sodium Sulphate)		)
(Glauber Salts))		)
Onion Juice	Heat.	Bad.
Lemon Juice	Heat.	Poor.
Saliva U.V.	Heat or .5% methylene blue. (Dilute Crystal Palace Marking Ink.)	Bad.
Starch. 1%	Heat or weak iodine	Fair.
Wax Paper. (To wrap up fruit)	Graphite or Charcoal	Simple and good. Can be used under typewriter, also to write on material and possible to type on material. Wax paper sometimes used to wrap gelignite.
Potassium Iodide. 1% solution (Apt to discolour)	2% gold chloride.	Good, but difficult to obtain. Allow Tincture of Iodine to evap. till colourless. Residue is Pot. Iodide.
Magnesia. Few grains dissolved in acetic acid.	Iron until paper is yellow. Wash in .5% silver nitrate. Iron again.	Very good but difficult development.
Soda/Salt. Paper impregnated with washing soda, writing done in salt.	Bathe in silver nitrate 5%. Wash/ Bathe in sulphuric) acid 10%. Wash/ Bathe in 3% ammonium sulphide.	} Fair } } }

SECRET INKS

Pyramidon.	Mixture of 2% potassium ferri-cyanide, and 2% ferric sulphate (freshly made)	Very good but used extensively by German Agents.
Potassium Thiocyanate. .5%	Ferric chloride 10%	Good. Hard to obtain materials.
Potassium Ferro-cyanide. (Visible unless v. weak)	10% ferric chloride	Bad. It always shows under iodine developer.
Molybdic Acid. (Apt to turn blue)	Heat	Bad.

MINOR TACTIC AND FIELDCRAFT

MINOR TACTICS AND FIELDWORK

Para-Military training is the basis of the type of warfare known as diversive or guerrilla warfare. Operations of this nature are usually carried out by bands of patriots in countries over-run by the enemy, and behind the lines. In the initial stages such bands may be unco-ordinated, and developed on the initiative of local patriot leaders. Later, they may be brought into closer touch, and may work in full co-operation with the field armies (cf. Russia).

While these operations are of necessity limited in extent, owing to the difference in size of the opposing forces, a small well trained and well led band of partisans can do damage to the enemy which is out of all proportion to the size of the band.

Three important features of this type of warfare are:

1. Speed and aggression in the attack, followed by quick get-away. SURPRISE IS ESSENTIAL.

2. The ability to strike at many points, either at the same time or at different times, in order to harass the enemy and keep him always on the alert.

3. All attacks must be directed against targets which, if destroyed, will bring about the maximum amount of damage to the enemy war effort -

   a) Directly and immediately, such as attacks on enemy headquarters during a battle.

   b) Indirectly; attacks on communications, supplies, or industrial production.

The results of such diversive attacks on the enemy can be far reaching:

1. Attacks on supplies, transport, or industries can slow down and partially disorganize the whole war effort.

2. Such attacks force the enemy to disperse his troops for police and garrison duties.

3. This lowers their morale and consequently their efficiency.

While the importance of this type of warfare is great, it is as well to consider its limitations.

1. It is not often possible, for reasons of security, for large bands to operate. This of necessity limits the scope of operations, and makes the selection of the right target vitally important.

2. Because the Germans fear this type of attack they take stern measures to stamp it out.

3. It is difficult to secure weapons, supplies and explosives.

4. It is difficult, and often impossible, to co-ordinate guerrilla operations into a concerted plan over a wide area.

In view of the factors outlined above, it is essential in guerrilla warfare operations that each soldier adheres to the following basic principles:

1. He must have complete knowledge of the country in which he is operating, or failing this, expert knowledge of how to make the best use of, and move about in, strange country.

2. He must have expert knowledge of all weapons used by his guerrilla band, and also if possible, full knowledge of as many weapons as possible used by the enemy.

3. He must give at all times complete obedience to his leader, and be absolutely devoted to the cause.

The nature of guerrilla warfare demands particular attention to:

1. FIELDCRAFT.

Since the element of surprise is essential in all particular operations, fieldcraft requires the greatest attention. In Depot School training students receive instruction in individual Fieldcraft. The Para-Military instruction carries this training further, and students are required to apply their knowledge to the infinitely more difficult job of collective fieldcraft. It is very much more difficult to conceal ten men than one, and very much harder for ten men to move about silently at night together.

The only way this can be achieved is for every man to concentrate the whole time on his own individual fieldcraft,

and remember that if he makes a mistake it endangers the
lives of all his companions.

Formations.

Any party of men moving across country should move in a
definite formation, not in a constantly changing huddle or a
straggling line. The reasons for this, and the essentials of
any formation, are to ensure:

a) Maximum use of available cover.

b) Permanent all-round defence.

c) Adequate communication between all members of the party,
   but particularly between the leader and his scouts.

A great many formations have been devised for use by the
regular army, some of which fulfil these requirements,
but most are unsatisfactory because they are impossible to
maintain either for a long distance or in broken country, and
very few really ensure the maximum use of available cover.
Chiefly for this latter reason S.T.S. do not use the diamond
and box shaped formations.

For a small body of men moving across any type of country,
either by night or by day, there are no better formations
than modified versions of single file. Scouts, according to
conditions and circumstances, must always be ahead of this
file. The main body, headed by the leader, follows on in
single file.

The intervals between the members of the party, and between the
scouts and the leader, depend entirely on the nature of the
ground and the limit of visibility. The scouts must be in touch
with the leader and in touch with each other; once they are
out of sight of the leader they are useless. Under the best
visibility conditions it is not desirable for scouts to be more
than 100 - 150 metres in front of the leader; in darkness or in
very close country 20 metres would be enough. The leader must
watch his scouts the whole time for any signal they may give
him - they are his eyes.

The only time when a considerable interval between members
of the main party is desirable is when, for instance, an
open hillside must be crossed in distant view of the enemy.
Here a close mass of men moving would be visible when widely
separated men would not. Each man of the party is detailed to
observe in a particular direction the whole time, and he must

be able to draw the leader's attention to anything that he sees with the least possible delay - a wide interval between members of the party makes this difficult.

When the party halts, it is automatically covered by the scouts, to ensure that it is not taken by surprise. This should be an invariable rule, whatever the reason for the halt.

Also, whatever the reason for the halt, the whole of the main party must immediately get into cover. The practice of halting for discussion in exposed places is very common in training, and is a very serious fault. As soon as the leader realises that a halt is necessary, whether because he is off his route and must use the map, or because he has reached the end of a bound and must wait for the scouts to observe, he must immediately get his party into a position where they cannot be seen. This is all the more important if the halt is in order to study the map - the white flash of a map can be seen at a great distance, and at no time should more of it be exposed than is absolutely necessary.

2. <u>MAP DIRECTION FINDING</u>.

Very often the partisan force will be so familiar with the country that the use of maps and compasses will not be necessary. But the time may come when the band is forced to operate in unfamiliar territory. Therefore, the partisan fighter must be adept in the handling of maps and compasses, and he must bear in mind that unless he makes his observation (while reading the map or compass) from behind cover, he runs a serious risk of giving himself away. Fieldcraft will therefore play an important part in direction finding.

3. <u>WEAPONS</u>.

<u>Pistols, Sub-Machine Guns, Grenades</u>.
The partisan fighter must have complete confidence in the weapon with which he is armed. He must regard it as a weapon which, if necessary he can use to force his way to the target to accomplish his task, or to destroy any enemy who attempts to prevent his withdrawal.

Should his weapon become useless, he must be ready and able to use his hands, or any other weapon which may be available.

He must learn to take care of his weapons, and to check up before he starts to ensure that his weapon is working, and that he has sufficient ammunition. This ammunition must be carried so that it is readily available.

4. EXPLOSIVES.

If explosives are carried, the maxim "The Demolition must not fail" will be borne in mind the whole time. Therefore:

a) All the charges and other stores must be prepared very carefully and completely before setting out.

b) Full allowance must be made for the possibility of casualties, i.e., a complete duplicate set of demolition stores should be carried, and every single man in the party should be equipped to do some damage on his own if plans miscarry.

While at the Para-Military School students will carry out a number of day and night schemes, and will have practice in planning small operations of the type mentioned above.

It will not be possible to achieve complete realism in targets and the military background, such as would be the case in the field. Every attempt will be made, however, to make schemes realistic.

Students will only get the maximum benefit from schemes if they use their imagination, and carry out the scheme as if it were a real operation. They must never do anything in a scheme which they would not do in the field.

TACTICS OF SMALL RAIDING PARTIES

1. <u>INTRODUCTION</u>.

   This lecture is designed to cover the tactical action of
   a small body of men attacking a guarded objective with
   explosives or incendiaries. It is not intended to cover the
   action of an individual or a very small party carrying out an
   operation by stealth alone.

   The target for such a raid might be any worth-while objective
   which may be destroyed by demolition or by fire. Raiding
   parties may, of course, attack objectives which it is more
   convenient to destroy by some other means. In general,
   the tactics of the raid will remain the same, though the
   composition of the party and individual action will naturally
   differ.

2. <u>THE COMPOSITION OF THE PARTY</u>.

   The remarks which follow have in view a basic party of 10
   men, but are applicable to much greater numbers.

   In an attack such as we have visualised above, the factors to
   be overcome to achieve success will be essentially:

   a) the enemy guarding the objective, and
   b) the objective itself.

   In addition, the party must reach the objective in safety,
   must be undisturbed while the work is done, and must withdraw
   in safety. The composition of the party follows logically
   upon these points.

   <u>Leader</u>: First, as in any operation, there must be <u>a leader</u>,
   who controls the entire operation. Among other things, it
   is his job to see that the men chosen for the various jobs
   outlined below are suitable for their work.

   <u>Sentry Party</u>: Second, there must be a small force whose job
   is to deal with the enemy at the objective. This we call
   the sentry party, since the sentries are the only people who
   will in all cases have to be dealt with in some way. Although
   in a great many cases the plan will be to avoid the enemy
   altogether, the sentry party must be prepared to kill them in
   case of emergency. The sentry party prepare the way for the

<u>Demolition, or Assault, Party</u>, whose job it is to effect the actual destruction of the target. They must be undisturbed while at work, and this is looked after by the

<u>Covering Party</u>. Their job is to see that while both the sentry party and the demolition party are, in turn, at work, they are not surprised by unexpected enemy – or in some cases to engage and delay an expected enemy.

These are the essential components of the party, and will vary in strength according to the strength of the objective and the number of men available. An estimate of exactly how many men are required for any piece of work must always be formed by the leader.

The exact action of these various components we shall now discuss in detail.

3. <u>ACTION AT THE STARTING POINT</u>.

   a) While the main body is assembling, the Covering Party will be responsible for all-round defence.

   b) The leader and sub-leaders (if any) will make a careful check of all demolition stores, weapons and equipment, and their proper distribution amongst the various members of the party.

   c) The leader will make a final check that no man is carrying any incriminating papers or documents, or any loose articles liable to make a noise, e.g. coins, keys, half-full match boxes, half-full water bottles, etc.

   d) Each man's personal camouflage, if this is being used, will be checked.

   e) Watches should be synchronised.

   f) Last but not least, check that each man knows his orders.

4. <u>MOVEMENT TOWARDS THE OBJECTIVE</u>.

The formation recommended (already referred to in previous lectures) is that of single file, with scouts ahead. The number of scouts used will vary with the number of men available. Three is the maximum. Behind them, at a distance varying with the visibility and possibilities of communication with the leader, come the main party, whose movement they are safeguarding. The scout's job is to make certain that any enemy, or difficult features of the ground, are made known to the leader before he stumbles upon them unaware, and to ensure that the party follows the best available route. The scouts are drawn from the covering party.

The main party will usually be disposed as follows:

In front is the leader, in communication with his scouts; behind him come part of the remainder of the covering party, so that the comparatively defenceless demolition party are sandwiched between the two sections of the covering party.

The demolition party will be carrying stores which are sometimes heavy; they will also require their hands to be free at the objective, so that they cannot be encumbered with bulky weapons. They must be treated largely as passengers during the advance, though they will retain responsibility for observing in a certain direction, as already outlined in the lecture 'General Movement by Day'.

Whether the sentry party is also sandwiched between two sections of the covering party, will depend on how the leader has armed them. If they are to kill silently, they must also be unencumbered with bulky weapons, and the same considerations will apply to them as apply to the demolition party. If they are to kill the sentries by fire, they will be adequately armed and may bring up the rear of the party – though in all cases the rearmost man should also be the second in command of the party.

The party moves forward by bounds – this was also discussed in an earlier lecture – and at any time when the party is stationary, the covering party should take up position to protect it as it would at the objective.

5. THE RECONNAISSANCE POINT.

The leader, either from personal reconnaissance or from information received, will have previously selected a point from which to make his final reconnaissance. This we term the "recce point". At a convenient place some distance short of the recce point the leader will leave his party under cover and protected by the covering party, and will himself go forward alone to make his final reconnaissance. In cases where this final reconnaissance cannot well be done by one man only, he may send a second or third member of the party to deal with those areas which he cannot himself reconnoitre.

The object of this final reconnaissance is to ensure that no change in the situation has occurred which might upset the

leader's plans. When it is finished he will return to his
party and either issue necessary amendments to his orders or
tell them that his original orders stand.

6. DISPOSITIONS AT THE OBJECTIVE.

The leader's next action is to place the various components
of his party in position for the attack. First, the covering
party will be placed. Their positions must afford the maximum
field of view and of fire and should also afford cover to the
sentry party themselves should they need assistance - thus
making certain that the sentries can in no case interfere.
Where the ground makes this double function of the covering
party impossible, there must be one section of the covering
party, whose function at the objective is solely to cover the
sentry party, and then revert to a normal covering function.
Communication signals between the covering party and the
leader will have been previously arranged - also the exact
action to be taken by them in the case of enemy approach or
other circumstances visualised by the leader.

Next, the leader will despatch both the sentry party and the
demolition party simultaneously. The sentry party will be
sent to previously determined positions from which to deal
with the sentries. The considerations which affect the method
by which they will do this are discussed in detail in the
next lecture. Even when the plan is to avoid the sentries
altogether, the sentry party should be in position to deal
with them in case of emergency.

The leader will aim at getting the demolition party as close
as possible to the objective, ready for immediate action when
the signal for assault is given. If this is not done there
will be a delay between the signal and the laying of the
charges, which may just give time to the enemy to locate and
cut off the party's withdrawal.

If there is no specific reason against it, the leader himself
will usually be with the demolition party, where he can
control the actual destruction of the objective, without
which the operation has failed.

7. ACTION AT THE OBJECTIVE.

We assume that the various sections of the party are now in
their final position and waiting for the attack to start.
This action starts immediately the sentry party have killed

the sentries, or, if they are to be avoided, when the leader gives the word that the coast is clear.

In a case where the sentry or sentries are killed by fire, the sound of that shot is the signal for the assault to go in. Whether the shot was fired by the sentry party or the sentry will not matter, for if it was fired by the latter, the covering party (see above) will kill him immediately.

Simultaneous action now takes place. The demolition party, under the immediate control of the leader, move quickly in and place their charges. The sentry party, whose job is now finished, take up position as an inner perimeter covering party. If a simultaneous attack upon the guardroom which supplies the sentries is part of the plan, this attack also goes in upon the same signal. The actual drill for such an attack is described in the next lecture.

As soon as the placing of the charges is completed, the leader will give his signal for the withdrawal. If the killing of the sentries has been done by fire, this signal may be an overt one, such as blasts upon a whistle. If, on the other hand, the killing has been done silently, or the sentries have been avoided, there will so far have been no noise and a delayed action charge will have been used, so that the party is well off the scene of action when the explosion takes place. In this case the signal for withdrawal must therefore be such as to arouse no suspicion; as will also have been all previous signals.

8. <u>WITHDRAWAL</u>.

As soon as the signal for withdrawal is given, the party will withdraw in the following order:

First, the demolition party, who, being lightly armed, must at all costs avoid contact with the enemy, and with them the sentry party who have formed an inner perimeter covering party and will now act as scouts to the withdrawing demolition party. Last to withdraw will be the covering party proper, who have heavier weapons and can bring more fire to bear in case of necessity. They will follow the demolition party as soon as they are certain that the latter are off the ground. They will keep a constant watch to the rear, but must on no account open fire upon any relieving enemy unless certain that they are detected.

The whole party meet at a rendezvous at a safe distance from the objective. Here the leader checks his party, makes certain that they are all present, reforms them into the order of march as for approach, or orders a dispersed withdrawal from that point.

A dispersed withdrawal by night is extremely difficult if the various members of the party are heading for the same place, because their routes are liable to approximate, and in the dark it is difficult to tell friend from foe. Thus, the party may individually be pinned to the ground, each man thinking the other's to be enemy searching for him.

The leader will have ordered a time limit for arrival at this rendezvous after which any member of the party not present will be considered a casualty.

9. COMMUNICATIONS.

The whole question of signals is considered to be of such importance that it is dealt with in a separate lecture.

10. DEALING WITH CASUALTIES.

Casualties present a far greater problem to the raiding party than to the ordinary soldier. Since it is absolutely essential that the raiding party should be off the scene of action as soon as their job is done, the most satisfactory method is probably to arrange a subsequent rendezvous not far away, to which wounded will make their way if capable of doing so. The leader should state in his orders the location of this emergency rendezvous and at what time (preferably during darkness on two successive nights) it will be visited by the search party. Where it has been possible to arrange this, medical stores may be left in advance at this R.V., and the search party should be equipped for carrying a wounded man or men. In the majority of cases it is improbable that the leader will be able to make any arrangement for any who are too seriously wounded to reach this rendezvous.

11. TIMING.

An operation must be most carefully timed if it is to succeed.

a) If more than one party is operating, the attack and any demolitions must be simultaneous. Ample time must be allowed for all parties to reach their objective.

b) Ample time, greater than the amount estimated, must be allowed for the approach, and especially for the sentry party to get into final position.

c) A margin must be allowed at the objective for unexpected incidents (i.e. for the changing of the guard if the time of this is not previously known).

d) Meteorological data must also be studied.

12. <u>WEAPONS</u>.

Although the details of the plan usually decide what arms are to be carried by the sub-sections of the party, certain general principles apply to all raiding parties of this type.

Every man in the party should be armed with a knife, and it is usually possible for every man also to carry a pistol as a reserve weapon against emergency. If a pistol is to be carried at all, it is worth while to carry not less than 3 magazines.

<u>The Leader</u>, although in a demolitions raid he will be operating with the demolition party at the target area, will probably not handle the charges himself. He can therefore carry a sub-machine gun, which will be the only automatic weapon with the demolition party.

<u>The Sentry Party</u> will be armed according to the method by which it is intended to deal with the sentries, and their subsequent covering party function must be looked upon as secondary. For example, if the sentry is to be killed silently, it is useless to encumber the party with a sub-machine gun; if he is to be killed noisily, the possible nearness of approach to the sentry will decide whether the weapon should be a rifle or a sub-machine gun. (The ranges at which these weapons should be relied upon for this purpose are discussed in the next lecture.) The leader must also decide whether in the circumstances it would be advisable for his sentry party to carry grenades.

<u>The Demolition Party</u> must confine themselves to small, light weapons, since

a) they may already be carrying heavy stores, and

b) they will require their hands to be free at the target area. Knives, pistols, grenades.

<u>The Covering Party</u>. In theory, the heavier the weapons employed by the covering party, the better. It is, however, often impracticable for a light machine gun, say, to be carried successfully over a long and stealthy approach. Where

the leader decides that this is possible, the L.M.G. is the
ideal weapon in that it has both range and volume of fire,
and can deploy and pin down interfering enemy as no lighter
weapon can. In default of an L.M.G., sub-machine guns, at
least one rifle to do any accurate shooting that may be
required, and grenades, form the covering party's weapons.

All the above are general considerations and must be modified
according to the particular operation in question. Grenades
are best carried in belt pouches, with the grenades across the
back, where they do not cause discomfort when crawling. Men
carrying sub-machine guns should carry as large a number of
magazines as is possible in view of their other commitments.
It should be remembered that magazines are noisy things to
carry unless some arrangement is made to guard against it.

13. <u>DEMOLITION CHARGES AND STORES</u>.

The Demolition Party will naturally be responsible for the
main demolition charges and means of initiation, although if
the total weight of explosive is large and the distance to be
covered considerable, it may be necessary to distribute the
stores over the whole party during the approach. To ensure
success for the operation, however, the following stores
should always be carried:

a) 1 complete duplicate set of charges carried by the
   covering party;

b) A spare means of firing the charge(s) to be carried by
   every member of the party.

In an attack on any industrial target where opportunities for
doing damage to machinery and installations other than the
main target are likely to present themselves, it would be
a good idea to equip the non-demolition members with extra
small charges, say 1 lb. each.

DEALING WITH ENEMY PERSONNEL AT THE OBJECTIVE

In almost every scheme or operation one of the deciding factors is the nature of the defences on the objective. Of these defences the personnel play the most important part, since no wire or other obstacle is insurmountable if undefended.

In an operation involving demolition of the objective, the immediate personnel to be dealt with will be sentries. They can be dealt with as follows:

1. They can be avoided altogether, and a short delayed action used for the demolition.

2. They can be killed silently, so that the guard and other supporting troops are not aroused. In most cases a short delayed action would be used here too.

3. They can be shot or dealt with by grenades. In this case a delayed action could not be used, because there would be every chance of its being discovered and removed.

What governs the choice of general method from the above three? The main considerations are these:

Methods (1) and (2) are used when the noisy killing would result in a fight with a force too strong for the attackers. They are usually impossible to employ by day.

Method (1) would be used only where the sentry's beat or position does not efficiently guard the objective, so that to kill him is merely an extra danger and difficulty to the operation.

Method (2) would be used where noisy killing would bring a strong enemy force on to the scene of action too quickly for the operation to be completed. (Remember that the operation includes the withdrawal.)

Method (3) would be used when either (a) the guard-room is a long way off and therefore could not interfere or (b) the guard is small enough to engage and destroy, and the support troops could not arrive in time to interfere. In this method the shot or shots killing the sentry should be the signal both for the attack on the guardroom and the placing of the charges. The

guardroom (if it is to be attacked) is dealt with as follows:
Two men take up position as near as possible to the windows and
wait for the signal of the shot. Immediately they hear it they
throw their grenades through the windows, keep down while the
grenades burst, then dash into the room with sub-machine guns.
While waiting for the signal, grenade safety pins should be eased
but not withdrawn. In daylight the man (or men) detailed to
shoot sentries should try to get within 50 yards with a rifle or
even closer with an S.M.G. for certainty. While a trained sniper
may feel certain of success at much greater ranges, remember
that the whole operation may depend on the killing of the sentry
with the first shot. At night, according to the light available,
S.M.G. or pistol - never a rifle - can be used at very close
range, i.e. a few yards only and sufficiently close to be able
to see the effect of your shot and to complete the killing at
point blank range if necessary.

Remember that the enemy's communications decide how quickly he
can get help from the supporting troops. Therefore, if you can,
destroy communications at the last moment. If you destroy them
too soon, before you are ready to attack, the destruction may be
discovered and a party sent to investigate.

General Considerations.

Guards are changed at intervals - in cold weather more often
than in warm weather. In Norway, guards are often changed every
half-hour. This factor must be taken into account and mentioned
in the orders; if it is not known it must be found out by
observation.

The N.C.O. i/c guard will visit the guard during his tour of
duty at least once; this must also be taken into account because
a dead guard is just as dangerous if he is discovered while the
party is on the job, as a live one. There is also the orderly
officer who may come round on a tour of inspection at any time.

The party will have to approach near enough to the objective to
observe the sentry. When they have studied the routine they will
then select their opportunity.

Supposing that the guard has a tour of duty of 2 hours and is
visited once during that tour by the N.C.O. When he comes on
duty he will be sleepy and partly blinded by the light of the
guardroom -this will wear off after about 1/2-hour. However, he

will gradually be roused by the cold and at the back of his mind there is always the thought of the N.C.O.'s visit.

The N.C.O. perhaps visits him at the end of the first hour. This will make him temporarily more alert but afterwards he can relax again and then he thinks only of the end of his tour of duty, now drawing slowly but steadily nearer. This is the time when a sentry is most off his guard - and although no hard and fast rule can be laid down, on a tour of duty of two hours, experience has shown that the period between 1 hour and 1-½ hours after he mounts is the worst time of a tour of duty. At this time the minutes seem to drag intolerably and the difficulty of keeping awake is most serious. The German Army is making use of Sentry Companies to guard lines of communication, etc. in occupied countries. These consist of older troops and young troops and are not to be described as first class. But of course this is by no means the rule.

The party must therefore decide to make its attack:

a) Either when the sentry is still seeing badly after being mounted and is still sleepy, or

b) After the N.C.O. has visited him and he is relaxing again and counting the time till he is relieved.

A sentry must be most carefully observed before he is attacked. An opportunity will always present itself and must be seized upon at once. The sentry may lean his rifle against something to rub his hands or to have a run off. Or if he doesn't do that he will sling it over his shoulder. No sentry is alert all the time, especially when he has been on the same job for some time.

When the sentry has been noiselessly despatched, one man at least must watch the guardroom afterwards in case the N.C.O. comes out again or the orderly officer turns up.

APPENDIX.

NOTE ON GERMAN SENTRIES.

FRANCE.

1. Camps and large store dumps are guarded mainly by Sentry Coys., usually of older troops and not first line troops.

2. Important objectives are protected by wire and wooden searchlight towers, containing a searchlight and M.G. (French pattern) at the four corners. (See fig.)

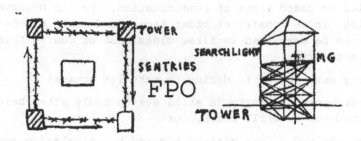

3. The sentries walk towards each other and patrol the perimeter so that if they are out of sight of each other it is only for a very short time. They meet under the towers.

4. The guard-room may be some way away but it is connected by 'phone to the towers and to the nearest H.Q. troops.

5. The guard commander relieves each sentry separately, marching him back to the guard-room and returning with his relief.

6. If the alarm is given the search-lights go on and the guard automatically turns out.

7. The sentries do not always stick to the perimeter but may patrol some way from it if they thus obtain a better view.

8. Bridges are usually guarded by outlying posts in the fields or gardens with M.G.'s.

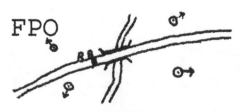

Road blocks are built near the bridges connected by telephone to the next one along the road.

If the bridge is a big one there is usually a sentry under or on the bridge as well.

9. Aerodromes are guarded by standing patrols at various points and there are rarely sentries on individual aircraft.

10. Headquarters in towns are inside a good house, with patrols going round at intervals.

AMBUSHES

1. DEFINITION.

A trap to catch and destroy a moving objective; more usually a vehicle or vehicles.

2. SUITABLE OBJECTIVES.

a) Supplies.

Food, ammunition, fuel, essential spare parts such as tires, etc.

The destruction of the stores carried by the vehicles will usually be of much greater importance than the destruction of the vehicles themselves, since, in war, the loss of a few vehicles is negligible.

The importance of the above supplies will always be qualified by the following considerations:

i) Whether the intended recipients are relying upon these stores to continue their particular effort.

ii) Whether the stores will be of use to the partisans themselves. Thus, for example, it is possible that the destruction of tires, petrol, or spare parts may render a number of vehicles immobile; or the destruction of ammunition or food might render a besieged enemy incapable of continuing their resistance.

b) Personnel.

The ambushing of troops on the march is rarely possible to the partisan, nor, unless their destruction served an immediate end, could they be considered a worth-while objective. Should these troops, however, be those specifically employed against partisan activity, their destruction might be said to serve an immediate purpose, or, if they were reserve troops moving up for a particular action, their destruction, or even delay, might be of great importance.

In general, however, the following personnel may be said to be the most worth-while objectives:

    Luftwaffe personnel;
    High grade staff officers;

Despatch riders, who may be carrying papers of importance.

The effect of ambushing the latter may be considerable. The moral effect of the <u>complete disappearance</u> of despatch riders will be great; large guards will have to be provided, thereby leading to further dispersal of enemy forces; documents will be lost that may cause delay or disruption of enemy action.

c) <u>Summary</u>.

Attacks should be carried out against supplies rather than against personnel, unless the latter are of great importance. The destruction of the German soldier is the job of the Army proper, and for the partisan to engage enemy troops is usually too risky a procedure.

3. <u>SCOPE</u>.

Scope is strictly limited by enemy tactics in the particular district where the partisan may be working, and the composition and organization of enemy convoys. Particularly does this apply to the <u>interval between vehicles</u> both in daylight and in darkness. It can be taken as axiomatic that in districts where Allied air attack is to be feared, convoys will – if they proceed in daylight at all – move with wide intervals between the vehicles. This interval may be as much as 300 metres. In such cases it is clearly extremely difficult for a small party to attack a convoy of even four vehicles, except by treating each vehicle as a separate ambush. The possibilities of 'cutting out' the last vehicle in the line will in such a case be worth considering.

As in all partisan operations, the leader must form an accurate estimate of the number of men required for the work, and an objective requiring a larger force of men must immediately be ruled out as far as he is concerned.

Under this heading we must consider the probable composition of Axis convoys. It is difficult to lay down many general rules owing to the difference in the amount of interference which the enemy expects in different districts. Some points, however, will remain constant.

a) Even in the case of a single vehicle which is an important objective, there will <u>always</u> be an outrider. In districts where no partisan interference is expected this will often be a motor-cycle at some distance ahead of the vehicle, varying with the type of country through which he is progressing. In the case of a heavy convoy in a district where attack is to be expected, the outrider may be an armoured car; or even, in guerrilla-ridden countries like Russia, a tank. The job of this outrider is to try to locate trouble before the convoy reaches it.

b) In the case of even the smallest convoy carrying important supplies, there will be guard troops on one or more of the vehicles.

c) The whole convoy will have certain definite orders as to action in case of attack.

4. <u>NECESSARY INFORMATION FOR AN AMBUSH</u>.

This should try to establish the details of the general rules outlined above.

a) A time and place at which the convoy may be expected and its route;

b) The speed, and interval between vehicles;

c) The numbers and composition of the convoy;

d) The type of vehicle used as an outrider or other covering force;

e) Guards - the fire power which they can bring to bear immediately;

f) The enemy's orders in case of attack.

All except (f) above may probably be found out by observation several days before the attack is made, although the time and composition of a convoy can never be relied on.

5. <u>TACTICS OF THE ATTACK</u>.

Boiled down to its essentials, the ambush requires:

a) Something to stop the objective;
b) A suitable place in which to stop it;
c) The choice of the best time to attack;
d) Man to effect its destruction.

These four headings will be considered separately:

a) <u>Something to stop the objective:</u>

This heading may be roughly divided into means that require the use of explosives and those that do not.

Under the first heading are the following, though it must be realized that an almost infinite variety of methods are possible, dependent upon the type of country, the ingenuity of the individual:

  i) Mining the road at a culvert or small bridge.
 ii) Mining the road by excavation (only possible in country roads without a macadam surface.)
iii) Pulling a charge across the road at the last moment and firing it as the leading vehicle of the main convoy passes over it.
 iv) Blowing some obstacle into place on the road, such as trees or rocks.

In all these cases the charge is fired electrically at the critical moment.

Normal concealed anti-tank mines, or other home-made mines, which the vehicle itself initiates.

Under the second heading - those which do not require explosives - the following may be mentioned. Again, an infinite variety is possible according to the circumstances.

  i) A tree may be partly sawn through and pulled down with rope at the critical moment.
 ii) Some vehicle, such as a farm cart, may be pulled, or pushed, or released across the road from a concealed position or a side alley.

There are also various methods, which, although not genuine obstacles to progress, will have the effect of stopping the convoy. It must be remembered, however, that should the action not go according to plan, the leading vehicle of the convoy may realise that the door of the trap is not genuinely closed and may make an exit and getaway.

  i) Artificial headlights used at night.
 ii) A mirror used in the same circumstances. Nothing less than a mirror of wardrobe size would be of any use.
iii) Live stock driven across the road, or, in larger quantities, driven down the road.
 iv) A blanket on a string or rope, hung across the road to obscure the vehicle.
  v) Dannert wire drawn across the road at the last moment.
 vi) Dummy anti-tank mines, such as plates inverted.

vii) Some large and recognisable object of value lying in
the road.

Since, as we shall see when considering the tactics proper,
the outrider must always be allowed to pass through the
trap, it is obviously much more difficult to place these
objects in position at the correct moment.

b) <u>A suitable place in which to stop the objective:</u>

The first considerations under this heading must be those
which facilitate the stopping of the convoy, and the second
will be those that facilitate its destruction.

The considerations which affect the choice of site from the
point of view of stopping the convoy will be these:

i) Either a bend or a rise in the road, so that the road-
block (and possibly the attacking force itself) will
not be seen by the leading vehicle of the convoy until
it is right on top of it. Thus, the obstacle can be
placed immediately the outrider has passed, instead of
at the moment when the leading vehicle of the convoy
proper reaches the desired spot.

ii) A road from which it is not possible for the vehicles
to make a cross-country detour past the obstruction –
i.e. a sunken road, a road out high into the side of a
hill, or one bounded by water upon one side and, say, a
rock face upon the other. (N.B. If the convoy is going
fast at the time when the first vehicle encounters the
obstacle, there will be a greater likelihood of the
rear vehicles piling up upon the front ones and thus
helping the attackers. It is, however, easier both to
stop and to estimate the positions of vehicles when
they are going very slowly – i.e. up a very steep hill,
or round a hairpin bend).

To facilitate the destruction of the objective:

i) Concealment for the attacking force, both from view
and from fire.

ii) A line of approach to these positions from the rear.
The positions should never be occupied from the front
because cover may be obviously displaced.

iii) A line of withdrawal covered and leading to some safe
place.

iv) There must be no cover for the enemy guards if they leave the vehicles – i.e. steep unclimbable sides of a ravine, or an open space which can be swept by fire.

Summary: Ideal place may be said to be a sharp bend in a road which has upon the one side a wide open space and upon the other steep rising ground with sufficient cover to hide the attackers. A very great advantage is secured by being above the convoy, in that ditches, etc. no longer represent cover to the enemy; it is more difficult for the enemy to direct accurate fire steeply upwards; it is easier for the attackers to throw hand missiles; a wider field of fire and of view is usually obtained; and it is difficult for the enemy to "come to grips". Whether it is best for the attackers to be all upon the one side of the road or upon both, will depend upon:

i) Possible safety from each other's fire;
ii) Possible lines of withdrawal in the event of the action having to be broken off.

c) The choice of the best time to attack:

A good many of the 'variables' of an ambush are affected by the time of day or night chosen. The main points affected are these:

i) The speed of and interval between vehicles. At night they will generally move slowly and closed up. By day they will move strung out at various intervals and as fast as roads permit.

ii) The concealment of the attackers and their trap – this is plainly much easier by night.

iii) The action itself – this requires a certain minimum of light for the best use of all weapons against the objective. This could of course be produced by flares at night, but the attack is likely to be less confused if carried out by dawn or evening light.

iv) The withdrawal of the attackers – it may be of importance for the attackers to have a good period of darkness to cover their withdrawal. In this case a late evening attack would be indicated.

v) Enemy resistance and morale. The enemy's morale is likely to be at its lowest in early dawn after driving through the night.

d) <u>Men to effect the destruction of the objective – the disposition of the party:</u>

i) <u>Look-outs</u> must be posted at strategic points to give warning of the approach of the convoy or of other traffic from either direction. With the additional function of signalling the approach of the objective, their role is identical to that of the normal covering party. They must be able to contact the leader by visual signal or by chain of signals.

ii) <u>Forward Party</u>, will be forward of the road block party and will deal with the outrider, who has first been allowed to pass through the trap. This party will be at the point which it is estimated the outrider will have reached at the moment the convoy is halted. When its work is complete, the forward party will take position as an extra covering party in the forward direction.

iii) <u>Road Block Party</u>, whose job is to place the road block (of whatever type) in position. The leader will be with this party and he will give the order for this or for the firing of the charge. With him will be sufficient men to deal with the first vehicle.

iv) <u>Rear Party</u>. Must prevent the rear vehicles from backing out or otherwise avoiding the trap; and they, together with the rear covering party, will prevent the enemy guards in the rear vehicles from organising opposition or working round behind the attackers. It may be necessary to form a second road block to close the trap at the rear – the leader will decide whether this is necessary, in accordance with the nature of the ground.

v) <u>The Remainder of the Party</u> will be disposed so as to cover the maximum "spread" of vehicles within the limits of the trap. Where the exact composition of the convoy is known, men should be detailed to deal with each specific vehicle, – but never forget that it is impossible to determine <u>accurately</u> the point at which each individual vehicle will come to a halt.

Snipers should be included in each group with the primary object of picking off:

– the drivers,
– any officers
immediately the convoy has come to a halt.

Weapons.

   i) An L.M.G.. which work independently of detailed
      orders, and which will open fire upon any particular
      point of resistance which appears to be developing. It
      should be sighted to have the maximum field of fire
      over the whole of the ambush area.
      (An anti-tank rifle would be of considerable value
      but is both cumbersome to carry - especially on the
      withdrawal - and also comparatively difficult to
      obtain).

  ii) Rifles for the snipers as detailed above.

 iii) Sub-machine Guns for all members of the party who have
      a direct role of attack upon the vehicles.

  iv) Pistols as reserve weapons (as previously mentioned in
      "Raid Tactics" Lecture).

   v) Grenades. Mills Grenades are useful for dislodging the
      enemy from behind vehicles where they may attempt to
      shelter. The Gammon Grenade should put any lorry or
      car out of action if a direct hit is secured upon the
      fore part.

  vi) Incendiaries. Molotov bottles or phosphorus bombs are
      useful for setting fire to the vehicles.

6. ACTION TO BE TAKEN WHEN THE CONVOY IS APPROACHED.

   a) The approach is signalled by the look-out - either
      directly or by relay. Signals must previously have been
      arranged to indicate that the convoy is greater or lesser
      than has been expected, and a clear signal that the convoy
      is unexpectedly too great for the attacking force. A
      different interval between the vehicles to that which has
      been expected should also be catered for.

   b) From this moment until the firing of the charge, or
      dropping of the obstacle, every man must keep perfectly
      still and invisible to the enemy.

   c) When the leading vehicle of the convoy proper reaches the
      selected point, the leader will give this order.

   d) The firing of the charge (or placing of obstacle) is the
      signal for general action. Simultaneous fire with all
      weapons, except Mills Grenades, will be opened. Mills
      Grenades must have their own definite and limited time,
      also on signal from the leader, during which the remainder
      of the party keep under cover to avoid casualties from

splinters. The snipers will concentrate upon drivers and
officers, the sub-machine gunners upon the enemy guards
accompanying the convoy.

7. ACTION TO BE TAKEN IF ALL OPPOSITION IS IMMEDIATELY WIPED OUT.

Anyone approaching the vehicles to carry out a search must
be detailed for this job by the leader beforehand and he must
only proceed to the road on the cease fire signal from the
leader. He must be covered by weapons still in position on
the ground.

There must not be a general stampede down to the road by all
the attacking force.

The search party must be speedy and thorough and the
searchers should be told beforehand what to look for.

The vehicles can then be set on fire, if tactically advisable,

a) Will it bring on pursuit?

b) Is it feasible to take possession of the vehicles?

8. ACTION TO BE TAKEN IF OPPOSITION DEVELOPS.

The ambushing force must not fight a pitched battle. Once
they do, they run the risk of being pinned to the ground by
enemy fire.

Hence the leader must have a signal for breaking off the
action should such a contingency arise, and in his plan he
must say what action is to be taken in such an event.

NOTE: At all times scouts must be in position in front and
rear of ambush to warn of the approach of any traffic
or assistance.

9. WITHDRAWAL.

a) If no opposition develops: As soon as the work is
completed the party must withdraw to a rendezvous at
convenient distance from the scene of action. In fixing
this rendezvous, the leader must envisage the possibility
of his party having to carry heavy stores taken from the
vehicles. These have to be hidden not far from the spot
and called for at a safer time. Also, owing to their
weight, particular attention must be paid to the likelihood
of the party leaving tracks in soft ground, or dropping
small loose stores that will show the enemy the route of

withdrawal. A "dog-leg" withdrawal, or even acuter change of direction, is advisable where possible.

b) If opposition develops: Automatic weapons must cover the thinning out of the party – e.g. the light machine gunner will be the last to withdraw and will attempt to do so unobserved by the enemy in order to give himself a few minutes' grace. Smoke may be used to advantage, but the wind must be in the right direction.

10. <u>AMBUSHING TROOPS ON THE MARCH.</u>

As mentioned in the first section of this lecture, it must be appreciated that only in certain cases is it worth while to ambush troops on the march; i.e. when their destruction will have an immediate effect. To destroy enemy troops, except in very large numbers – which is beyond the scope of the partisan – has comparatively small results.

There may, however, be cases in which the destruction of troops would have good results. The following are instances:

a) If patrols are sent out to attack or locate partisans.

b) To hold up troops advancing to a definite objective, e.g. reserves going into battle. The necessary dispersal on ambush will slow them down.

c) In country districts where there are very few troops (Cf. Yugoslavia).

d) To attack morale, and increase the size of enemy parties when they go out.

The principle remains the same – let the covering force, e.g. scouts, etc., through, and attack the main body. Have picked snipers to kill off the officers, N.C.O.'s and men with automatic weapons. Remember that when passing through a defile the Germans very often have flank guards. (Cf. Norway).

ATTACKING AN ENEMY OCCUPIED HOUSE

NOTE: The following lecture deals with an attack by partisans on a particular building, e.g., an enemy headquarters, with surprise as the principle aim.

An attack on a house converted into a strong point is more in the nature of a military operation when this attack is expected, and is therefore not dealt with in this lecture.

While the attack on an isolated building may form part of an operation for the clearing of a village or town it has nothing to do with street fighting as such, for which there is a specialised drill.

In attacking any occupied house or any building there are several important rules which apply in all cases:

a) There must be a detailed preliminary reconnaissance of the approaches to the house and the house itself. If direct personal recce is impossible, a reliable agent's report might be accepted. The latter should include, however, an accurate sketch.

b) There must be a definite plan of action to which all must adhere. Once the house has been entered complete control of the party by the leader is impossible, and therefore everyone must know the plan and its object.

c) If casualties are to be avoided, speed and aggression must be used as soon as the action has begun.

d) As in all guerrilla projects, it is essential that every allowance be made by the guerrilla leader for the original plan miscarrying. Steps will always be taken in advance to overcome difficulties if and when they arise, and the leader will always be prepared for the worst.

1. THE RECONNAISSANCE.

    a) The approaches.

        i) Good cover - if possible coming fairly close up to the house, at least near enough for weapons of short effective range to be brought to bear on all the exits.

ii) Good field of fire for all static weapons all round the house, controlling all the exits.

iii) Ground from the point of view of noise — any gravel paths, grass verges, lawns, piles of rubbish, noisy gratings, obstacles, e.g., buckets, brooms and ash bins.

iv) Surrounding walls, fences, hedges — can they be climbed or can a way be made through them? Must ladders be brought, or ropes, or are there such things on the spot?

v) Are there any buildings near which might be used by other enemy forces to influence the course of the action?

vi) From which direction can help come, and in which direction will it be impolitic to withdraw?

vii) Position and numbers of sentries — time of change over — a method of patrolling.

b) <u>The House.</u>

  <u>Outside</u>:

  i) Doors — location, and which way do they open? Are they usually locked or not?

  ii) Windows — do they open up or down, or on hinges, and if the latter, do they open inwards or outwards? How are they latched?

  iii) Drain Pipes — leading up to roof or upper stories —good ones usually go to the lavatories and the bath rooms, and they are generally not locked.

  iv) Gutters along the roof.

  v) Steepness of the roof and layout of the roofing. Skylights.

  vi) Are there any outhouses that would help to get on to the roof?

  vii) Cellars — low window or coal chute.

  viii) Chimneys — design.

  ix) Balconies and buttresses — for cover and for getting on to the roof and the upper floors.

  <u>Inside:</u>

  i) Floor plan — storey by storey. Size of rooms.

ii) Position of doors and the way they open.

iii) Staircases - have they any curves?

iv) Do rooms lead into one another? Are there any large built in cupboards?

v) Layout of the rafters.

vi) Composition of walls and ceilings.

vii) Composition of interior - will it burn?

Much of the above information can be found out by observation, but it is obviously much better if you can get hold of someone who has been inside the house, or better still, the architect or builder.

When you have this information draw a plan of the house, and if possible, get a scale model made.

2. <u>THE PLAN OF ACTION.</u>

The size of the force at your disposal will vary, and it is not possible to lay down rules for this, <u>but</u> your force will be divided into two parts:

a) The Covering Party - outside the house.

b) The Assault or Entry Party - to enter and clear the house.

Whatever the size of the party, and whether you have the advantage of surprise on your side or not, you <u>must have a covering party in position before you make a move against the house</u>.

a) <u>The Covering Party</u>.

The duties of this force are threefold:

i) To prevent any help being given to the defenders from the outside.

ii) To kill any enemy who may attempt to leave the house.

iii) To give the alarm in case of surprise enemy relief.

Therefore the covering party must be divided into:

i) Men to give warning of possible enemy reinforcements.

ii) Men to cover the exits from the house.

In the plan you will decide as far as possible in which direction you intend to drive the enemy, and your will post your covering party accordingly.

But remember that there must be a recognition signal which is known to all the party, in order to avoid having your own men shot if they should leave the building at any time.

If there are sentries round the building they must be silently eliminated first, or if they have to be shot, the attack must coincide with this. In this latter case the first shot fired by the sentry killers is the signal for the attack.

Telephone lines on the way in should be cut by someone who acts on the sound of the first shot, and not before.

b) <u>The Assault or Entry Party</u>.

Again it is impossible to lay down hard and fast rules, but in principle it will be composed as follows:

   i) 1 leader.

  ii) Men with automatics to cover the leader, and to cover doors inside the house while the attack goes on.

 iii) Bombers.

This question will be dealt with more fully under the heading "How to Enter".

3. <u>ENTERING THE HOUSE</u>.

a) <u>Where to Enter</u>.

   i) <u>The Front Door</u> - the most likely place for anyone to come in - hence - sure to be covered, and may have the guard sleeping behind it in the hall, or at any rate a telephone orderly or even a sentry. On the other hand, you will get immediate control of the hall and the foot of the staircase.

  ii) <u>The Back Door</u> - less likely to be defended, but certain to be covered in some way. Entry here should be easier than by the front door, and there will probably be better cover for the approach. But inside you are not usually in a very commanding position immediately.

 iii) <u>Windows</u> - this gives you more choice, but:
- you cannot enter so quickly,
- you form an easier target when you enter,
- you are silhouetted,
- you must jump down.

iv) <u>The Roof</u> - If you can get into the house from the roof, you have a definite advantage because you can drive the enemy down and prevent him from rolling grenades down on you. But it is very difficult to enter from here unless circumstances are particularly favourable, because:

- It is difficult to get on to the roof.
- When you are there it is not easy to get in unless there is a skylight.
- You are bound to make some noise when you are getting there.

v) <u>By Explosives</u> - use of H.E. to blast a hole in the wall -surprise effect good, but amount of explosive great.

<u>Conclusion</u>:

Unless conditions are particularly favourable, or you can distract the enemy's attention to allow you to operate from the roof, you will have to make your way in on the ground floor. The back door is the best place. We shall consider entry from the ground floor as the most likely course.

b) <u>How to Enter</u>.

i) <u>What size force to use</u> - The force that enters the house should not be too large and should be selected according to the design of the building and the number of tasks to be performed.

In principle it should consist of the following:

- 1 leader.
- 1 bomber.
- 2 entry or door men.
- 1 landing man.

But for a very large house more would be required, especially for covering duties.

ii) <u>Entry by the door</u> - The two entry men take up position on either side of the door while the leader and the landing man either cover the door from the front (if there is adequate cover) or from the side. The bomber is with the leader.

The door is then forced (either kicked or blown open with a small charge over the lock). The entry man then throws in a grenade and after waiting for it to explode, they dash into the house.

When they give the signal "Clear," the leader and the rest of the party enter.

When the entry men have crossed the threshold, they must not pause in the door way but should slip right and left and make their way across the hall to the staircase clearing any opposition as they go. Grenades may effectively be thrown through appropriate windows.

iii) <u>Entry by the windows</u> - A similar drill should be used as for the door but it is not as good a way of entering for reasons already stated.

iv) <u>Entry by the roof</u> - It is not proposed to outline any drill for this because the number of occasions when this will be possible in the case of an isolated house are few.

Should it be attempted, the following points should be borne in mind:

- An agile man can scale a drain pipe with a rope with which he can assist the other members of the party.
- Use of outhouses.
- Use of overhanging trees.
- Ladders found locally or brought by the party, i.e. light scaling ladders.
- Human pyramid.

But remember that a certain amount of noise is bound to be made and your move may be anticipated by the enemy. You must also guard against interference from the windows.

On the roof your only feasible means of entry will be through a skylight or by using a small charge.

c) <u>Action Inside the House</u>.

When the entry has been made from the ground floor, as soon as the party has entered, a sentry must be posted at the foot of the stairs, covering all the doors on the ground floors and the cellars. It may be found better to leave two men here to cover your back.

The remainder of the party with the leader, make their way to the top of the house and begin the systematic clearing of the house, floor by floor and room by room.

271

There are many advantages in operating from the top floor downwards:

i) Everything the attackers throw tends to fall on the defenders and everything the defenders throw tends to fall back on them.

ii) Any rushes the attackers make, being in a downward direction will give greater velocity to the attack and increased momentum, than any similar move made by the defenders.

iii) In a building invested from the bottom the defenders have one small chance of escape and will tend to put up a stiffer resistance, but when attacked from above, the normal means of exit are available and will in all probability be used. The covering party will then deal with the enemy as they leave the house.

Staircases. These are very difficult and dangerous because grenades can be rolled down on the attackers and it is difficult to reply. One man should cover the bottom of the staircase while the second dashes up the stairs as far as the first bend or the landing. He takes position there and the other man either joins him or passes him and makes good the next bound. A burst of fire over the head of the moving man will help to discourage the enemy.

Rooms. When clearing these the same drill as for entry applies. If the man who opens the door finds no opposition the leader enters and makes a thorough search. Cupboards and locked doors can be dealt with by firing the tommy through the wood. It is also a good idea to fire down through the floor. This will bring down large lumps of plaster on the heads of anyone in the room below.

Special care must be taken in long corridors with many doors not to be cut off or shot in the back. Work along corridors room by room.

When entering a room occupied by an unsuspecting enemy, either fling open the door and rush in or throw in a grenade.

Finally, two points of importance:

i) When carrying grenades ready for use don't take out the pin in order to save time - you may get wounded or fall and drop the grenade.

ii) When you have cleared the house you must have some signal to warn the covering party that you are coming out as they will not know the result of the attack.

STREET FIGHTING

INTRODUCTORY REMARKS.

The general principles of all fighting apply equally to Street Fighting, but penalties for mistakes are higher. Therefore, a very high standard of efficiency and thoroughness is essential.

Bear in mind that Street Fighting can be carried on by all arms (i.e. tanks, mobile artillery, infantry, aircraft - compare notes on the latest events at Stalingrad). Also, no hard and fast rule can be laid down as to which level above or below ground may form a decisive point in any action, as fighting may be carried out on the roofs of houses, upper storeys, at street level, and below street level - in sewers and basements.

No type of warfare demands such a high state of physical fitness and endurance as street fighting. All who take part must also be able to use, with ease and rapidity, different types of weapons one after another.

There can never be any definite rules in the use of formations and weapons in Street Fighting. In view of this, teaching at this school will be confined to general advice given on the various points which will assist those who might at some time be confronted with this type of warfare. They are:

1. THE APPRECIATION.

It is essential that a proper appreciation be prepared before any Commanding Officer can issue orders for the employment, to the best advantage, of the troops under his command. You must understand that, in both attack and defence, a number of principles generally apply, but these two aspects are, of course, completely different in their application to Street Fighting.

a) Defence.

The following points should be carefully noted:

i) It will never be possible to defend each building in a town of any size.

ii) Therefore, those buildings which it is decided to defend must be carefully chosen to fit in with the general scheme of defence.

273

    iii) The defence must devise suitable means of intercommunication.

    iv) Surprise and movement can be employed equally well in defence as in attack (there is nothing so demoralising to attackers as to find themselves attacked in the rear in narrow cramped quarters.

    v) As no prisoners can be taken, life must be sold at its dearest.

b) **Attack.**

This should include:

    i) The assumption that the advantage lies with the defenders.

    ii) That the attack must aim at surprise, speed, ingenuity, and forcefulness.

    iii) That any plan of attack must be sufficiently flexible to allow of it being frequently changed.

    iv) That any attack at dawn is generally expected.

    v) That any attack in the evening, just after stand down, is likely to succeed with surprise.

    vi) That streets, both main and secondary, will be avenues of death, and that approach should generally be made through back gardens, alley ways, etc.

    vii) Once several main objectives have been achieved, counter attack must be expected. Therefore, all points and attacking parties must be consolidated immediately once objectives are reached.

2. **THE PLAN**.

Taking into account the various factors briefly mentioned above, leaders of Street Fighting parties should remember that nothing must be left to chance in the planning of either defence or attack in this type of warfare. Remember also, that recognition signs on clothing, and intercommunication, not only between attacking or defending parties, but also with supporting troops (if any) who may be able to send reinforcements, are essential.

Finally, keep all plans for action as simple as possible and make sure that the most junior members of these parties understand the immediate objective in hand, so that in the event of casualties the plan of action will not fail.

a) Defence.

It is essential that a proper plan of action is drawn up
for the defence of any village, town or city, taking into
account the forces at your disposal. Bear in mind that
casualties will probably be heavy, and that all points
which are still being held may be cut off and liquidated,
one by one. Also take into account that very often the
best form of defence in Street Fighting is attack in the
enemy's rear or flank. This can be carried out by parties
specially hidden in sewers or basements, and timed to start
on receipt of a pre-arranged signal. The method of giving
the latter is, of course, open to difficulties, as the
noise prevalent in Street Fighting is shattering, and sound
signals will rarely be heard. Some other method, therefore,
should be employed.

It should not be difficult, provided there is time, to make
certain that strong points are suitably prepared against
enemy attack. Isolated buildings standing in their own
grounds form an easy target in Street Fighting. It is
more likely that the most easily defended buildings are
those upon which the enemy stumbles unexpectedly, and
against which there is not much covered approach where
the enemy can use surprise. Basements are usually excellent
places, if properly strengthened by pit props, sandbags and
stones. If on the corners of streets these command many
areas of approach, and can be used as deadly obstacles
in the path of the enemy, provided adequate fire power is
available.

Remember that in attack the enemy will almost certainly use
smoke, and therefore, in choosing any particular point bear
in mind that there may be a prevailing wind which will blow
smoke back upon the advancing enemy. It is also essential
that economy of fire power be preserved, and that an
advancing enemy be fired upon only at the last moment, so
that it is quite certain that the attackers will be killed
to a man if fire is brought to bear upon them.

A machine gun firing aimlessly down the street would only
give the defending position away to the attackers, who may
be under cover.

Camouflage also plays a very important part in
the preparation of strong points, and if used with
intelligence, can often result in the complete ambush of

the enemy. Remember also that all weapons should never be sighted on the same level, and that smoke will hang low; therefore, it may be of advantage to have some automatic weapons sighted high up on a building.

Remember also that if it is possible, buildings which are likely to be singled out by the enemy as objectives should be mined as a trap.

It is also essential that each man, as far as possible, shall be a self-contained unit. He should have with him his weapons, his ammunition, and above all, he should carry as many rations as he can within reason; no street fighter can afford to leave his post because "the rations have not arrived".

Finally, good team work, and the ability to fight on when cut off will very often turn seeming defeat into victory.

b) Attack.

The first principle to remember in Street Fighting attacks is that the enemy will be expecting you. Therefore, unless the force with which you are attacking consists of large numbers of tanks and other heavy weapons (and these we will not deal with here), you must employ surprise and ingenuity to the fullest advantage to achieve success.

Secondly, make absolutely certain that the signals or signs by which you give your orders for the attack and for co-ordinating your advance are heard and understood by all concerned. There have been in the past various schools of thought which deal with a recognised drill for the clearing of houses. This is not always possible without a very great deal of practice among regular troops, and therefore various methods must be considered, and not just a detailed plan of attack which may not apply, such as is laid down for regular troops. Remember that if you are going to use smoke it must be used in circumstances when it is advantageous to you and not to the enemy.

Make absolutely certain that the maximum amount of your fire power is used intelligently, and in a concentrated form, i.e., that it is brought to bear upon the objective which you are attacking. Covering fire, of course, must play a very important part in all attacks of this kind, and all taking part in Street Fighting, should be trained so that they will not be deceived by camouflaged enemy strong points. To develop a good eye for detecting these points is not easy, but it should be stressed that they are points which need careful consideration.

Note carefully the following points in clearing a house.

Houses should, if possible, be cleared from the roof downwards for two reasons:

i) Gravity fights on your side.

ii) A cornered enemy must fight. Therefore drive him towards the door rather than towards the roof.

Drill for entering a suspected house from ground level.

i) Place covering fire. Targets to include:

- Windows, Loopholes, etc. of the house itself.
- Windows, Loopholes, etc. of adjacent house.

ii) Party of 5 men, (commander, bomber, 2 entry men, 1 landing man).

Two entry men take up positions one on each side of chosen means of entry.

- *If by door or window it is forced or smashed in.
- *One entry man throws bomb in.
- Both enter.
- If room is clear or when they have cleared it the commander is signalled to aproach by a shout of CLEAR.

iii) Commander, bomber and landing man rush in. Landing man takes up position to cover stair or landing while commander and bomber make their way to top of house and commence search. Entry men search cellar (if any) and ground floor rooms. As the commander makes his way to top of house a burst of fire through the door, wall or ceiling of a suspected room has the effect of rattling any occupants and if fired down to a room usually has the effect of bringing down the ceiling on top of the occupants and setting up a thick cloud of dust.

NOTE: Should entry be forced by an explosive agency Drills ii) marked * may be omitted.

3. SPECIAL NOTE ON WEAPONS.

a) Do not forget that the defenders will, by using rifles and automatic rifles, whether firing from the rooftops and upper windows or from ground level, have the advantage over an attack based only on S.M.G. fire power. Therefore, whilst a percentage of S.M.G.s is essential for close-quarter fighting in the houses, etc. rifles and automatic rifles are also essential in order to prevent the attack being "outranged".

b) The safety pin should never be drawn from a Mills bomb or similar grenade until immediately before it is thrown. Many casualties have been caused by a man being badly wounded whilst carrying a grenade with the pin out. The grenade falls from his hand, and he is unable to deal with it.

OBSERVATION IN PARTISAN WARFARE

1. INTRODUCTION - THE IMPORTANCE OF OBSERVATION.

The secret of every successful operation is detailed and accurate information. Whereas in regular warfare such information is generally forthcoming from a higher formation, and the fighting unit has little chance to verify its accuracy, in irregular warfare the responsibility must rest upon the band itself. The observation cannot be too detailed - some small detail of the enemy's habits may prove to be the deciding factor when it comes to the actual operation.

2. CHECK-UP ALWAYS NECESSARY.

Information may become out-of-date very quickly. Therefore, no matter how trustworthy your information is or even if you yourself have reconnoitred and observed some days previously, a final "check-up" reconnaissance is always necessary. When a partisan band have themselves made the reconnaissance a day or two prior to the operation, the leader will make this final "check-up" as late as possible - sometimes on the operation itself. In this case he leaves the rest of the party a short distance back and goes forward to his "recce point", to satisfy himself that nothing has changed since the first observation was carried out.

3. OTHER TIMES WHEN OBSERVATION MUST BE CARRIED OUT.

Besides the reconnaissance of the target area and the route to it, observation will frequently be necessary during the actual movement of the party. Particularly, it is necessary at the end of each "bound", to ensure that there is no enemy on the ground which the party is about to cross. The value of surprise must lie with the agent and not with the enemy, and

when such observation is not carefully carried out, a whole
party may stumble into the arms of the enemy. In such cases,
when you are examining the ground for the presence of human
beings, look first for <u>movement</u>, because it is most easily
seen. Next, look carefully at anything that is <u>darker</u> than
its surroundings, and lastly, look at anything that is much
<u>lighter</u> than its surroundings or is of a very different
colour. If you are suspicious of an object – take no chances,
wait until your mind is made up. Never spend less than three
minutes in observation – a quick glance is useless, and
merely lulls into what may be a sense of false security.

4. <u>SEE WITHOUT BEING SEEN</u>.

To the agent there is little use in being able to see the
enemy if the enemy can also see him. Most people have thought
of the unlimited possibilities for observation that would be
open to an "Invisible Man", and this is what the agent must
try to be.

It is often possible to hide one's body behind something when
observing, but unless the head itself is in view, you will
not be able to see and might as well be back at home with a
glass of whisky. Therefore, <u>the importance of the camouflage
of the head cannot be over-estimated</u>. It is sufficient
to remember that without such camouflage close quarter
observation is virtually impossible. If there is a secret of
successful observation, this is it.

There are other details besides camouflage which are of great
help. When possible, observation should be <u>done round</u>, not
over, cover, and the head should be kept at <u>ground level</u>.
The human eye is unconsciously most receptive of movement at
its own level above the ground, and movement much lower or
much higher than this (i.e. at ground level or in trees) is
frequently overlooked. Opportunities for observation from
trees are comparatively few, and ground level has therefore
the most general application. The head, then, should be
kept as close as possible to the ground when observing
round cover, and only just enough of it exposed to allow
observation – it is quite unnecessary to expose the whole
head. If the head is not camouflaged, the exposed part of it
should be protected by a bunch of herbage held before it. If,
however, it is moving about much, no camouflage in the world
will prevent its detection. It is of the greatest importance
that the head should be kept as still as is humanly possible,

and when movement is necessary it should be done extremely slowly, an inch or less at a time. Remember, also, the rest of your body, and if you are lying down do not raise your feet over your back in order to get a change of position when you are getting stiff.

Any object of regular outline should be avoided as a place from which to observe - anything protruding from a smooth surface is very easily seen. During the last war it took the British a year to find this out - their trench parapets were beautifully regular and smooth, while the Germans' were rough and uneven and untidy, with many pieces of rubbish, old tin cans, loose sandbags, etc. scattered about on them.

5. <u>ARTIFICIAL AIDS TO OBSERVATION</u>.

Binoculars, or a telescope, are a great help in all observation.

A less obvious aid, but one that is even more useful, is a periscope, and where it is possible for the agent to acquire one, he should always do so. There are many varieties of periscope, the simplest of which - an arrangement of small mirrors of highly polished metal surfaces on a stick - can be home-made. At the other end of the scale are the periscope monoculars, giving a magnification of up to x 6. These were chiefly made for trench warfare, but it is possible that some are still in existence in the German Army. It is well worth while to construct a home-made periscope.

6. <u>"IF ONLY WE HAD MORE INFORMATION . . ."</u>

The items in a target area which will have the greatest bearing upon the operation are tactical considerations, and are fully dealt with in lectures on Appreciation and Planning. But it must be emphasized again that no detail is too small to be worth recording mentally, or in writing if the information is for the use of others. Things that at first sight may appear entirely insignificant suddenly assume a major importance when the plan is being made. If the slogan of "Know your enemy" can be directed at regular troops, how much more must it apply to the agent, who must always face an overwhelming numerical superiority. He must rely upon surprise and a <u>detailed</u> knowledge of the enemy to counteract that superiority.

For the same reason, anything that is not fully understood must be observed and investigated until it is. If in the last

war the first people to see gas-containing cylinders had
investigated their purpose, the first gas attacks would have
lost much of their terrible surprise value.

7. <u>GERMAN MILITARY SIGNS</u>.

However painstaking the individual, his information from
observation will be incomplete if he is unable to recognise
the common military signs and symbols used by the enemy. If,
for instance, a certain village is known to contain battle
H.Q. of a German Division, it would be extremely difficult
for the observer to distinguish it from the Brigade H.Q.,
which might be housed two doors away from it or across
the street - unless he is able instantly to recognise the
military symbol at the entrance to the house.

8. <u>OBSERVATION REPORTS</u>.

An observation report made for the use of someone else should
be made out in this form. On the first sheet, a sketch map of
the area under observation. Each feature of importance should
be numbered to correspond with a key at the foot of the map -
this is better than writing on the map itself, which is
apt to become confusing and obscured. Next, write a general
description of the area leaving out such details as you have
already made clear from the map. This description should deal
with 'constant' factors -features, that is, that would be the
same at any time of the day, <u>not</u> individual enemy actions
that have been noticed. When this is completed, give your
page a marginal column, and enter the times at which various
actions or activities have been noted, describing the activity
opposite to the time. If you are drawing deductions, other
than obvious ones, <u>state</u> that they are your deductions, and do
not represent them as proven fact. In describing the position
of these activities, it is possible to refer to the sketch
map, in this manner: "1455 hrs. The head of a German officer
was visible in the window at point 'o', or "1515 hrs. Two
private soldiers left the door at point 'f' and entered the
latrines at point 'd'. They then left the observation area by
the gate at point 'x'."

The report should not be long-winded, but make quite certain
that you do not sacrifice clarity and accuracy to brevity.

This type of observation report is intended to enable someone
else to attack a stationary target guarded by the enemy.

HOW TO BECOME A SPY

Observation reports dealing with movements of troops, vehicles, etc. <u>must</u> answer the following questions:

a) When. (date and time).
b) Where. (as exactly as possible).
c) What and how many. i.e. 14 Mk. IV tanks.
d) Direction and estimated speed, i.e. N.E. at 20 k.p.h; or towards 'Y' along road 'X - Y'.
e) Any other details. (As in other types of observation, no detail which time allows is too small to be of importance.)

Finally, Negative information, i.e. that no enemy A.F.V's. were observed in such and such an area - is equally important.

PRINCIPLES OF CAMOUFLAGE, CONCEALMENT AND DISGUISE - I

1. INTRODUCTORY.

As the word 'camouflage' is used in ordinary conversation, it covers pretty well all methods of deceiving the enemy, and is thus a very general term. In order to do a thing well, it is necessary to understand exactly what one is trying to do, and for this reason we sub-divide the general term 'camouflage' into three separate headings. These headings are:

> Camouflage proper;
> Disguise;
> Concealment.

2. DEFINITIONS:

Camouflage proper is often called the "general resemblance". That is to say that you deceive the enemy by melting into or mingling with your background, and are no longer noticeable at all. Example: the white 'snow-sniper's' suits used in Russia and Finland.

Disguise is often called the "special resemblance". That is to say that you deceive the enemy, although he does actually see you, because he mistakes you for some harmless or unimportant object. Example: The most obvious example is the German parachutists' use of nuns' and other female clothing. Less obvious, but still disguise, a man dressed in grey clothing may, in a country such as this, pass for a rock, even though he is not very near any other rocks. If you consider the number of objects in any countryside which a man could make himself resemble, it will be clear that disguise has almost as wide an application as camouflage proper.

Concealment is to hide behind something, so that you are actually cut off from view. No example is required, and since a man who is entirely concealed is somewhat functionless, we shall not discuss it further.

Having defined these words, it will be clear at once that all three methods can be used by a man simultaneously. For example: he may <u>disguise</u> his head as a small gorse bush, <u>camouflage</u> his body to disappear altogether, and <u>conceal</u> his feet behind something. But unless he knows this himself, he is liable to 'fall between two stools' and achieve nothing.

3. <u>METHODS OF ACHIEVING THESE RESULTS</u>.

   a) <u>Camouflage proper</u>.

   To the partisan, by far the most general application of camouflage proper is the use of background, as already broadly outlined in the lecture "Movement by Day". Get into the habit of thinking constantly of your background, and if there are others dressed as you are, notice against what backgrounds they appear to be invisible and against which backgrounds they look obvious. If you concentrate on this, you will find that almost unconsciously you choose, the whole time, backgrounds most like the clothes you are wearing. Where there is no background that is very like your clothes, use natural camouflage - that is, leaves, grass, heather, branches, etc. - to cover partially and break up the colour mass of your body. Pockets, button-holes, waist-band, collar - all these can receive and hold pieces of vegetation which will partially obscure your clothes and help you to mingle with your background. (When using natural camouflage, remember that under a hot sun it withers quickly, and may be worse than useless at the end of a few hours.)

   The whole question of colour in camouflage is extremely complicated, but there is one salient fact that should be remembered. The works of man are immediately recognisable by their <u>regularity</u> in colour, and also in outline. If you were to look at a garden lawn and were asked what its colour was, you would reply 'green'. But while green is certainly the predominant colour, you will find if you look more closely that there are not only many different shades of green, but also many other colours - browns, yellows, dark patches of shadow, etc. Remember, therefore, <u>solid colours always look suspicious</u>.

   Besides the question of colour, there are three more factors which make an object recognisable for what it is. These are:

     i) Shape in the flat, or outline.
    ii) Shape in depth.
   iii) Tone - that is, how light or how dark an object is.

284

These are considered in detail below:

i) <u>Shape in the flat</u>. This is determined by outline, or outside edge. If you cannot see the outside edges of the object, it becomes much more difficult to recognise. There are two general ways of destroying outline. One is to break up the outline by patches of different colours, so that it does not appear as a continuous line. This is usually called "disruptive painting", and is used on buildings such as aerodrome hangers, etc., as well as on camouflaged clothing. Note, however, that it is useless if it is just patches of colour on the bulk of the object: it must break up the <u>outline itself</u>. The other method is by adding on to the outline protruberances and irregularities that destroy the shape. On a man, this is best done with natural camouflage – leaves or branches or tufts of grass, etc. While on the subject of outline, remember that it is often possible to make the outline of your body and limbs resemble the outline of the objects around you, with very good effect. For example – rocks do not have branches, therefore when among rocks keep your arms close to your body. Trees do, and it is often possible to make your arms look like branches of a standing tree or roots of a fallen one. This is worthy of much more thought than it usually receives. Up a tree you will find about the best hiding place of all, as suprisingly few people ever look up into the trees they pass under. But here again, the outline of your body must be made to follow and resemble the outline of the trunk and its branches. Even a bare tree can be a good hiding place if this is remembered.

ii) <u>Shape in depth</u>. This is what makes an object appear solid – and is dependent upon SHADOWS and high lights. They are, in fact, the only factors that make a white marble statue recognisable from a white paper silhouette.

Shadows are the most difficult problem in the whole of camouflage, whether of man or an aeroplane factory, and always seem to find some way to reveal the true shape of the object, do what one will. But once their vast importance is realised half the battle is won.

HOW TO BECOME A SPY

Look at the man who is lying on the ground, or
standing against a wall. Wherever his body touches the
ground or the wall on the opposite side from which the
light is coming there is a shadow, wherever there is
a furrow in his clothing there is a shadow - there is
a shadow between his arms and his body, between his
legs, under his chin, and so on. These shadows give
him his shape -if they were not there he would appear
to have no arms, only one thick leg - in fact he would
become less and less like a man. It is for this reason
that "snipers' suits" are made as cloaks, without
arms or legs - so that there shall be no specifically
human, and therefore betraying appendages.

Now, one golden rule applies. The flatter an object,
the less shadow it gives; therefore an object with
sloping sides gives much less shadow than one with
straight sides. Try this with a match-box, with a
strong light coming from one side. Then bend out one
side till it is at a gentle slope - there will be no
shadow at all.

It is for this reason that large buildings that are to
be camouflaged so as to disappear into the landscape
are built with sloping sides - were they not, their
shadows would betray them. The same applies to the
camouflage of a man.

It will be seen immediately that the closer a man
presses himself against the ground or background he
intends to blend with, the less shadow he will cast,
and the more he will tend to disappear. Similarly,
if his arms are pressed to his sides, there is less
room for shadow that would fall between his arms and
body if the latter were hanging loosely, or if his
hands were folded on his lap. Again, a man sitting
with his legs stretched out on the ground in front
of him will be less visible if his legs are flat on
the ground than if his knees are slightly drawn up.
Ruckles in clothing, like, for example, the ruckle
formed by a battle-dress blouse at the waist also cast
a black shadow. If you are going to take up a position
from which to observe, for instance, try to arrange
both yourself and your clothing so that the absolute
minimum of shadows are formed - and think where those

shadows are likely to be. Some grass, heather, or other vegetation, is extremely useful to fill up these spaces where the shadows would fall, if you are to remain in one position for any length of time.

iii) <u>Tone</u>. This is often more important than colour, especially at a distance. An object of unusual colour is usually spotted at once because it is also of an unusual tone. Some extraordinarily bright colours can pass unnoticed if they are of exactly the same tone as their background – that is to say, if they would appear neither lighter nor darker in a photograph. As most backgrounds are much lighter in tone that one suspects, make it a general rule to keep a dark background whenever you can. You are <u>usually</u> seen because you are darker than your background.

PRINCIPLES OF CAMOUFLAGE, CONCEALMENT AND DISGUISE – II

1. <u>DISGUISE</u>.

Having realised that disguise is not necessarily a matter of wearing a false red beard or getting a stage cow, its possibilities increase considerably. But it will also be obvious that there are very, very few objects that are suitable for the disguise of a man's body <u>in movement</u>, and a man is much more often moving than stationary.

The chief application of the "special resemblance" therefore, is for use on the <u>head only</u>. As discussed in the lecture "Observation", it is often easy to hide the body behind something (conceal it), but a man is usually somewhat useless if his hand is also concealed.

Now is the time to realise that camouflage proper can very rarely be used satisfactorily on the head – it must be disguised. That is to say, it is very difficult to make the head blend into and mingle with its background – especially at close quarters, which is the range from which you should always try to observe – but it is comparatively easy to make it look like something completely different. This 'something different' may be anything from a small bush or a moss-covered stone to a tiny bucket or a pile of horsedung. One of the simplest of all means of disguise of the head is a sheet of moss, such as grows round trees roots, on stones, etc. It has two great advantages.

287

a) It is to be found everywhere in the world where there are either large trees or rocks;

b) It requires no making or work, as it can be taken off the ground as a solid sheet that will cover the whole head – a ready-made hat. Its use, among other types of camouflage and disguise, can be easily practised in this area.

If the head is to be disguised as a bush, let it be as large a bush as comfort and weight will allow. Every hat worn for operational purposes should be capable of receiving natural camouflage, that is to say it must have holes, or string, into which vegetation, etc. can be inserted or tied. This vegetation must not only completely cover the hat, but must also completely break up the outline of the head, by adding on to it. A large bush looks much less likely to be a man's head than something that is exactly the size and shape of a man's head.

Other methods of improving the disguise of the head are discussed later in this lecture under the heading of artificial camouflage.

2. ARTIFICIAL CAMOUFLAGE.

Artificial Camouflage, as applied to a man, was first developed for the use of snipers. We have already seen that it is impossible to render a moving object completely invisible by camouflage, and the sniper is one of the few men in regular warfare whose job it is to keep quite still.

Because of the shadow difficulties already discussed, snipers' suits soon gave place to snipers' cloaks, or to sheets under which a man could lie. In this way, the shadows which define a man's limbs were eliminated. These cloaks and sheets were sometimes very elaborate, and required long preparation, such as pouring molten rubber over the surface with which the sniper was required to blend, and then making the dried and painted rubber into a cloak.

All these methods are beyond the scope and opportunity of the partisan, but there are two simple forms of artificial camouflage which are well worth study and are within the opportunity of everybody.

The first of these is the sheet made of sacking. It is remarkably effective, frequently more so than the more elaborate types, and is very easy to construct. Sandbags, cut open and sewn together, form the basis. The sheet should be about 8' long and 4' wide, and the edges should be made ragged so that there will be a less obvious line where the sheet joins the ground. Next, rub the sheet thoroughly in the soil of the piece of country in which it is to be used, so that bare patches upon it will appear to be bare patches of soil. Then sew or tie on to it pieces of grass or other vegetation typical of the country. When used where there are sparsely vegetated patches of soil, this is extremely invisible, is easily carried rolled up. Since vertical surfaces always cast most shadow, the sheet must be drawn well away from the body at sides, <u>not</u> tucked in round the man, as is often the first instinct.

A variation of the above is a sheet which is <u>entirely</u> covered with vegetation down to the last inch, and is therefore completely indistinguishable from the ground around it when it is laid out like a carpet. In this case the sewing on the vegetation must be done on the spot, and the sheet is left spread out flat when its user leaves his observation post after dusk. Care must be taken that vegetation used does not wither quickly. Such a sheet is not easily portable, but in most types of ground it is entirely invisible, and can be treated as a static observation post.

It will be immediately obvious that this principle of sacking camouflage can be applied with great effect and much less labour to the camouflage or disguise of the head alone. In this case, a sort of balaclava helmet is made of the sacking, and it is completely covered with vegetation sewn on to it, or with a sheet of moss as previously described under the heading of disguise. When used as a 'lining' to the moss it has the advantage of excluding insects.

A second type of artificial camouflage within the opportunity of the partisan is the use of camouflage truck nets. These are common to all belligerent armies, and vary little in type. In principle, they consist of string netting dyed green or parti-coloured, and hessian tape in various colours (called in the British Army 'scrim') is provided to tie on in short lengths to represent leaves, and to break up the general colour mass. Truck nets are remarkably easily stolen, and have a wide application. They can be used as is the sheet to camouflage a man lying down, can be draped over him among vegetation while he is in a standing position, can be used to camouflage any object that must remain in the open and be invisible to the enemy, or can be used as a screen through which to fire an L.M.G., for example, when ambushing a convoy. Their effectiveness is out of all proportion to their simplicity and ease of use, and are worth much consideration in irregular warfare.

Of the same principle as net camouflage are veils to cover the face, which have already been discussed in the lecture "Movement by Day".

There is no reason why ingenuity should not improve on these few types of simple artificial camouflage, but it must be remembered that the partisan does not have access to unusual materials.

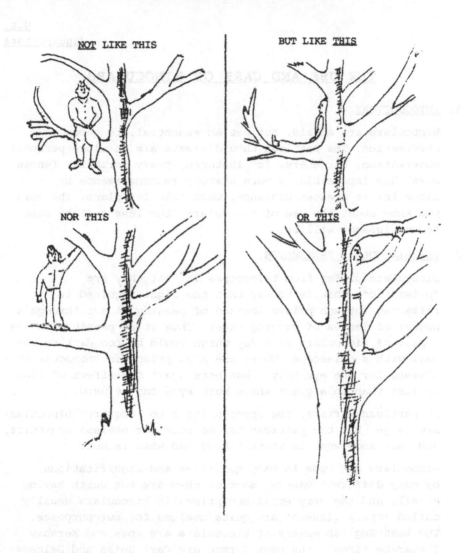

NOT LIKE THIS

BUT LIKE THIS

NOR THIS

OR THIS

RECTANGLE — BIG SHADOW

SLOPE — SMALL SHADOW

THE USE AND CARE OF BINOCULARS

1. INTRODUCTORY.

   Binoculars are an aid, but not an essential, to good observation. The partisan should always aim at close personal observation, but where, for instance, heavy perimeter fences make this impossible, a more sketchy reconnaissance by binocular at greater distance, must take its place. The more you know about the use of binoculars, the less sketchy such reconnaissance will be.

2. THE BINOCULARS THEMSELVES.

   Binoculars differ from telescopes in that they are "prismatic", that is to say that the light required is refracted through prisms instead of passing direct through a number of lenses of varying power. Thus it is possible to use a pair of binoculars on a day which would be too dark to see well with a telescope. There are also prismatic "monoculars" - glasses for one eye only - but here again the effect of light is less than in a glass where both eyes can be used.

   In partisan warfare, the opportunities to 'acquire' binoculars are large. But the partisan has no room for useless souvenirs, and must know what is worth taking and what is not.

   Binoculars are made in many qualities and magnifications, by many different makers. Some of them are not worth having at all, and the very small non-prismatic binoculars usually called 'opera glasses' are quite useless for our purposes. The best English makers of binoculars are Ross and Kershaw (separate firms), the best German are Carl Zeiss and Dalmeyer (also separate firms).

   Binoculars are made in magnifications from 4 to 25 - anything smaller than 4 being in the nature of an 'opera glass'. The natural tendency in most inexperienced people would be to plump for the 25, in that they could remain more than five times further away from the enemy than if they plumped for the 4. But there are other equally important considerations.

   The main factors are these:

   a) How much do they magnify?

b) How much light do they let in - that is, how easy to see
with are they on a dark day? This factor is called the
"light equivalent".

c) How large are they? Are they easy to carry?

Now we immediately come up against an important consideration -
the greater the magnification the less the "light equivalent"
and the more bulky and awkward are the glasses to carry. So
perhaps the 25's are not the best after all.

Most binoculars - all good ones - have their dimensions
written somewhere on them, usually on the 'shoulder', and
they are written in this manner:

8 x 25

or

10 x 50

The first figure is the number of magnifications, the second
is the number of millimetres across the object glass (the
big lense at the opposite end from the eye-piece). The "light
equivalent" is obtained by dividing the first figure into the
second and squaring the result. Thus the "light equivalents"
of the examples are 9.5 (approx.) and 25. The greater the
"light equivalent" the more use the binoculars are under poor
light conditions. Those with very low "light equivalent" are
only useful in bight sunny weather.

So we see that to have a high "light equivalent" there must
be a large object glass, and that immediately makes for
bulk. These are the problems which confront both the makers
of binoculars and the partisan leader who would equip his
band. Were they more generally understood there would be less
grumbling over the quality of binoculars issued to Armies.

Try, then, for the glass of medium dimensions - a
magnification of 8 or 10 and a "light equivalent" of not less
than, say, 10, and the higher the better as long as the glass
is still easily portable. The Carl Zeiss light-weight 10 x
50, carried by many German officers, may be said to be the
ideal binocular for general purposes. The peace-time price
of these in England was something over £50, and in the first
years of this war they were changing hands at over £100.

3. FOCUSSING.

Binoculars are focussed by a small wheel, which is usually
central, between the eye-pieces, but may be on each eye-piece

separately. A third variation is that in which the central wheel focusses the right eye only, and the left eye is focussed by screwing the eye-piece itself. In all cases it is useful to put a small mark showing where the "infinity" focus for your own eyesight is.

4. <u>THE CARE OF BINOCULARS</u>.

    a) All good binocular lenses are made of highly polished glass which is <u>soft</u>. This high polish is essential if the best results are to be obtained, and it can only be retained by <u>careful</u> cleaning. Thus, a piece of chamois leather, silk, or well-washed 4x2 should always be carried either in the binocular case or the pocket-book, and used for this purpose. First flick off the dust that may be on the outside of the glass, then clean with a gentle circular motion. <u>Never</u> touch the glass with finger or thumb.

    b) If the glass is allowed to get damp, fogging inside the lenses will result. To cure this, lay it in the sun or in a warm room, but do not let the metal get hotter than body temperature, or the Canadian balsam which fixes the lenses in most high class binoculars will melt and the glasses will fail to focus properly. When working parts get wet, they must be dried and slightly lubricated before the glasses are put away. Rifle oil will do for this purpose.

    c) Unless there are very special reasons for it, don't use your binoculars under conditions which are certain to get them wet. They may become useless before you have learnt what you want to know, and they will be useless for some time.

    d) Carry binoculars <u>on your person</u>, either in their case or in a <u>clean</u> pocket. Dust and dirt must be kept from the lenses. Keep them on your body when travelling in lorries, etc. - jolting shifts the prisms and destroys accurate focussing.

    e) Never attempt to strip binoculars, unless you are an expert.

5. <u>SPYING WITH BINOCULARS</u>.

    a) <u>Steadiness</u>: Always use a rest when you can, it is most important to keep the glasses steady. If you cannot rest the glasses on anything, press the edges of the eye-pieces against the top of the eye-sockets (not enough to cause discomfort). This gives a steadier result than is otherwise possible without resting the glasses. Every man must suit himself with regard to position. When you cannot rest the glasses, try to get both your elbows on to your knees, to form a tripod. A man will very rarely spy standing up unless his is observing over cover, when he will be able to rest the glasses.

b) <u>Technique of searching ground</u>: When searching a given sector of ground, divide it into fields of view – don't let your eyes wander aimlessly over it. Work slowly, allowing each field to overlap. Do not pass on from any unexpected or unusual object without trying to find out what it is and why it is there. Don't look at the same object for too long. If you can't make something out, rest your eyes, and look away from it and then look back quickly. On the other hand, don't give it up because you have not been able to make it out the first time. Light conditions are constantly changing, and what was invisible at 1100 hours may be quite plain at 1105. The keenest vision is at the edge of the eye – do not keep the object you are studying in the centre of the field of view. Visibility is best after rain, owing to the refraction of light from raindrops.

c) Binoculars cannot give the same perspective as the naked eye, and the following points, which are caused by this slight distortion, must be remembered:

  i) "Dead" ground is not easily distinguishable, i.e. glasses have the effect of flattening out the ground.

 ii) Distances between objects in line <u>ahead</u> appear smaller than they really are.

iii) Distances between objects in line <u>abreast</u> appear greater than they really are.

d) <u>DANGER</u>!

If you don't make some sort of a shade to cover the object glass, your position will be given away to the enemy in sunny weather by the flash. Its size must vary with the size of the object glass. Make them with paper, cardboard, or anything more permanent that you are able to get. When nothing is available, the hands can be cupped to form an extension to each object glass, but this is not entirely satisfactory.

G.
Appendix I
February 1944

PROTECTION OF RAILWAYS AND ROADS

The number and strength of guard troops and sentry posts depends on the number of bridges, tunnels, etc., to be guarded and the nature of the terrain. Under average conditions a battalion is necessary per 100 kilometres of track or road, of which 2 men are required per kilometre for local protection, with the remainder on patrol duty or acting as reserves.

Each company takes over a given section, piquets of 2 N.C.O.s. and 10 men being entrusted with the protection of specific points (the N.C.O.s. relieving one another, with 9 men for sentry duty and reliefs and 1 man in reserve for special duties).

Heavy weapons are distributed among the various sub-units.

Battalion and company commanders' headquarters are usually located with the reserves in the centre of each section. Piquets and reserves occupy strong points with a good field of fire and protected by barbed wire. In guarding railways a locomotive coupled to a truck is held ready at the strongpoints garrisoned by the reserves; in the case of roads, M.T., from which all baggage has been cleared, is kept ready at these points.

Vital points such as bridges are guarded by a single sentry by day and by double sentries at night. In the case of long bridges or of tunnels sentries are posted at either end, while covering parties may be employed too where dead ground conceals the approaches. Extra sentries may be posted below the bridges at night time (at the bridge piers).

Energetic patrolling is carried out by day on both sides of the road or railway - sometimes with cyclist patrols. Foot patrols make contact with one another during the night by moving along the permanent way* or keeping to the roadway.

Special attention is given to testing fish plates, bolts and rail joints and a good look-out is kept for explosives secured to the inner flanges of rails and for any disturbances of the ballast such as would indicate the laying of mines.

---

* A band of partisans specialising in track destruction on the Leningrad front recently gave a quarter of an hour as the interval of time elapsing between the passing of sentries.

Draisines are at times employed for purposes of inspection or for supplying posts. An armoured draisine is sometimes sent ahead of transport trains instead of a pilot engine.

If sufficient troops are available, patrols are sent off deep into the country on either side of the railway or road to search villages and question their inhabitants. (This practice appears to have arisen as a result of the order given to partisans not to withdraw more than 20 kms. from the main lines of communication).

Crops or woods adjacent to railways and capable of affording cover to guerrillas are often burnt or cut down to a width of 200 yds. or so from either side of the line. Farms adjacent to the railway may for the same reason be evacuated or burnt down. The inhabitants of villages adjacent to the railways are made responsible for safeguarding the line in their neighbourhood.

G.
Appendix II
February 1944

INTERCOMMUNICATION IN THE FIELD

The best plan may be made ineffectual by an insufficient amount of attention being paid to the question of intercommunication.

The subject is of paramount importance to both regular and irregular forces but it presents far greater difficulties to the latter, since, in most cases, stealth and silence are their watchwords by day and by night.

In every partisan operation it is absolutely necessary that the leader should, in making up his orders, visualise in advance every possible occasion and circumstance when it may be necessary for himself or any member of the party to communicate with any one or more of the remainder; he must be satisfied that the signals arranged are adequate under all circumstances and known to all who may need them.

THE TWO MAIN TYPES OF SIGNALS.

All signals that will require to be given during a partisan operation can be roughly divided into two types:

a) Those which need not be concealed from the enemy.

b) Those which must not warn the enemy of the presence of the users.

TYPE (a).

The signals falling into this category are those which start a noisy action, those which are given during it continuance, and those which mark its end.

Signals of this type do not usually present serious difficulties. The signal for the opening of the action may, for instance, be a shot or a blast on a whistle. The main consideration is that some action on the part of the enemy shall not be mistaken for the leader's signal, e.g. all German sentries are equipped with whistles; it may be, however, that the action could be arranged to start on the particular sound being produced by either side, if production by the enemy automatically means that he is aware of something being amiss, e.g. a shot from the sentry.

Another consideration is that all members of the party for whom any signal is intended must be able to hear (or perhaps see) it, no matter how much noise or confusion there may be in the course of the action.

Visual signals (by hand, arm, flag, etc.) are only dependable if the men for whom they are intended are looking towards the signaller at the time, and therefore a preceding audible signal may be necessary to attract their attention; subject to this limitation, however, visual signals are useful.

In spite of the fact that signals of this type are overt, it is nevertheless desirable that the range at which they can be seen or heard should not be unnecessarily extended further than is essential for them to be noticed by the party; if this latter requirement is satisfied, the smaller radius at which they are obvious, the better.

TYPE (b).

Signals falling into this category, "stealthy" signals, present much greater difficulties and require both forethought on the part of the leader and constant rehearsal by any of the party who may, in any eventuality, need to use them.

They can be conveniently divided into two kinds:

i) Those that are not sufficiently loud or visible to be heard or seen by the enemy.

ii) Those which have to be received over some distance and therefore will be heard or seen by the enemy but must not make him suspicious.

In considering (i), very careful thought must be given by the leader to the distances at which either audible or visible signals are likely to be perceptible by the members of the party under different weather conditions. For instance, a low hiss as a danger signal will be inadequate on a wet night with a high wind; likewise, in a ground mist, visual signals from a look-out who is giving warning of the approach of a convoy may be useless.

It may be necessary for the leader to duplicate, audibly and visually, a certain signal under this heading, in order to cope with differing circumstances, e.g. the danger signal: it is quite likely that circumstances may arise when it is possible to make quite safely a movement of the band but not the slightest sound, and vice versa.

It is not possible to specify as being superior to others any particular sound designed to reach the ears of the members of the party but not those of the enemy; a hiss, click of the tongue, or various air-noises in the mouth, etc., are all useful, according to circumstances and weather conditions.

Recognition signals can never truly come into this category since their use necessarily implies either that the party is separated and endeavouring to rejoin, or that the user is not certain of the identity of the person to whom the signal is directed.

In considering (ii) – these which have to carry over some distance and will therefore be heard or seen by the enemy, but which must not make him suspicious – it will immediately be clear that, in the majority of cases, they will be audible signals, and usually the only possibilities will be animal or bird sounds with some characteristic to distinguish them from the genuine sound: this characteristic may be some slight variation of note, usually at the end, or may be repetition in a prescribed order or with definite intervals.

A sound will therefore be chosen that is:

a) Probable in the particular locality, i.e. do not choose a hyena for use in Europe, or a cock crowing in the middle of the desert.

b) Not likely to attract attention in itself, e.g. a dog barking is always a suspicious sound and may cause investigation by the enemy.

c) Not too difficult to learn, and one of which the genuine version can be heard by the members of the party and rehearsed by those who will use it.

Suitable sounds will therefore vary with the country and district in which the party is operating. Sounds for use by night must be confined to those animals and birds which are normally noisy be night, and the same applies to signals for use by day.

Specimens are:

By night: owl.   By day: wood pigeon.

Endless possible sounds could be listed and the above are quoted as examples only.

GENERAL.

Once an audible signal has been chosen which imitates a natural sound, it must be rehearsed until the leader is satisfied that all members of the party who may possibly need to use it are capable of producing the sound realistically whenever required, and that all the party can recognise it. He cannot be satisfied on this point unless he has listened carefully to the genuine sound for comparison.

It is always better for signals conveying different meanings to be entirely different sounds and not merely diverse multiplications of the same sound: this avoids the possibility of a man hearing only part of a signal and acting accordingly, e.g. hearing two out of four blasts on a whistle and quite rightly carrying out some different action for which two blasts had been the prescribed signal.

All signals should be kept as short and uncomplicated as is consistent with their being received and understood.

The use of string or cord has been advocated by some people as a means of intercommunication and of keeping in touch within a small party moving in single file on dark nights. As a means of intercommunication it is not very satisfactory: the circumstances of its use imply that it will almost certainly be tugged and pulled at moments when no signal is intended, either through someone stumbling in the dark or through the cord itself being caught up in some obstruction, but as a means of keeping in touch it is quite good -the cord should have knots along its length corresponding with the number of men. Use can also be made of a cord as a previously laid guide-line in difficult going in darkness, e.g. through a thick wood or across a ford. In a previous lecture we recommended that every man should carry on an operation a length of at least four yards of stout string: by tying these together a suitable cord can be made for use as either a guide-line or a contact-line.

MINOR TACTICS
APPENDIX I
January 1944

RECCE OF GROUND & SELECTION OF ROUTE

All Fieldcraft and Minor Tactics are a means to an end – their purpose is to enable you to reach your objective undetected, or to withdraw from it in safety. These lectures contain general considerations applying to all operations requiring stealth; the actual tactics of different types of operations are discussed in detail in other lectures.

"Fieldcraft" has been defined as "the art of being like an animal in its own terrain" – which implies a complete familiarity with the ground over which one is working. Since we are often operating in country which is strange to us, the importance of recce is clear and cannot be over-estimated.

If recce is to be of real value, there must be a clear idea what is to be looked for and what the recce may be expected to decide.

Recce of the ground should always decide the following factors:

1. The best route (both for advance and withdrawal).
2. The best clothing and personal equipment.
3. The amount of time necessary.
4. The establishment of bounds and landmarks.
5. The organization of all-round defence.

These points may be considered in detail as follows:

1. The factors affecting the choice of route:

   a) Enemy dispositions – guards, patrols, system of
      communication, wire, proximity of local troops, etc.

   b) Other features to be avoided. These include roads, paths,
      houses (particularly farms, where there are always dogs
      and other domestic animals to announce arrival), any
      place where there is any congregation of either wild or
      domestic animals or birds, and all skylines. If careful
      attention is paid to the latter on recce, it will very
      rarely be found necessary to cross a skyline. A place will
      almost always be found where there is a fold in the ground
      forming a "double skyline" (that is the skyline is not
      truly continuous, one part of it being behind the other),
      or where there is sufficient natural cover for the body
      never to appear in silhouette.

302

c) <u>The presence or absence of cover</u>. The route chosen should afford the best cover during the <u>latter</u> stages of the approach when close to enemy. The most frequent mistake is that of choosing a route affording good initial cover, but little or none when it is most needed. In choosing the route, the aim should be that the party should be invisible from as many directions as possible for as long as possible, and that it should always be near enough to cover to be able to "melt away" if surprised. This implies that "broken" ground should be chosen, not open ground, and that the lowest part of that broken ground should be followed the whole time, even to a matter of inches. Always try to keep <u>something</u> between you and the enemy, even if it will only just hide you.

d) <u>The position of the sun</u>. To approach by a route that will place you between the enemy and the sun, particularly when the sun is low in the morning or evening, is of great advantage. To have a sun low in your eyes as you approach is to be avoided at all costs.

2. <u>The best clothing and personal equipment</u>:

a) <u>Clothing</u>. Certain general principles will always apply. The clothing should be of neutral colour and tone. Tone (that is, how light or how dark it is) is of more importance than colour. There must be no bright objects, such as buttons, belt buckles, etc., which may glint in the sun. No clothing should be worn which will make movement noisy even at the closest quarters, – i.e. leather may creak, metal objects may chink together, stiff material – such as a mackintosh – will rustle. Clothing should be looked over for loose buttons, etc., which might come off when crawling. Duplicate brace buttons are advisable – a man who is holding up his trousers with one hand is helpless. The distance and the type of ground to be covered will decide whether soft or hard shoes should be worn – boots are always clumsy and should be avoided when possible. Shoe covers (two pieces of sacking or other material to wrap round the feet) or a thick pair of socks which may be pulled on over the shoes and secured round the ankle, may be carried to facilitate silent movement on road or pavement or rock. Places on the route which might make the carrying of such special equipment necessary, should be looked for on the recce. The face and hands <u>must</u> be veiled or darkened, unless direct bluff is either contemplated or may be necessary in an emergency. This last consideration is fully discussed in the lecture "Appreciation". Methods of veiling and darkening the flesh are discussed in the next lecture on Minor Tactics.

b) <u>Personal equipment</u>. Nothing must be carried which is unnecessary. Personal equipment must be cut down to a minimum, and unnecessary objects mean extra bulk, weight, noise and possible loss of security. The following are always useful, and should be carried independent of personal taste or the necessities of the particular operation decided by the recce.

 i) A knife, capable of being used either as a utility or offensive weapon. As an offensive weapon the ordinary clasp knife can be improved by sharpening the back of the blade for a short distance below the point.

 ii) A match-box, full, because a half-empty box rattles. If there are only a few matches in the box the lower part of the box should be filled out with grass or other material.

 iii) Some money - paper when possible - because coins in the pocket are noisy.

 iv) A length of at least four yards of stout string. This may be used for any purpose from tieing up a man to preparing a booby trap or stretching across a path to give warning of a man's approach.

 v) A watch, worn on the wrist, where it will not get crushed when crawling.

 vi) A compass, worn on a string round the neck, but carried down the <u>back</u>, where it will not cause discomfort when crawling.

 vii) Some first-aid equipment on the lines of the British First Field Dressing.

The length of the operation and the type of ground will decide what type of quantity of food (or water) should be carried.

3. <u>Timing</u>.

In training, it will be found that the greatest number of operations fail due to inadequate attention being paid to timing. The greatest and most detailed attention should

be paid to this on recce and the time taken to cover the
ground on recce must be carefully noted. Whenever possible,
the amount of time finally allowed for the operation should
be greater than has appeared strictly necessary on recce.
In open country the normal walking speed of a man is
approximately 100 yards in one minute; nothing less than
double this amount of time can be expected in an operation
requiring stealth. Crawling may lengthen the time to as much
as half-an-hour for the same distance, when really difficult
ground has to be crossed, and all these things must be taken
into consideration when finally computing the time necessary
for the operation. During training it is useful to note
constantly the amount of time taken to cross various pieces
of ground, and to measure distances with the eye and compare
them on the map.

4. The establishment of bounds and landmarks.

This is absolutely necessary on recce - failure to do so
will frequently result in loss of direction when crossing
difficult ground, and the failure of the operation. Two
purposes are achieved by the establishment of bounds:

a) Maintenance of direction.
b) Ensuring observation of ground immediately to be crossed.

The ground to be covered should be divided into sections,
the end of each section or bound being a landmark easily
recognisable from any direction. The necessity for this
will be clear when it is remembered that it is not always
approached from the expected direction, and that it is often
impossible to raise the head above ground level when moving
towards the objective. When each landmark is reached, the
ground between it and the next should be thoroughly observed
before it is crossed. Observation is fully dealt with in the
next lecture.

5. The organization of all-round defence.

Nothing can ever obviate the necessity for all-round defence
at all times. Danger does not always come from the expected
direction and the advantage of surprise must lie with us and
not with the enemy. When the force is composed of several
men, each must be allotted an angle or direction for which he
is responsible at all times, whether at halt or on the move,
and his attention must never stray from this direction. When
alone, a man must constantly be looking all round him all the
time, never allowing himself to become preoccupied with one
direction to the exclusion of others.

<u>Recce by field-glasses or telescope</u>. When recce is conducted by field-glasses or telescope, the following points should be remembered:

a) "Dead" ground is not easily distinguishable, i.e. glasses have the effect of flattening out ground.

b) Distances between objects in line <u>ahead</u> appear smaller than they really are.

c) Distances between objects in line <u>abreast</u> appear greater than they really are.

d) In bright weather, flash may be produced by the object glass which will give away the position of the observer unless a shield or shade is used. Such a shade should not be less than 15 cms. long for an object glass of 50 mms. or 10 cms. long for an object glass of 30 mms. The shade may be made of brown paper or cardboard, or other material available. When nothing else is available, the hands may be cupped to form an extension or funnel to each object glass.

e) The ground to be searched should be divided into sections, and each section searched from flank to flank. Each travel of the glass should overlap the previous one.

f) A greater degree of steadiness can be obtained by pressing the eyepieces against the upper part of the eye-socket and resting the elbows, thus forming a wedge.

In all cases where the leader of a party is unable to carry out a personal recce, he should arrange for a written Route Report, with sketches or sketch-maps of the ground. This is fully dealt with in the lecture on Route Reports.

(At the end of the lecture, the Instructor should repeat the five points to which particular attention should be paid on recce.)

GENERAL MOVEMENT BY DAY

1. Formations.

   Any party of men moving across country should move in a
   definite formation, not in a constantly changing huddle or a
   straggling line. The reasons for this, and the essentials of
   any formation, are to ensure:

   a) Maximum use of available cover.
   b) Permanent all-round defence.
   c) Adequate communication among all members of the party, but
      particularly between the leader and his scouts.

   A great many formations have been devised for use by the
   regular army, some of which fulfil these requirements,
   but most are unsatisfactory because they are impossible to
   maintain, either for a long distance or in broken country,
   and very few really ensure the maximum use of available
   cover. Chiefly for this latter reason we do not use the
   diamond and box shaped formations.

   For a small body of men moving across any type of country,
   there is no better formation than single file with scouts
   ahead.

   In speaking of formations we have in mind here a basic sized
   party of 10 men but the formation applies equally well to
   larger or smaller parties. When, however, a party of 20 or
   more men are concerned it is better in any case to form into
   two parties and rendezvous, as for any stealthy operation a
   party of such a size is unwieldy.

   This formation complies with the three requirements mentioned -
   particularly it ensures that the whole of the main body use
   the cover chosen by the leader, which is extremely difficult
   to ensure in an extended formation. Only the scouts use high
   ground, and that only enough to ensure the safety of the party
   they are preceding. In a box or diamond formation, on the
   other hand, the flank men must constantly be using ground where
   there is no cover, in order to maintain their position in the
   formation.

The intervals between the members of the party, and between the scouts and the leader, depend entirely on the nature of the ground and the limit of visibility. The scouts <u>must</u> be in touch with the leader and in touch with each other – <u>once they are out of sight of the leader they are useless</u>. Under the best visibility conditions it is not desirable for them to be more than 100-150 metres in front of the leader, but in darkness or in very close country, only contact with the leader can decide the maximum distance. The leader must watch his scouts the whole time for any signal they may give him – they are his eyes.

The only time when a considerable interval between members of the main party is desirable is when, for instance, an open hillside must be crossed in distant view of the enemy. Here, a close mass of men moving would be visible when widely separated men would not. Each man of the party is responsible for observing in a particular direction the whole time, and he must be able to draw the leader's attention to anything that he sees with the least possible delay – a wide interval between members of the party makes this difficult.

When the party halts it is automatically covered by the scouts, to ensure that it is not taken by surprise. This should be an invariable rule, whatever the reason for the halt.

Also, whatever the reason for the halt, the whole of the main party must immediately get into cover. The practice of halting for discussion in exposed places is very common in training and is a very serious fault. As soon as the leader realises that a halt is necessary, whether because he is off his route and must use the map or because he has reached the end of a bound and must wait for the scouts to observe, he must immediately get his party into a position where they cannot be seen. This is all the more important if the halt is in order to study the map – the white flash of a map can be seen at a great distance and at no time should more of it be exposed than is absolutely necessary.

2. <u>Use of background</u>.

Where there is no cover, background can be effectively used, provided that the following points are remembered:

a) In any ordinary neutral-tinted clothing a man at a distance looks <u>darker</u> than his background. This can easily be demonstrated by watching a man cross a hillside which is partly light and partly dark coloured. Therefore, always keep as dark a background as you can.

b) The colour of the face and the hands is unnatural to any landscape and by their position on the figure easily define the object as a human being. They should, therefore, always be blacked or veiled. It is not enough to black the face only, as is so often done - the hands must be darkened also. Any mixture used for blacking should not contain oil unless in the smallest quantities, to make it adhesive - a oily surface shines and catches the light. Veils have the advantage that they can quickly be discarded if there is any chance of passing as a friend. The best material for veils is fine mesh black or green muslin net, and it should be soaked in hot water for some hours to remove its starchiness. If this is not done it will make a constant rustling noise round the head, which makes hearing difficult. The veil should be of double thickness over the whole face except for a belt of single thickness running round the front from ear to ear. It is not sufficient to leave eyeholes of single thickness as it will be found that vision is very much restricted at the sides. The veil must be made to tie on securely or it will be easily displaced when crawling or passing through thick cover.

c) Any swiftly moving object is very easily seen - movements should be slow and smooth.

d) Shadows flatter the resemblance between you and your background - keep to the shadows wherever possible.

3. Crawling technique.

When both cover and background fail, it is necessary to crawl. Crawling is usually performed in a very haphazard way due to a lack of clear understanding of what the crawler is trying to achieve.

The primary consideration is whether you are crawling to:

a) avoid being seen;
b) avoid being heard;
c) avoid both.

Each requires a different technique and unless this is clearly understood the result can never be satisfactory.

a) When crawling to avoid being seen, the whole body should be as close as possible to the ground. Since there can be no head without a body following it, and no rump without a head preceding it, it is quite useless to keep one part of the body low unless the rest of the body follows suit – the strength of the chain is the strength of its weakest link. Every part of the body, including the face, must touch the ground. Movement is effected by fingers and toes (left and right alternately, not together) the arms being stretched out immediately in front of the body. This is commonly called the "flat" or "snake" crawl.

b) When crawling to avoid being heard, the "bear" crawl should be used. It is so called because a bear leaves one set of footprints only, like a biped, the hind feet being placed exactly in the imprint of the fore. In the case of the man, the knees are placed in the exact positions of the hands, which have first carefully felt for and removed any noisy material on the ground.

c) When crawling to avoid both being seen and heard, a compromise technique is required. The fingers of both hands are interlocked under the chest, and at each forward movement the body is lifted just clear of the ground, assisted by the toes of both feet moved together. As in position (a), the head is kept as close to the ground as possible and the body is lifted no higher than to allow its clear passage without a dragging sound.

The smaller the surface area the body presents to the enemy, the less likely it will be to be detected – therefore when crawling always face the enemy if possible.

4. Observation.

Observation is necessary at the end of each bound, to ensure the safety of the ground which the party is about to cross, it is necessary when approaching the objective and it is necessary on recce. Never spend less than three minutes in observation – a quick glance is useless and merely lulls into a sense of what may be false security. The thing to look for first is movement because it is most easily seen. Then look carefully at anything that is darker than its surroundings; lastly at anything that is much lighter than its surroundings. If you are suspicious of an object – take no chances; wait until your mind is made up.

If there is more than one in the party, the observer's rear should be covered by another member of the party. His attention is fully occupied with the direction in which he is observing and he is vulnerable to attack from behind. The aim of observation is to see without being seen, and, if this can be achieved, the greatest possible advantage has been secured over the enemy. Since the most prominent feature will be the head, <u>the importance of its camouflage or disguise cannot be over-estimated</u>. The head can be camouflaged either by natural or artificial means but it must be done thoroughly. Two blades of grass do not make you invisible, nor is it enough merely to cover the head if the outline of its shape still remains. If natural camouflage is used (i.e. herbage, etc.) it should be used plentifully, so that no part of the headgear remains uncovered and the head can be exposed down to the level of the eyes without fear of recognition. It should be remembered that natural herbage dies quickly and, especially in cases of plants which have very light-coloured under-sides to the leaves, may be very visible when dead. The simplest of all means of natural camouflage of the head is a sheet of moss and has two great advantages. First, it is to be found everywhere in the world where there are trees or rocks; second, it requires no making or work as it can be taken off the ground in a solid piece that will cover the whole head – a ready made hat. Artificial camouflage of the head is a hat that is constructed to look like something else, and is dependent upon personal ingenuity. It is rarely as satisfactory as natural camouflage.

When possible, observations should be done <u>round</u>, not over, cover, and at <u>ground level</u>. The human eye is unconsciously most receptive of movement at is own level above the ground, and movement much higher or much lower than this level (i.e. in trees or at ground level) is frequently overlooked. The head, then, should be kept as close as possible to the ground when observing round an object, and only just enough of it exposed to allow observation – it is quite unnecessary to expose the whole head. If the head is not camouflaged, the part of it that is exposed should be protected by a bunch of herbage held before it.

Any object of regular outline should be avoided as a place from which to observe – anything protruding from a smooth surface is very easily seen, (instance British and German trench parapets 1914-16).

The greatest of all aids to observation is a periscope, which allows the observer to see without exposing himself at all. Periscopes are not generally obtainable, but a rough one is not difficult to make. Thousands of these were home-made for the coronation of the present King - consisting of a simple arrangement of mirrors on a stick. (Demonstrate model).

The movement of the head during observation must be extremely slow - the head must be raised inch by inch and lowered again in the same way - any quick or jerky movement attracts attention at once.

5. Animals and Birds.

In addition to the possibility of your own movements being detected by sound or sight, the likelihood of deduction of your whereabouts from disturbed animals or birds must not be overlooked. This applies to disturbance of both domestic and wild animals and birds. Sheep when alarmed run and huddle together, staring in the direction of the object that has frightened them; domestic geese set up a great noise and walk in the direction of the intruder - to cite two examples only. Wild animals and birds, being more generally distributed and more difficult to avoid, present a great problem. Rooks at a rookery will set up a great commotion and rise high over the trees when their territory is invaded; wood pigeons fly out of the trees with a clapping of wings. Magpies, jays, jackdaws, etc., all have their own unmistakable alarm notes. In arable land the movement of game-birds will often locate the position of a man accurately. Hares, which have a preference for crossing open ground when disturbed, also betray the position. A piece of rabbit-infested ground without a rabbit to be seen means that someone has passed that way recently. Instances can be multiplied beyond the scope of a lecture. Many dangers of this sort are difficult to avoid, but ground where there are known to be definite congregations of animals or birds, i.e. sheep-ground, rookeries, rabbit warrens, etc. should be avoided in the choice of a route.

Remember that these things will not betray you only, they will also betray the enemy if you pay attention to them. An obviously alarmed animal or bird should always make you suspicious until you know the cause of it.

There is also much to be deducted from the ground. A man will not always leave footprints, but except on the hardest ground

he will always leave some mark of his passage – the grasses
are bent, a rock is marked where a nailed boot has scratched
it, some moss is rubbed from it, a wisp of wool is left on
barbed wire; but these things will not be noticed unless
they are looked for. The subject of human footprints is too
specialised a subject to go into in detail, but some points
are worth remembering.

6. <u>Footprints</u>.

a) <u>General</u>. A small amount of loose soil is always thrown
up by the heel and the toe, forward in the first case,
backward in the latter. The amount of soil is in direct
relation to the speed of travel. The most marked impression
is left by the outside of the back of the heel and the
inside of the toe. The faster the travel, also, the closer
laterally the right and left foot, and the straighter the
feet are pointing.

b) <u>Walking</u>. Average pace slightly over 30". If a small man
taking long steps, heel indentation is deeper. Carrying
a heavy load feet are wider apart laterally, toes pointed
more outward, steps short, indentation deep especially
at toe and outside edge of foot. A stout man leaves a
similar track, but less indented at the toes, the track
more regular with less divergence. The height of a man is
usually about six and one-third times the length of the
imprint of his naked feet. A lame man takes a short step
with his <u>lame</u> leg, not his sound one.

c) <u>Running</u>.

i) <u>Trained runner</u>: Indentation of toe deep, possibly no
heel mark. Distance between paces up too 6 ft. for a
6ft. man. Prints in straight line, no outward turn of
toes.

ii) <u>Untrained runner</u>: Heel print deep as well as toe print,
heel pointed less straight, noticeable divergence in
straight line of track. The same track will be shown by
any man running under stress of great emotion or mental
confusion.

d) <u>Freshness of tracks</u>. In very fresh tracks the loose earth
thrown up will look darker than the surrounding earth,
edges of print sharp, not rounded by rain or wind. Broken
vegetation will not have begun to wither at the break,

which becomes noticeable after a few hours, varying with the weather. Bent grasses will not have recovered upright position. Age of tracks may be known from effect of rain showers when these have been recent. Best practice of all is look at your own footprints at varying times after you have made them and in varying weather conditions.

e) <u>Tire Tracks</u>. Most important consideration is which way they are going. Most certain way is by crossing or overlapping of front wheel tracks by rear wheels. Over a bump tracks will momentarily broaden out at the far side, as the tire takes the downward bump of the chassis. Position of the tracks on the road are also an indication, especially when cornering. In the case of a bicycle, direction is more easily distinguishable, as rear wheel more often crosses or obscures front wheel, especially uphill as the forward position of the rider causes more wobble. The faster the travel the straighter the line.

7. <u>Summary</u>.

There can be no passengers in a party. Every man has a job to do all the time, and unless at a halt for rest, he must never relax. If training is to be useful, this idea must be applied throughout it. The slackness of one man can ruin the value of a training scheme for a whole party. Training here is intensive, and time on schemes cannot be wasted.

MINOR TACTICS AND FIELDCRAFT

GENERAL MOVEMENT BY NIGHT

Much of the Lecture II (Movement by Day) applies also to Movement by Night, but because at night our primary aim is SILENCE, there will be certain differences, but not as far as formation goes.

We recommend the Single File formation for use in all light conditions. At night this formation will, however, be closed up to whatever degree may be necessary to ensure control of his party by the leader.

The differences will particularly affect the route - the type of ground over which we want to move.

1. <u>Factors influencing the choice of route</u>.

    a) <u>Best type of cover</u>.

    As in day work, the route should give the best cover in the latter stages of the approach, but a different type of cover will be required. SILENCE is the keynote – therefore the thickest cover will very rarely be the best. Ground that is silent to move over, will then be the first consideration. On a very dark night nothing else need be thought of. If it is a little lighter, <u>keep a dark background</u>. If it is a very bright moonlight night the considerations will be the same as for day operations. If there is a likelihood of searchlights or Verey lights being used, keep close to cover that you can get behind quickly. Remember that the direct route is a bad one nine times out of ten.

    b) <u>Features to be avoided</u>.

    Particularly these will be any features that may give you away through <u>noise</u>. Any farmyard, and place where domestic animals are confined, is a death trap. Where there are known to be dogs, the direction of the wind must be remembered too. Ground that is noisy to move over <u>must</u> be noted on recce and avoided on operation. Avoid all skylines and water – they are of equal importance. It is less easy to tell when one is silhouetted at night than in daylight, but you are even more obvious to the enemy. A

315

party moving along the side of a piece of water is bound to be silhouetted from some angle – this applies even more to the sea. Avoid the most obvious route or approach –this is where the defence will be strongest.

c) <u>The Moon</u>.

Always find out the times of its rising and setting, and do not rely upon visibility being good while the moon is up. Remember that the slightest change in light conditions at night has a much greater effect on seeing than in daylight, and that they can change very quickly. Approach by a route that gets the moon behind the enemy – just the reverse of the route you would choose with the sun in daylight.

2. <u>Clothing for Night Work</u>.

The colour of the clothing is not important if the tone (that is, how light or how dark it is) is neutral. Very dark clothes are bad – when you see a man at night it is because he is even blacker than his surroundings. Wear nothing that is very dark or very light. Any form of shininess must be avoided, and things that will shine when they are wet. There must be nothing that will be noisy in movement – no squeaking shoes, creaking leather braces, etc. Mackintosh material is bad because it rustles when moved. Rubber or rope-soled shoes are the best – when this is not possible, carry shoe cover as described in the last lecture. The face and hands must be darkened or veiled. Even on a very dark night, when this would seem unimportant, there is the danger of a sudden light. Unless the face and hands are darkened this will show you up at once.

3. <u>Personal Equipment</u>.

In addition to the personal equipment mentioned for day work, the following should be carried:

a) A stick. This enables the ground to be felt carefully before you, which is very necessary on a really dark night. This must not have a metal ferrule, which is noisy. If an old bicycle tube is available, the whole stick can be encased in it and tightly bound. This prevents sharp noise when the stick knocks against anything. The stick may also have a lead-loaded head as a weapon of silent offence.

b) A small pocket torch and one spare battery. The torch can be encased in a section of bicycle tube in the same way, to avoid jingling against other objects in the pockets, or it can be bound with rags. A home-made arrangement on the glass, so that the aperture can be varied from a pin-point to the whole area of the glass, is advisable.

c) Watch and compass with luminous dials. The watch is best worn on the wrist, with face against the skin instead of outwards. The compass in the way recommended for day work.

d) Some cough lozenges or sweets to suck. This prevents coughing.

Again, as in day work, nothing must be carried which is unnecessary. Care must be taken that there are no noisy objects in the pockets and it is the duty of the leader of a party to make sure of this himself. Jump up and down on the floor and see if there is any other noise than that of your feet.

4. Timing and Communication.

Accurate timing is the only substitute for direct communication, which is exceedingly difficult by night. A very careful estimate of the amount of time necessary to cover each piece of ground should be made. When moving silently in favourable country the index figure of 50 yards in one minute is a useful one to remember. But however accurate the timing, signals remain absolutely necessary, and must be arranged, practised and rehearsed before any scheme or operation. The essentials of a signal for use at night are that it should be sufficiently loud to be certain of being heard, and that it should not sound like a human being. The signal of a dog barking, most often used by students, is not good, because a dog barking is in itself a suspicious thing. When an animal signal is used there must be some way of distinguishing it from the genuine animal - i.e. it must finish in a particular way or be given in a certain rhythm. The sounds usually made are so unrealistic that this is not necessary, but that is not our aim. There must be a signal for danger, a signal for dispersal, a signal for simple recognition and a signal for halting.

5. All-round Defence at Night.

The same principle applies as in day work. Each man in the party must have a permanent responsibility for an angle or direction. But the whole party may easily blunder into danger if one golden rule is not followed - STOP FREQUENTLY AND LISTEN. Again and again in training, students blunder right into enemy which they should have detected had they followed this one simple rule. It is the only way to ensure that the ground in front of you is safe, and its importance cannot be stressed too much. During these halts for listening, each man keeps his attention on the direction for which he is personally responsible. To make this system work well, the whole party must be closed up well, so that no man is far separated from the the rest of the party. On a dark night, even the scouts will be separated from the leader by no more than a pace or two, and the main party will be close enough together to touch one another. If the operation is a long one, and the party halts for rest and sleep, they must be covered by a proper covering party the whole time. There should be two awake for every one asleep, so that a fight can be put up even if the covering party itself is taken by surprise.

6. Use of Field-glasses at Night.

Good use can be made of field glasses at night if they are of a sufficiently high "light equivalent". The "light equivalent" is arrived at by dividing the number of magnifications into the measurement of the object glass in mm and squaring the result. The number of magnifications is given first on all glasses, the measurement of the object glass second, i.e. 8 x 30 or 10 x 50. The "light equivalent" of the first would be 14 (to the nearest decimal); that of the second would be 25. A "light equivalent" of about 10 is necessary for use at night.

7. The Technique of Individual Movement.

When ordinarily walking in the daytime, one is, without being conscious of it, constantly stepping over small obstacles, lifting the feet where there is a step up, and so on. It is impossible to do this at night because it is impossible to see the ground in front of one's feet. Therefore the only way to avoid constantly tripping over small objects is to lift the feet much higher from the ground than one does in daytime - almost a mark time action - and shorten the steps accordingly. This also avoids the noise made by the feet brushing through long grass or other herbage, and is the basis of all silent movement in the dark. Carelessness is at the root of all noisy movement, and it is impossible to be careful when moving fast, so all movement should be slow. The full weight should not be placed upon the foot until it has been tested lightly - this does not take much time and avoids breaking large sticks, stepping in large holes and so on. The foot should be pointed straight – the "Charlie Chaplin Walk" presents a larger area of frontal surface and is noisy.

The rubber-cased stick, mentioned under "Equipment", will be found of great assistance in moving across rough ground.

If there is noisy ground to cross, wait for a "counter noise" – some car, train, a gust of wind – anything that will cover the noise you make.

Recognition of noisy and silent ground.

The following rule is not invariable but it is very nearly always true except of artificial surfaces. Noisy ground looks dark-coloured, silent ground looks light-coloured. This is due to the fact that the dark colour is almost always due to a number of small shadows and means that there are small objects like sticks, herbage, stones, etc. on the ground. Where there are no shadows the ground must be smooth, and therefore silent.

8. The Best Use of the Senses at Night.

It is important that the best use should be made of what remains of sight. The degree to which men can see in the dark varies greatly. It should be the job of a leader to find out the degree of night sight which each of his men possesses and use them accordingly. Certain foods do improve sight at night, but only over too long a period to be much use. There are, however, certain things to be avoided, and alcohol is the most important. It should never be drunk the day preceding a night operation.

A man's normal powers of sight are not recovered fully for at least half-an-hour after coming out of artificial light into the dark.

Staring at an object for too long is to be avoided. If you stare at an object that you cannot see plainly, the eyes begin to play tricks – the edges blur and there seems to be movement where there is none. Many a shot has been fired and position given away for this reason. If you are suspicious of an object, concentrate on listening, giving it a rapid glance at intervals. By this means any change in its shape or position is much more easily detected. It is sometimes easier to see an object if you do not look straight at it but a few degrees off it.

Any bright light, such as a flare, searchlight, etc., will rob you of your sight for some minutes. Therefore, close your eyes when there is a likelihood of being dazzled. The moment after such light is extinguished is useful for any quick movement, while the enemy is partially blinded. Remember that at night or in a mist, small objects nearby are apt to look like much larger objects further away. For example, a bunch of thistles seen from ground level ten yards away may look like a big bush or tree a hundred or more yards away.

Hearing at Night.

This, more than any other sense, must be relied on to replace sight, and the aim should be to achieve the acute analytical hearing of a blind man. This can only be done by constant and conscientious practice, trying to analyse sounds in the dark, and obtain a clear mental picture of what is going on without any use of sight. It can be practised by closing the eyes in the daytime, and trying to understand what is going on round about you as a blind man does. Human ears are badly placed for hearing. Animals may be roughly divided into animals that pursue and animals that are pursued, and each of these main groups have their ears placed in the way most suited to their needs. Thus a hare or rabbit is able to turn its ears almost completely to the rear, a fox or wolf almost completely forward. Thus by facing the direction of the sound, a human being is not getting the best use from either ear - one ear only should be turned in that direction.

Hearing is the most acute when the mouth is slightly open - and when not trying to see at the same time, each sense being at its best when operating alone.

A loud explosion has the same effect on the hearing as a flare or other bright light has upon the sight. The deafening effect is greatly magnified when the teeth are clenched, which is the comman reaction, because of the greater vibration thus produced. The mouth should be slightly open, and should the explosion be expected it is always best to cover the ears. In the same way that the moment after a dazzling light has subsided is a good moment for moving (because the enemy is blinded) the moment after an explosion is a good one for noisy movement that has to be made, because the enemy is deafened.

Sound travels much more slowly than sight. The speed is 360 yards per second, but varies according to temperature and altitude. It is quicker in summer than in winter, quicker at low altitudes than high. The quickness of your movements must compensate for this time-lag, i.e. if you hear a round being slipped into the breach of a rifle, it may be half-way to the man's shoulder by the time the sound reaches you.

Sound travels more clearly on a gentle wind than on a gale or when there is no wind at all. Fog also helps sound, rain deadens it. Fog has rather the same effect on sounds as it does on sight - a faint noise close by sounding like a louder one further away.

Some substances are powerful sound conductors, in the same way that some are electricity conductors. Still water and wood are two of the most dangerous.

Touch.

It is important that the sense of touch should be constantly practised, both in order to be able to obtain a mental picture of ground and objects by touch alone, and also to acquire dexterity which does not depend upon eyesight. When preparing a demolition, for instance, it is impossible to show the smallest light - the whole job must be done by the sense of touch alone. Unless it is constantly practised the handling of objects by touch alone will be clumsy and noisy, which spells certain failure.

HOW TO BECOME A SPY

CROSSING OF OBSTACLES

The route chosen for the approach to any objective should obviously as far as possible avoid all obstacles - by which term we mean fences, hedges, roads, rivers, walls, etc. - in fact any natural feature which will either slow up movement or, as in the case of roads, constitute a danger point on the route. But there will always be obstacles to be crossed on almost any route to a worthwhile objective, and although these vary so greatly that no law can be laid down for the treatment of each, certain general principles will always apply.

1. Preparing obstacles for crossing.

   Owing to the importance of absolute silence, whenever possible obstacles should be prepared for crossing during the reconnaissance of the route. That is to say, if there is a gap to be made in a hedge, an easy place to be found at which to get over a wall or to ford a stream, this must be done beforehand and MARKED in some way to make it easily recognisable at night. How clearly it can be marked must, of course, depend on the risks of the enemy noticing it. If it is not possible to do any preparation on recce owing to lack of time or nearness of the place to enemy posts, there is one invariable rule - one or, if necessary, two men should on the actual operation prepare the obstacle for crossing whilst the others cover. A disorganised rabble passing through a hedge or fording a stream by different routes is as great an advertisement as a brass band.

   Finally, a previously prepared obstacle must be approached with as much caution as a rendezvous, as it is always possible that the enemy may have found it.

2. Methods of crossing various obstacles.

   a) Wire Fences.

      Contact with stretched wire causes a vibration audible at a great distance in the direction in which the wire runs, and detectable by touch at an even greater distance. Any contact with the wire must therefore be avoided. When visibility is no consideration, the fence may be vaulted by placing the hand

322

on the post or staple only, or it may be possible to crawl underneath the lowest strand if there is a likelihood of being seen. Reconnaissance should always establish the best point at which to cross an obstacle and, if possible, preparation of the obstacle should be done at the same time - i.e. removal of a wire strand in an inconspicuous way, or the scooping of a depression in the ground so that it is possible to crawl under the lowest strand.

b) Hedges.

When it is necessary to cross a thick hedge, a hole through which to pass must be prepared either at the time or on the recce. When this is done on the actual operation, one man only must prepare the hole, while the others, if any, wait under cover until it is complete.

c) Roads.

There are several possible methods of crossing roads and in the case of a party it must be understood by everyone beforehand which method is to be used. The factors affecting the choice of method and of the point at which to cross are quite different for light and darkness. Visibility is the main consideration in daylight or bright moonlight; silence in darkness.

Points at which to cross.

In daylight or bright moonlight, ideal points to cross would be either through a culvert or drain under the road, provided there is cover on either side, or on a bend with thickly covered rising ground on either side of the road. In the latter case, if the size of the party allowed it, a man would be sent to watch the road from each skyline while the main party crossed, rejoining them at a prearranged signal. At night, a culvert is, of course, an excellent point. On a country road another good point is where two hedges cut the road at right angles to it - these will form a good background both for the approach and movement away from the road, but the main consideration will be silence unless visibility is good.

Method of Crossing.

The main question, if no culvert or drain is available, is whether the road should be crossed by the party in one body or whether only one man should cross at a time. This must mainly be decided by the likelihood of surprise by the enemy. There are points for and against each method and it is up to the leader to decide which is the more suitable method in the particular circumstances.

Crossing in one body - factors for:

i) No waste of time.

ii) A shorter time during which there is anything for the enemy to see.

- factors against:

i) A large bunch of men is more easy to see and more likely to catch the eye.

ii) If the road is ambushed or covered by fire, the whole party can be destroyed by one burst of fire. All the eggs are in one basket.

The reverse of these circumstances is true for the other method.

If only one man crosses the road at a time, an interval must be decided by the leader. 10 seconds is the interval most commonly used. The party will not move off until the last man has crossed. It sometimes happens that there is no very suitable spot for crossing a road, and that this must be done within actual view of the enemy, though probably at a considerable distance. It must then be decided whether it is better to:

i) Crawl across the road and rely upon extreme slowness of the movement to escape detection. This would be possible when a) the road was narrow and traffic infrequent; b) in failing light.

ii) Wait for something to happen which will momentarily distract the enemy's attention and then cross the road rapidly in one body.

The choice of a method can only be decided by conditions at the time - i.e. light conditions, traffic, whether heavy rain, etc.

d) Walls.

Here there is the skyline danger and sitting or standing on the wall must be avoided. For ordinary walls, either -

    i) Throw one leg across, lie on top of the wall flat and roll over, keeping as low as possible.

    ii) "Dive" on to wall and roll over.

For high walls, some method as taught in P.T. must be used, or a ladder or rope with a grapnel.

<u>Other Methods</u>:

Use creepers, overhanging trees, fruit tree wires, staples, crevices, or make a pile of logs or boxes until the hands can reach top. Other things: Improvised ladder, old gates, doors, garden seats, trellis work, old bedsteads.

The best thing of all to do is to avoid high walls whenever possible.

e) <u>Water</u>.

    i) <u>Rivers</u>.

When the stream is deep and slow moving try to find a ford. A good point to cross is at a bend - there is often a gravel bottom and firm ground on both banks. Also it is more difficult for people to see you.

Use driftwood or floating vegetation to camouflage the head. If you swim, try to land amongst rushes or beneath overhanging trees. But ensure that the bank is not too steep to climb.

    ii) For swiftly flowing streams, cross in shallows where the water flows over pebbles, i.e. a small rapid but never <u>above</u> a fall. Avoid large boulders and never jump on to rocks over which water is flowing. A rope is a great advantage and a sound safety precaution. If you swim, start higher up than the point at which you aim to land and swim diagonally across, allowing the current to carry you down.

f) <u>Barbed Wire</u>.

    i) Double Apron Type -

       - Cut lower strands with wire cutters and crawl through. If alone cut near pickets and hold long strands in other hand. If there are two of you one man grasps wire and the other cuts <u>between</u> his hands - cut close to pickets to avoid noise.

- It is sometimes possible to climb carefully through the wire, but avoid touching upper wire with pack or clothing.

- Throw coat or sacking across, or wire netting and climb over.

- One man to lie across while others crawl over him.

ii) Dannert Wire - by careful manipulation it is possible to crawl through by separating the coils.

iii) If it is not necessary to be silent, any of the methods of vaulting wire as taught in P.T. will do.

iv) Beware of the possibility of fence being electrified - look for insulators on pickets.

DEMOLITIONS

DEMOLITION SYLLABUS

PERIOD NO. 1.

Lecture. GENERAL INTRODUCTION TO THE COURSE.   1 Hour.

    1) Introduction and simple theory of Explosives.
    2) The explosives used.
    3) Safety precautions.

PERIOD NO. 2.

Lecture.   PREPARATION OF A CHARGE AND   1 Hour.
               WATERPROOFING FIRING SYSTEM.

  1) Preparing the Charge.

    a) The Explosive.
    b) The Primer.

  2) Preparing the Firing System.

    a) Safety Fuse.
    b) The Detonator.
    c) Igniters used with Safety Fuse.

  3) How to fire the Charge.

  4) Waterproofing the Firing System.

PERIOD NO. 3.

Practical.   FIRING SMALL CHARGES..   2 Hours.

To practise the lessons taught in Periods 1 and 2.

  1) Cutting and Lighting Safety Fuse.

    a) Fuse.
    b) C.T.I.
    c) Match.

  2) Firing Detonators.

    a) Crimping with teeth.
    b) Using Crimpers.

  3) Firing Primers.

      Prepare firing system as in 1 and 2 and use to fire
      primer.

4) Firing 1 cartridge '808'.

> Each student to prepare firing system. Then tape primer to charge of '808' and fire on any suitable object.

5) Waterproofing.

> Autumn Crocus. Each student to prepare one Autumn Crocus.

6) The Pull Switch.

> Each Student to ignite safety fuse, using pull switch. Then to re-set and use on schemes.

PERIOD NO. 4.

Lecture.   PLASTIC AND '808' .   1 Hour.

1) Nobles' '808'.
2) Plastic Explosive.
3) Making up P.E. and '808' into a charge.
4) How much to use.
5) Placing the charge and fixing to the target.
6) Double initiation.

PERIOD NO. 5.

Practical.   FIRING SMALL CUTTING CHARGES   1 Hour.
                         ON METAL

Students to work in pairs. To prepare small charges to cut:

1) Angle Irons - 1 cartridge '808' cut to shape.
2) Rails.

> a) 2 cartridges '808' placed vertically and fired.
> b) 2 cartridges P.E. moulded.

3) Channel Irons - 2 ¾ lbs. P.E. or '808' joined by thin strip for web. (2 charges to be made up).
4) Solid steel bars or steel cable approximately 3" diameter. 9 cartridges P.E. or '808' per cut.
5) Steel plate - Demonstrate strip charges of 4 cartridges P.E. Demonstrate:

> a) Firing at 2 cartridges P.E. and '808' with rifle.
> b) Tamping.
> c) Slow speed '808'.

PERIOD NO. 6.

Lecture.   DETONATING FUSE.   1 Hour.

1) How to recognise detonating fuse.

DEMOLITIONS

2) Use of detonating fuse.
3) How to make up a charge with detonating fuse.
4) Taping on the detonator.
5) Simple methods of linking charges.

    a) The junction box.
    b) The straight main.

6) Linking charges in series.
7) Detonating fuse as a substitute for a primer.

PERIOD NO. 7.

Practical.   USE OF DETONATING FUSE.   1½ Hours.

1) Students in pairs to prepare and fire primer in plasticine charge using double tail 1' detonating fuse and double means of initiation.

2) Students in pairs to prepare 5 rail cutting charges '808' (2 cartridges) and fire by junction box. Detonating fuse 2 double rails. Primer in each charge.

3) Students in pairs to prepare 5 rail cutting charges P.E. 3 double tails detonating fuse using knot in lieu of primer. 12' straight main. Detonators at each end of main.

4) Practice for speed - students to work singly.

    a) Junction Box.
    b) Straight Main.

Plasticine charges - 10 charges.
15' double straight main.
3' double tails for a) Junction Box.
                  b) Straight Main.

Check knots.

PERIOD NO. 8.

Lecture.   STANDARD CHARGES.   1 Hour.

1) Introduction.
2) Flexible standard charges (1½ lb. and 3 lb.)

    a) How to make up.
    b) How to fire.
    c) Splitting standard charges.

3) Rigid standard charges.

a) The ½ lb. clam.

b) The general purpose charge.

4) Use of standard charges as bulk explosive.

5) Steel and cast iron.

PERIOD NO. 9.

Practical.   MAKING UP STANDARD CHARGES.   1½ Hours.

Each student to:

1) Fill and assemble 1 Clam.

2) Make up IV2 lb. and 3 lb. Standard charge.

3) Split the standard charges made in b). (Plasticine to be used).

4) Examine general purpose charge, insert detonator and detonating fuse.

PERIOD NO. 10.

Practical.   MAKING UP AND FIRING LIVE   2 Hours.
                       STANDARD CHARGE.

1) Each student to make up 1½ lb. standard charge in moulded '808' – use wooden mould and soften '808' in hot water.

2) Fire split 1½ lb. charges on channel irons, bringing tails together for one and using straight main and series method for remainder.

3) Fire 2 clams filled P.E. on suitable metal.

4) Each pair of students to prepare one general purpose charge for linking to straight main.

PERIOD NO. 11.

Practical.   MAKING UP AND PLACING CHARGES IN   1 Hour.
                       THE DARK.

Students in pairs prepare 5 1½ lb. plasticine charges. Place on suitable target and link to straight main of double detonating fuse. Charges to be inspected and checked.

PERIOD NO. 12.

                       PRACTICAL TEST.   1 Hour.

PERIOD NO. 13.

Practical.   LINKING AND FIRING OF LIVE CHARGES.   2 Hours.

DEMOLITIONS

1) Students in pairs to make up 5 1½ lb. standard charges of P.E.
2) Charges to be cut in half, making 1¼ lb. charge per student.
3) Each charge to be placed individually on suitable metal target and joined to straight main.
4) Practice for speed with dummy charges using straight main.
5) Each pair of students to fire 2 linked general purpose charges on channel iron or girders

PERIOD NO. 14.

Lecture.   THE RAIL CHARGE.   1 Hour.

1) Train derailment.
2) How to make up the rail charge.
3) Preparing the firing system.
4) How to place and fix the charge.
5) Fixing the rail charge in the dark.

PERIOD NO. 15.

Practical.   PREPARATION OF THE RAIL CHARGE.   1 Hour.
Each student to prepare dummy rail charge complete with fog signals and dummy detonators. Test on dummy track and then use for Period 16.

PERIOD NO. 16.

Practical.   MOCK DERAILMENT.   1 Hour.

Use charges prepared in Period 15.

PERIOD NO. 17.

Practical. NIGHT WORK WITH STANDARD AND RAIL CHARGES. 2 Hours.

Each pair of students to prepare:

1) 1½ lb. standard charge in plasticine with two magnets for fixing.

2) 1 rail charge complete with fog signal.

Practise fixing of rail charge on dummy track and linking of standard charges to 15' main. Check carefully for faults.

PERIOD NO. 18.

Lecture.   THE TIME PENCIL AND LEAD DELAY.   1 Hour.

1) The time pencil.

  a) Description.

b) Range of delay.
c) Drill for setting in operation.
d) Method of attaching.
e) Short-comings of the time pencil.

2) How to waterproof the time pencil.
3) The lead delay.

PERIOD NO. 19.

Practical.   USE OF THE TIME PENCIL.   1 Hour.

1) Each student to operate time pencil according to correct drill.
2) Each student to prepare charge two cartridges '808' with primer and fire one 10-minute pencil on rail.
3) Each student to prepare primer with detonating fuse and fire by taping on two pencils.
4) Each student to waterproof one pencil and detonator with balloon.

PERIOD NO. 20.

Lecture.   INCENDIARIES I.   1 Hour.

1) Where to start fires.
2) How to start fires.
3) Simple matches.

   a) The lb. M.L. Flare.
   b) The paraffin tyesule.

4) The wick.
5) The target.
6) Ventilation.

PERIOD NO. 21.

Lecture.   INCENDIARIES II.   1 Hour.

1) The firepot.
2) The 2½ lb. thermite.
3) The pocket time incendiary.
4) The No. 77 Phosphorous grenade.
5) Attacking petrol and oil.

PERIOD NO. 22.

Practical.   INCENDIARIES.   1 Hour.

1) Demonstrate M.L. flare, Tyesule, Firepot, 2½ lb. Thermite and P.T.I. burning inside a wooden structure to compare

burning effect. The wooden structures should be made up from dry planks and should have two sides roughly 3' square, the ends nailed to a 6" plank, leaving a 5" space between the two sides.

2) Students in pairs prepare Incendiary Parcel - 2 M.L. flares (quick match removed) + 6 Tyesules + 2 Time pencils.

3) Each student to work one P.T.I. Demonstrate effect of one strapped to bottle of paraffin or 50/50.

4) Demonstrate No. 77 Phosphorous Grenade as means of starting fire and add bottles of 50/50 or paraffin.

5) Demonstrate attack on petrol wagon - Can 50/50 or paraffin:

   a) Flares lit separately.
   b) Flares linked by detonating fuse to charge.

Note: Use loop of detonating fuse to hole can. This should be enclosed in plasticine block charge. For

   a) Fire with 30 secs, safety fuse.
   b) Lead detonating fuse to Flares and use 10-minute pencils.

6) Demonstrate effect 2½ lb. Thermite on petrol can - good way of attacking petrol cans in dumps.

7) Students practise fitting C.T.I. to Firepots or linking with Orange Line. 10 Firepots. 20' Orange Line. Demonstrate use of No. 77 with slow burning Bickford and detonator, included in and fired by link system to catch anyone trying to put out fire.

PERIOD NO. 23.

Practical.   STANDARD CHARGES ON CASE IRON   2 Hours.
                       AND GIRDERS.

Students working in pairs to prepare 5 1½ lb. charges in P.E. Then:

1) Demonstrate the effect of a standard charge (or part of it) on cast iron.

2) Use remainder to cut girder.

3) Use General Purpose Charge for cutting girder.

PERIOD NO. 24.

Lecture.   THE LIMPET AND HOW TO ATTACK SHIPS.   1 Hour.

1) Attacks on shipping.
2) The Limpet.

3) The A.C. Delay.
4) Drill for preparing and fixing limpets.
5) Drill for linking limpets.
6) Aids to the placing of limpets.
7) Attacking ships with limpets.

    a) General rules.
    b) Ocean-going ships.
    c) Canal barges.

PERIOD NO. 25.

Practical.   LIMPET DRILL.   2 Hours

Students in two squads.

Squad 1 - a) Carry out full fusing drill for limpet.
        b) Link 5 limpets with detonating fuse.
Squad 2 - Practise use of placing rod.

Squads change over at half time.

PERIOD NO. 26.

Practical.   MISCELLANEOUS.   1½Hours.
1) Gammon Grenade.

    a) Each student to assemble 1 complete Gammon Grenade using plasticine for charge.
    b) Throwing practice.
    c) Demonstrate effect of grenade filled '808' fired on armour plate - note scab.

2) General Purpose Charge as a grenade.

3) Tyre Burster.

    a) Practise laying echelon with no detonators in.
    b) Assemble with detonator and demonstrate action by allowing plate to fall on bursters.

4) Demonstrate:

    a) The Pressure Switch for train derailment.
    b) The Release Switch as a booby trap.

PERIOD NO. 27.

Revision.   MAKING UP STANDARD CHARGES.   1 Hour.

PERIOD NO. 28.

Revision.   QUICK PLACING OF CHARGES IN THE DARK.   1 Hour.

DEMOLITIONS

Revision.   INCENDIARIES.   1 Hour.

PERIOD NO. 30.

                     FINAL TEST - Written.   1 Hour.

PERIOD NO. 31.

                     FINAL TEST - Practical.   1 Hour.

          SPIGOT MORTAR   1½ Hours.

Practice in setting up and firing both with trip wire and
time delay. Explanation of various uses in the field.

RAILWAYS

Lecture 1.   Destruction of Rail Communications.

  1) Train derailment.

     a) How a locomotive moves on the track.
     b) Types of track.
     c) Derailment to block the track.
        i) With explosive.
        ii) Without explosive.
     d) To destroy a specific train.
  2) Suitable sites for derailment.
  3) Systematic rail cutting.

Lecture 2.   Attacking Rolling Stock.

  1) Locomotives.
     a) With explosives.
     b) Without explosives.
  2) Running Sheds and Turntable.
  3) Cranes.
  4) Wagons and Coaches.
  5) Signal Communications.

This period can be done in conjunction with a visit to a
railway marshalling yard.

H.2.
November 1943.

HOW MUCH TO USE

1. GENERAL REMARKS.

   a) Number of charges. - In all demolition work the number
   of charges should be kept to the minimum compatible with
   economy of explosive and the attainment of the desired
   effect.

   "THE DEMOLITION MUST NEVER FAIL."

   b) Degree of accuracy required. - It is not necessary for
   the charge required to effect a given demolition to be
   calculated with greater accuracy than to the NEAREST
   POUND, or in the case of mined charges 25 LBS. (i.e. one
   tin of Ammonal). While waste of explosive should never be
   countenanced, especially as supply must necessarily be
   limited, nevertheless the risk of failure to carry out a
   complete demolition in order to save small quantities of
   explosive is NEVER JUSTIFIABLE. A small margin of safety
   must therefore be left, even under ideal conditions, since
   small irregularities may easily occur in the strength of
   explosives or the security of fixing.

   "THE DEMOLITION MUST NEVER FAIL."

Conditions will sometimes arise in the field for which no
allowance is made in the following formulae. In such cases a
too rigid adherence to these formulae must be avoided, they
should be taken more as a guide than as a hard and fast rule.
When in doubt, err on the side of overestimating the charge
required.

   "THE DEMOLITION MUST NEVER FAIL."

2. CLASSIFICATION OF CHARGES.

Charges may be divided into three main classes, the
characteristics of which are discussed below. There is no
marked line of division among these classes, and compromise
among them will often occur in practice.

   a) Cutting Charges. - The explosive is placed superficially,
   and acts chiefly through shattering action at the instant
   of detonation. Hard substances are very susceptible to the

336

sudden blow produced on detonation; thus for steel work and similar hard materials this class of charge should invariably be used. In the case of masonry, however, the amount of explosive required soon sets a limit on the thickness which it is economical to attack with cutting charges, and compels the use of other methods.

b) <u>Mined or Buried Charges</u>. - The explosive is placed underground, and acts through lifting and pushing action due to the expansion of the gases formed on detonation. Explosive is most efficiently employed in this manner, since its full effect is developed.

c) <u>Concussion Charges</u>. - This is a modified form of mined charge, in which an enclosed air space replaces solid tamping, and the lifting action of the explosive takes effect through the pressure of displaced air ("blast") on the containing walls.

3. <u>APPLICATION OF CHARGES</u>.

a) <u>Steel and Iron</u>. - Can only be cut with a cutting charge; though girders may be greatly damaged by the twisting caused when their abutments are demolished by mined charges.

b) <u>Masonry</u>. - A thickness of not more than 5 or 6 feet may be attacked with a cutting charge. When this thickness is exceeded, the employment of a cutting charge becomes uneconomical and unreliable. Masonry is normally attacked by the use of "borehole" charges. This, however, necessitates the use of special tools, and must suffer from the amount of time and labour required.

c) <u>Timber</u>. - Owing to its tough and fibrous nature, timber requires an even larger cutting charge than masonry for members of equal size. But, owing to the ease with which holes can be bored in it, it can be demolished fairly easily by small "borehole" charges.

4. <u>FIXING OF CHARGES</u>.

a) <u>Cutting Charges</u>. - The charge should cover the full breadth of the surface to be cut, and be in direct contact with it. The cross-section of the charge should be as nearly as possible in the shape of an inverted "U" where explosives of a plastic nature are employed. In the case of slab explosives, the cross section of the charge should

be as nearly as possible square. This arrangement will
ensure that the maximum shearing effect is produced.
All portions of the charge must be in close contact;
sympathetic detonation, even in the case of dynamites,
CANNOT be relied upon. Incomplete detonation means
incomplete destruction.

"THE DEMOLITION MUST NEVER FAIL."

The charge as a whole must be firmly fixed to the object to
be destroyed.

c) Concussion Charges. - Principally employed in the
destruction of buildings. An explosive with a low velocity
of detonation should be used. Charges should be placed
if possible against an essential part of the structure.
It is important that all doors, windows and chimneys
through which air can escape should be closed. Charges in
adjoining rooms should not be placed opposite one another.

5. CALCULATION OF CHARGES.

a) Cutting charges. -

Steel or iron rounds:

$C = 2/3d^2$ Slabs G.C. or T.N.T.

$C = 4d^2$ oz. of P.E. or "808"

(Minimum charge 2 ozs.)

Where C = Weight of charge in slabs of G.C. or T.N.T. or
weight of charge in ounces of P.E. or "808"

d = the diameter of the round in inches.

Use this formula for cable or "steel wire rope", and for
hollow rounds.

Steel or iron plates:

$C = 1/8bt2$ Slabs G.C. or T.N.T.

$C = 3/2bt2$ ozs. P.E. or "808"

(Minimum charge 2 ozs.)

Where C = Weight of charge as above

b = the full breadth of the plate

t = the thickness of the plate in inches.

DEMOLITIONS

Calculation for girders or "R.S.J.'s" must be dealt with by the intelligent application of the above formula to every portion of the section on which it is desired to cut.

b) <u>Mined charges</u>. -

Behind masonry abutments or retaining walls and in rock and masonry:

C = DV50 lbs. of Ammonal or T.N.T. powder.

Under roads or in hard ground (i.e. clay, chalk, etc.)

C = DV100 lbs. of Ammonal or T.N.T. powder.

In soft ground (i.e. sand, peat, etc.)

C = DV200 lbs. of Ammonal or T.N.T. powder.

Where C = weight of explosion in lbs.

D = diameter of required crater in feet.

c) <u>Timber cutting charges</u>. -

Hard Woods (i.e. oak, teak, ash, etc.)

$C = 3D^3$ slabs of G.C. or T.N.T.

Soft Woods (i.e. larch, fir, pine, etc.)

$C = 3/2D^3$ slabs of G.C. or T.N.T.

All Woods

$C = 2D^2$ lbs. of P.E.

Where C = Weight of charge in lbs.

D = Diameter in feet.

GENERAL DESTRUCTION

1. <u>TRANSPORTATION FACILITIES</u>.

   1. <u>ATTACKING RAIL TRANSPORT</u>.

      a) <u>Importance of Targets</u>. Main object to delay traffic and reduce the number of locos. and rolling stock available to enemy.

      b) <u>Methods</u>. Derailment – systematic rail cutting – attacks on stationary locos., station facilities – signals and communications.

      c) <u>Derailment</u>. Two main methods are:

       i) To make a gap in the rails.

      ii) By obstruction to cause the flange of the train's wheels to ride up on top of the rail and go off the rail.

      Trains are self-destroying targets:

       i) <u>With H.E.</u>

         – Using Fog-Signals or Pressure Switches and 2 linked charges of 2 – 2-½" cartridges, make train itself fire the charges so as to cut out a piece of rail at least 1 metre long ahead of the engine.

         – Using the same system but placing the charges at the last minute so as to avoid a pilot-engine. In this case firing could be done by short Bickford fuses or as before.

         Remember to take care of 'check' rails, if any, as well, and note the effect of a steeply banked curve in counteracting centrifugal force.

      ii) <u>Without H.E.</u>

         – By <u>displacing a rail</u> on the outside of a bend.

         – By <u>obstructions</u> in crossing-points, i.e. fishplates or crowbars in the "diamond".

         – By interference with facing-points, i.e. a 1" nut tied to the face of the switch-tongue. (This method only works at hand-operated points at remote places or in sidings.)

d) <u>Tactical considerations for derailment.</u>

   i) Tunnels and long cuttings best for derailment to cause delay.

   ii) Steep embankments or entrances to bridges are good sites for derailment of a particular train.

   iii) In principle, choose a place difficult to reach except along the permanent way.

   iv) Attack the <u>outside rail on a bend</u>. The only exception would be where a curve is so well 'banked' that there is a better chance of derailing the train <u>inwards</u>.

   v) Try and make the derailment part of a concentrated plan, i.e. one of several derailments on interdependent lines and include an attack on the break-down train, cranes, etc.

   vi) Cut telephone wires.

   vii) On a double track railway direct derailment so as to tear up and block both tracks, i.e. attack the <u>outside rail of the inner track</u>.

e) <u>Locomotives</u>. Forms of attack on stationary locos.

   i) <u>With H.E.</u>

     - ½-lb. charge on cylinder head where piston-rod enters - always attack same cylinder on all locos (they are not interchangeable).

     - ½-lb. charge to cut connecting-rod - squeeze into web at little end.

   ii) <u>Without H.E.</u>

     - Flatten copper lubricating tubes.

     - Remove corks and needles from big-end bearings.

     - Smash the governor of the brake-pump with a hammer.

     - Put rags or fluff into the water-tank of the tender.

     - Introduce Vulcastabs (concentrated soap tablets) into the water-tank.

f) <u>Running-Sheds and Turntables</u>.

   i) Run a loco. (under steam) into turntable pit.

   ii) Unscrew plugs or bungs of lubricating oil barrels to cause waste and loss.

g) <u>Cranes</u>.

Insert ½" bolts or pieces of steel rod between 2 successive pairs of teeth on the main gear wheel, so that they will catch and strip the teeth when the driving wheel is engaged. Pack in with grease.

h) <u>Water Columns</u>.

Overshut the valve so as to break the spindle.

i) <u>Wagons and Coaches</u>.

Attack a collection of wagons with fire if possible. (See Vol. II)

j) <u>Signals, Communications</u>.

   i) Cut signal and telegraph wires over a wide area or outside an important junction.

   ii) Smash "block-instruments" in signal-boxes.

   iii) Start a fire in the lower half of the signal box, there is likely to be a good draught there.

2. <u>ATTACKING ROAD TRANSPORT</u>.

a) <u>Roads</u>.

Owing to quantity of stores required to block effectively, not usually suitable target. If stores are available, and local conditions render certain road 'bottlenecks' good targets, CRATER - rather than blow debris down on to the surface of the road. The former usually takes far longer to repair. Make use of drain pipes or culverts.

b) <u>Bridges</u>.

   i) Rail.

   ii) Road.

   iii) Aqueducts.

<u>Beware Reinforced Concrete</u>.

Attacking STEEL bridges - cut all MAIN load-bearing members. Charges placed so that heaviest section is free to fall.

Attacking BRICK or STONE bridges - cut arch ring - or pier - or both.

Point out difficulties, i.e. quantity of stores required, length of time bridge will have to be in your uninterrupted possession - speed with which enemy bridging company can erect temporary structure.

Possibilities AND difficulties of mining abutments. Explain theory of abutment face being line of least resistance of your mined charges.

Consider H.E - time - and equipment required.

c) Road Transport.

Emphasize size of target. Most effective method of destroying car or truck is to place a one-cartridge magnet charge on top of the petrol tank. If this method is impossible - place CLAM on cylinder block.

For diesel-engined military vehicles, place CLAM on crankcase.

Rail Communications)
Shipping) Already dealt with.
Canals and Inland Waterways)

d) Armoured Fighting Vehicles.

Cavity charge above petrol tank or engine. Solid charge in between sprocket and track.

3. ATTACKING MILITARY INSTALLATIONS.

a) Guns.

For Static Guns (not A.A.) a cylindrical charge fired in breach.
For A.A. Guns attack elevating shaft and/or traversing ring.
For Mobile Guns attack axles (wheel bearings).

NOTE: Cradles and carriages less easily replaced than barrels, jackets and breach blocks.

b) Inflammable Supplies and Buildings, etc.

   i) Commodities: e.g. Cotton, Sugar, Rubber, Celluloid, Paper, Timber, etc.
  ii) Small Arms Ammunition.
 iii) Equipment and Clothing.
  iv) Warehouses, Docks and Wharves.

Consider the possibilities of causing dust explosions, i.e. neutralize preventive measures, and start small fire, or detonate small quantity of ammonal. The following are very susceptible: - Wheat Flour Mills, Grain Elevators, Cereal Mills, Wood Sawmills.

c) <u>H.E. Filled Shells. Bombs and Explosives</u>.

More easily detonated than burnt. Don't count on detonating wave jumping large gaps between separate dumps. Place small charge, i.e. CLAM on EACH dump.

4. <u>ATTACKING OIL INSTALLATIONS</u>.

a) <u>Petrol, Crude Oil. Kerosene</u>: All quite likely to ignite with flash from detonation - <u>even</u> so have <u>some</u> incendiary.

b) <u>Heavy Fuel Oils</u>: High flash-point - therefore charge plus long burning incendiary with 'wick' required, i.e. The 'Tar Baby'.

NOTE: i) How can you tell whether a tank is full or empty?

    ii) How can you tell whether a tank contains oil or petrol?

   iii) Neutralize elaborate FIRE precautions.

    (i) Get someone to tell you!

    (ii) Smell of petrol vapour round Petrol Tanks - and Oil Tanks have heating coils round inlet valves.)

c) <u>Attacking Storage Tanks</u>.

  i) <u>Tanks below ground</u> extremely difficult to tackle.

  ii) <u>Above-ground Tanks</u> are often surrounded with anti-blast brick walls and inaccessible except near the inlet valve. In principle the method of attack will always be to get the fuel out into the air, having arranged an incendiary parcel or several individual incendiaries to receive and set fire to the fuel. This can be done either by:

   - Cutting a hole in the tank with H.E. (a special charge is needed for this and specialist instruction would be given at a later stage to students requiring it - or

   - By mechanical means, i.e. opening valves and unloading joints in outlet pipes.

Note that the quickest way of setting fire to oils with a high 'flash-point' is to pour paraffin over the surface and then throw lighted rags in from the windward side.

iii) The easiest fuel targets are undoubtedly the smaller, mobile tank wagons such as <u>Railway Tank Wagons</u>, <u>Road Wagons</u> and <u>Airfield Filler Tanks</u> or "Bowsers", for which an ordinary 1-lb. charge of H.E. is quite sufficient -placed on the underside and used with an incendiary.

5. <u>ATTACKING AIRCRAFT</u>.

a) Place 1-½-lb. charge as near as possible to a fuel tank. Best positions as follows:

<u>Single-engine (Fighters)</u> .

   i) In the cockpit under or behind the pilot's seat. (Latter position accessible in the ME 109 via a locker behind the pilot's head and in the F.W. 190 via the port side inspection door.

   ii) On the fuselage skin under the pilot's seat fastened by tapes.

b) <u>Using the Altimeter Switch</u>. Attack aircraft in the air with 1 - 1-½-lb. charges inserted into one of the many available spaces and in contact with a main structure member, e.g. in the tail unit, rear fuselage, machine gun or cannon space, undercarriage recess.

c) Sniping with rifle and tracer ammo. during the 2 hours after an aircraft has landed in winter holds definite possibilities of igniting the petrol, if not of exploding the petrol vapour, German aviation spirit becoming explosive between -5 degrees C. and a lower limit.

<u>Gliders</u>. Vulnerable to Incendiaries: place inside the fuselage if possible.

6. <u>ATTACKING INDUSTRIAL INSTALLATIONS</u>.

In attacking machinery, bear in mind that the majority of main frame components of most machines are made of CAST IRON, and, in consequence, the value of being able to distinguish CAST IRON from STEEL.

Hints:

CAST IRON	STEEL
i) Much rougher before painting.	
ii) Smooth curves.	Sharper angles.

iii) Smooth surface.	Ridge(s) of weld metal.
iv) Raised lettering.	Name plate.
v) Sweeping curves on lugs.	Lugs and/or protrusions fitted at sharp angles.
vi) CHISEL TEST: Flake.	Peel.
vii) Bolt holes machined and 'SPOT FACED'.	Bolt holes just drilled.

Also, of course, there is the possibility of encountering CAST STEEL. However, it is not normally used for machine FRAMES, as it is, i) expensive, ii) difficult to cast, iii) only used where heavy stresses or strains will be encountered – or where excessively high pressures will have to be withstood.

Take as good example of Cast Iron target the Bearing Pedestal of a <u>RUNNING</u> Generator. Two 'sausage' charges: one on each corner of the short side, about one third of the way up from the base, will wreck the pedestal, also cause the rotating part of the generator to drop on to the casing. As this part will probably be rotating at high speed, the damage will be extensive.

<u>Industrial Structures</u>.

Some typical industrial structures common to Power Stations and Factories, etc:

a) <u>Coal Handling Plant</u>:   Essential where it is required to handle large quantities of coal very quickly.

   i) Coal conveyers: <u>The higher</u> from the ground the better, i.e. further to fall! Attack towers and supports.

  ii) Skip-Hoists: Again – the higher the better. Attack supports.

 iii) Wagon Tipplers: Impossible to handle large quantities of coal quickly without these. Attack with charges immediately below bearings at either end.

b) <u>Cranes</u>: <u>Cranes, Dockside or Cranes mounted on Structures</u>: Very good target, always attack as many as possible at same time.

DEMOLITIONS

Method recommended:

  i) For fixed cranes cut all legs at base and a section out
  of two legs on whichever side the crane is required to
  fall.

  ii) For mobile cranes (more common) only necessary to cut a
  section out of the two front (dockside) legs.

c) Transformers: Information essential in order that attacks
                  are confined to important transformers.

Identify transformers by Oil Cooling Tank on top. Also –
three main types:

  i) Cooling Tubes round Winding Casing.
  ii) Corrugated Cooling Surface to Casing.
  iii) Separate Banks of Radiators at right angles to plain
  casing, on very large transformers.

ATTACK – all types by placing charge (Standard Sausage for
i) and iii) a charge moulded into the corrugation for ii))
in centre of long, low-voltage side (less insulation) about
one quarter of the way up. Use incendiaries to ignite oil,
provided they do not interfere with the amount of H.E.
carried.

IMPORTANT: Do not confuse Transformers with Switch-Gear,
which is very often non-essential, and therefore a bad
target.

d) Wireless Masts: Triangular type resting on ball and socket
   joint, comparatively easy to fell.

ATTACK – Cut sufficient Tie-Bars connecting 'stays'
to concrete anchors to make mast fall across station
equipment.

FINALLY, stress that although High-Tension Pylons would
appear to be good targets, in reality they are NOT.
Reasons: Towns and factories almost invariably have
alternative sources of supply. (ii) Very short time
required to arrange emergency supply, i.e. probably less
than 48 hours.

Taking these points into consideration, it is advisable
only to attack H.T. Pylons when very large widespread
attack is possible.

THE ESSENTIAL FACTORS OF FIRST AID IN THE FIELD

AIM.

To preserve life, hasten recovery or prevent aggravation of injury concerned.

INTRODUCTION.

First Aid is the assistance given at a time of accident, making use of available material. Improvisation especially in the field is usually necessary, for example, the use of sticks, rifles, etc. for splints, handkerchiefs and various articles of clothing for dressings.

In dealing with an injured man one must at once:

a) Determine the nature of the case,
b) Decide what treatment is required according to circumstances which, in war, are liable to complicate, and in some cases prevent the ideal treatment being carried out. However, in most cases it is possible to strike a happy medium, by first of all patching up the wounded man, and then going out to complete the job in hand.

It should be the duty of all at the present time to know the essential facts about first aid to the injured. Lives are more precious than ever, so, not only must we learn to kill the enemy, but also learn the fundamental facts of emergency treatment in order that we will be in a position to save the lives of others and our own selves, that we may live to fight another day.

The following notes deal primarily with first aid in the field where in many cases elaborate medical and surgical equipment will not be available.

WOUNDS.

There are five main types:

1. Abrasions   Slight injury - unimportant from first aid
                            point of view.

2. Lacerated Wounds.   Ragged edges, usually extensive damage to
                            tissues; bleeding is not always great as
                            vessels may be torn irregularly.

3. Incised Wounds.   Regular edges, tend to bleed freely,
                            caused by cutting instruments.

348

4. Contused Wounds.   Caused by blunt instruments. There is
                       much bruising giving rise to swelling and
                       discolouration.

5. Punctured Wounds.   Caused by penetrating instruments, e.g.
                       knives, bayonets, bullets. May give rise
                       to serious damage in deeper structures.
                       Such a wound may become infected
                       (poisoned).

COMPLICATIONS OF WOUNDS.

When a man is wounded, three main things have to be fought:

1. Bleeding.   2. Shock.   3. Blood poisoning.

1. Bleeding or Haemorrhage.

This is perhaps the most important subject in first aid. In
order to carry out treatment efficiently it is necessary to know
a few facts about the blood and its circulation.

a) Blood.

The average man has 10 to 12 pints of blood. The fluid
portion is the serum which clots when it is outside the body,
thus assisting in the arrest of haemorrhage. The remainder of
the blood consists of red corpuscles which carry oxygen to
the tissues, and white blood corpuscles which tend to destroy
germs.

Death is likely to take place if a quantity of blood is
lost. The rapid loss of a pint of blood may be fatal, but a
similar loss over a period of minutes is not likely to cause
death.

The above facts indicate that speed is an all important
factor in the treatment of haemorrhage.

b) Course of the Main Blood Vessels.

It is necessary to have a mental picture of the positions
of the arteries, names are unimportant. (This subject will
not be referred to in detail, the essential points will be
illustrated by means of a chart.)

c) Pressure Points.

These are located over a bone background so that pressure may
be effective. In severe bleeding it may be necessary to apply
pressure at these points in order to prevent arterial blood
to reach the wound. The points are as follows:

Carotid - at lower part of neck
Facial - as it passes over the lower jaw
Occipital - at the bank of the head
Temporal - in front of the ear
Subclavian - above the collar bone
Axillary - in armpit
Brachial - by fingers under inner edge of biceps
Radial and Ulnar - one either side of the wrist
Femoral - in centre of groin
Popliteal - behind knee
Anterior Tibial - in front of ankle
Posterior Tibial - on inner side of heel bone

(A practical demonstration will be given on the above.)

The above pressure points can be easily located by means of feeling the pulsations in the artery, e.g. Radial Artery at wrist.

d) <u>Characteristics of Bleeding</u>.

   i) <u>Capillary Haemorrhage</u>: Blood is red, bleeding is not serious.

   ii) <u>Venous Haemorrhage</u>: Blood is dark red, and tends to flow from the end of wound farthest from the heart. Can be quite severe.

   iii) <u>Arterial Haemorrhage</u>: As the blood pressure is high in the arteries, blood tends to escape with more force. It spurts out on each contraction of the heart. The blood is bright red. This type of bleeding is most dangerous, and treatment must be carried out without delay.

<u>TREATMENT OF ARTERIAL HAEMORRHAGE.</u>

1. Lay patient down and raise the injured part.

2. Apply a pad directly on the wound and tie in position with a firm bandage. The pocket field dressing is suitable for this. It may be necessary to improvise, e.g. handkerchiefs, ties, etc. In most cases bleeding can be controlled by the above means.

3. If bleeding is obviously very severe, then immediate digital pressure may have to be applied to the respective pressure point until the necessary dressings are procured, e.g. an incised wound severing the femoral artery in the thigh, pressure must be applied at once to the groin by means of both thumbs.

4. If direct pressure over the wound fails to control the haemorrhage, then other methods must be employed. What is called "pad and flexion" may be used if the wound is situated well below the knee or elbow. In the case of the lower limb a large pad is placed behind the knee and the leg bent so that the back of the heel practically comes in contact with the back of the thigh. The limb is fixed in position by means of a "figure of eight" bandage. In the case of the arm the pad is placed in front of the elbow.

5. It may be necessary in some cases to apply a Tourniquet, which is merely a constricting band, which is placed between the wound and the heart in order to cut down the flow of blood. Improvisation again has to be carried out. A small flat stone covered by a handkerchief, a tie and piece of stick, pencil or pen are required. The pad formed by the stone is placed over the artery and the tie or handkerchief fixed in position round the limb, incorporating and pressing on the pad. A half knot is made and the pencil is used to twist the tourniquet tight. The tourniquet in itself is a dangerous thing if care is not employed, liable to cause death (gangrene) of limb if left in position too long or applied too tightly.

Rules for Tourniquet.

1. Don't tie too tight. Stop twisting when bleeding is controlled, do not give two or three extra turns for luck. Too much pressure may damage the main artery to limb.

2. Relax pressure every fifteen minutes.

3. Never leave a man alone for any length of time with the tourniquet in position if it is at all possible. Gangrene is likely to set in after six hours.

4. Elevate limb if there is time.

WARNING. Many wounded were aggravated in the last war through improper use of tourniquets. They are seldom required and should only be applied to the arm and thigh. If a man is bleeding from the neck, do not apply a tourniquet!

2. Shock.

In any serious injury shock is liable to develop, especially after wounds caused by gunfire, bombs and explosives. From the first-aider's point of view it is a very important subject, because he can do much to prevent its onset or if it has already developed he can help to control the condition.

It is caused primarily by failure of the circulation, the blood pressure falls, the man becomes pale, cold, and the skin is clammy. The pulse at wrist is very feeble, his lips and ears take on a bluish tint. His breathing is shallow and sighing. Death soon follows if action is not taken.

TREATMENT OF SHOCK.

1. Relieve pain. This can be done by making the patient comfortable, e.g. fixing up injured limb by means of splints and bandages. Morphia, gr. ¼, may be given. 1 tablet under tongue allowed to dissolve slowly.

2. Keep patient warm, cover with blankets and coats above and below. You may be required to take off some of your own clothing. If circumstances allow get the patient under cover. Hot water bottles should be obtained.

3. Hot drinks, such as hot sweet tea. DO NOT GIVE ALCOHOL if patient is still exposed to the elements.

4. Keep at rest in a recumbent position.

5. If haemorrhage is present then, of course, it must be arrested before anything else is done.

3. Blood Poisoning.

All wounds are contaminated, that is, they contain a certain amount of dirt which usually harbours bacteria (germs). The only clean wound in the proper sense of the word is the incision made by the surgeon on the operating table. In the latter case his hands and knife are surgically clean, and likewise the skin of the patient.

A wound that is contaminated is very likely to become infected, which means that the germs proliferate and invade the tissues. Any large wound is considered to be infected if it has not been cleansed within six hours of receiving injury. This cleansing, however, is a job for the surgeon in hospital. In the field it is well nigh impossible to clean a wound.

Prevention of blood poisoning in the field consists of covering the wound with a dressing as sterile as possible. If there is obvious dirt on the surface and on the surrounding skin, this may be removed by running water, preferably boiled and allowed to cool. Penetrating foreign bodies such as stones, bomb fragments, etc. should be left in situ. The patient should then be transported to hospital where the wound can be dealt with. Circumstances may prevent this last move, in certain circumstances it may be permissible to carry out a more thorough cleansing of the wound. Soap and water are the safest preparation to use. Iodine must never be applied to a large wound as this not only destroys some of the germs, but also tends to kill the white blood corpuscles which play a big part in defending the body from infection. Chemical antiseptics give a false sense of security for the above reason.

WOUNDS - PRINCIPLES OF TREATMENT.

1. Arrest bleeding - treat shock.
2. Remember danger of removing imbedded fragments - this may cause further damage and bleeding.
3. Cleanse - depending on circumstances.
4. Apply dressing (field) and fix in position.
5. Apply some support if wound is extensive.

FRACTURES.

There are two principal varieties:

1. Simple - where bone alone is damaged.
2. Compound - where bone, tissue and skin are all damaged.

a) Evidence of Fractures.

   i) Pain, swelling and tenderness.
  ii) Loss of rigidity - giving rise to disability and unnatural mobility.
 iii) Crepitus - caused by fragments of bone scraping together.

b) Dangers of Fractures.

   i) Increased damage, fracture may become compound, or damage to nerve or blood vessel.
  ii) Shock.
 iii) Infection.

c) Treatment of Fractures.

   i) Prevent further damage by rest, correct posture and fixation.
  ii) Shock.
 iii) Proper transport.

e) Compound Fracture.

   i) Arrest haemorrhage.
  ii) Cover wound.

iii) Do not replace protruding bone. <u>Carefully</u> fix limb by splints or sling.

<u>SPLINTS</u>.

Provide support, proper alignment, and prevent movement. They must be strong and stiff, e.g. sticks, rifles, newspapers rolled, etc. and of the proper length. The splint should incorporate the adjacent joints to the fracture. For example, in a broken forearm, the splints should come beyond the elbow and wrist.

<u>Method of Application</u>.

a) Pad with something soft, and prepare ties which are placed around limb and splints so as to avoid the actual site of fracture.

b) Use gentle, sustained traction to get limb in good position. For example, broken thigh bone, pull gently on ankle until injured limb lies along sound limb.

c) Fix splints in position, making certain that they do not press on arteries and thereby interfere with blood supply. For example, in arm feel for pulse of wrist.

<u>Fractured Spine</u>.

Caused by crushing or fall. Two cardinal symptoms:

a) Paralysis of limbs.
b) Loss of sensation below the break. Patient does not feel pin-prick.

If in doubt treat any severe back injury as a fracture.

<u>Treatment</u>.

Great care must be taken in moving the patient as further damage may be done. Keep back as rigid as possible.

<u>Transport</u>.

If unconscious or neck is broken, carry face up. If neck is injured apply large pad behind the neck and place head slightly back.
If conscious and back is broken, carry face downwards.

<u>Transfer to Stretcher</u>.

Several bearers required so as to move patient en bloc.

A few special injuries liable to occur in war will now be dealt with, and the important points of treatment mentioned.

DEMOLITIONS

<u>War injuries to Face and Jaw</u>.

Dangers: i) Haemorrhage. ii) Breathing may be interfered with. Haemorrhage usually can be controlled by local measures, remember pressure points.
Breathing is interfered with on account of the tongue falling back into the throat.

<u>Practical Application</u>.

  i) Transport face downward.
  ii) If conscious, get patient to hold his tongue forward by placing his finger in mouth.
  iii) Bandage under chin over top of scalp.

<u>Chest Injuries</u>.

Caused by bullets, bomb fragments, etc. May be small, or very large gaping wounds, exposing lungs.

<u>Treatment</u>.

  i) Sit patient up.
  ii) Complete rest essential.
  iii) Apply dressing to wound.
  iv) If gaping wound or if air is obviously being drawn through wound, a large pad, soaked if possible in sterile water, should be applied to form an airtight dressing. This will give much relief and in many cases will save life.

<u>War Injuries of Upper Limb</u>.

There are three factors to be considered:

  i) Haemorrhage. If limb is smashed, or shot away, or if bleeding comes from main artery, then tourniquet may be applied. In other cases use pad and bandage.
  ii) Wound. Field dressing.
  iii) Fracture. "Splint 'em where they lie". Splints may be used or in some cases the arm may be fixed to the body to immobilise it.

<u>War Injuries of Lower Limb</u>.

Bandaging the legs together is good emergency treatment when no splints are available.

Thomas Splint ideal for serious injury to thigh. Saved many lives in Great War, because it reduced pain and thereby cut down the incidence of shock.

Injuries around knee tend to be serious and should be evacuated to hospital at once. First aid - apply dressing and immobilise.

War Injuries of Head.

Keep patient quiet. Adjust patient's clothing and posture. Assist breathing by holding jaw well up, by pressure under chin. Do not attempt to give fluids. Bleeding alarming but not serious as a rule. Pad and bandage will control it.

Compression may result following head injury. Symptoms may be delayed. Patient becomes unconscious some time after injury. Pulse becomes very slow.

It the above symptoms are noted every endeavour should be made to get the patient to hospital. In most cases a trephining operation is indicated.

War Injuries of Abdomen.

Keep patient flat on his back. If wound gaping, draw knees up, raise head and shoulders slightly. Give nothing by mouth.

If intestines protrude through the wound, cover with a large dressing, preferably soaked in salt solution (1 teaspoonful to a pint of water). Keep dressing moist.

Eye Injuries.

If the eye is obviously seriously damaged, apply a simple pad, fixed by a bandage round head and keep patient lying flat in order to reduce pressure on injured eye.

FIRST AID IN ASPHYXIA.

E.g. Drowning, foreign body causing choking.

TREATMENT.

Artificial Respiration. (This will be demonstrated).

FIRST AID IN BURNS.

1. Patient trapped in a burning room. First aid worker should apply wet handkerchief over mouth and nose and crawl along the floor, keeping flat to avoid flames, pull the patient out. If asphyxiated (breathing practically stopped) carry out artificial respiration.

2. If clothes on fire lay patient down, and cover with coat or rug to smother flames.

3. Patient in contact with electric current:

   a) If possible break circuit. Push patient off by means of dry stick, rescuer standing on some dry non-conductor, e.g. wood, newspaper.
   b) Artificial respiration.

c) Treat burns.

4. Patient with scalds caused by burst boilers or pipes:

   a) Do not expose burned surface.
   b) Treat for shock.
   c) Exposed burn covered with clean dry sheet or dressing.
      First aid preparations, e.g. tannic acid, are seldom
      required, they usually interfere with ultimate treatment.

Albucid made up in tubes is perhaps the safest application
if medical attention is likely to be unavailable for several
hours. This might be carried in operations.

General Treatment of Severe Burns.

Wrap patient up both below and over him, give hot drinks.
Shock is the great danger. Local treatment to the burn is not
so important.

Burns of Eyes.

Wash eye with water, plenty of it.

Chemical Burns.

Dilute chemical with large quantities of water, and remove
contaminated clothing.

Acid Burn.

Wash with soda bicarb. solution (1 teaspoonful to a pint of
water).

Alkaline Burn.

Wash with equal parts of vinegar and water.

In all the above injuries remember that SHOCK must be guarded
against.

TRANSPORT OF INJURED PERSONS.

As a rule, transport is bad for the patient who has been
seriously injured, but in many cases it is necessary.

Splinting and bandaging should be carried out before any
attempt is made to move the men with severe wounds.

(Various methods of transport will be demonstrated, e.g. -
hand carrying and improvisation of stretchers, etc.)

PHYSICAL TRAINING—SYLLABUS

1st WEEK
6 PERIODS:

1. Trained soldier's Tables 1.
2. Ropework. Standard Climbing (P.T. Kit)
3. Preliminary groundwork.

2nd WEEK
6 PERIODS:

1. Trained soldier's Tables 2.
2. Ropework. Standard Climbing (P.T. Kit)
3. Progressing groundwork.

3rd WEEK
6 PERIODS:

1. Special Tables.
2. Ropework. Standard Climbing (P.T. Kit)
3. Advanced groundwork, landing from heights, horsework.

Each period will be divided approximately into three parts. Thus variety will be obtained and boredom must at all cost be eliminated.

PHYSICAL TRAINING—LECTURES

Physical training throughout the course is progressive and leads up to the final stamina tests of the Assault Course and the 24 Hour long distance Trek.

The object is to increase the general physical fitness of the students and to fit them for their course at S.T.S.51. With this in view special attention is paid to the following:

a) Physical Exercises - P.T. and games to make students supple and to increase their all-round bodily fitness.

b) Tumbling - to break the fall when landing from any reasonable height.

c) Rope work - to strengthen the arms and in particular to enable students to pull themselves up, i.e. to lift their own weight.

d) Crossing of obstacles - so that men shall not be held up either when they are approaching their objective nor when they are getting away.

e) Hill work - incidental to all training - but excellent for strengthening ankles.

The time of day during which P.T. is carried out will depend upon the various seasons of the year.

The course culminates in an obstacle course - perhaps better called an Assault Course or Combined Training Course. In this, students are confronted with specially designed and natural obstacles spaced over a course, which also includes firing with all the weapons they have used during training. The layout of the various courses varies, but each one is basically the same. Each course is based on a narrative scheme. Points are awarded for time, shooting, and ability and style in crossing obstacles.

This is a valuable exercise for assessing the stamina as well as the determination and progress of the students.

Combined with the long hill trek, the assault course gives instructors a good indication both of a student's physical stamina and of his character under difficult conditions.

CLOSE COMBAT

2. Disarming.

   Method A.
   Method B.

3. Searching a prisoner.
4. Taking a prisoner away.
5. Securing a prisoner.
6. Defence against downwards or sideways blow.
7. Gagging a prisoner.

CLOSE COMBAT

LECTURES

PREFACE.

1. Designed to teach how to fight and kill without firearms. Since the course includes the use of the knife, "close combat" is not strictly correct. "Silent Killing" is a more appropriate description.

2. Time available to students is limited. It is essential, therefore, to confine the teaching to what is simple, easily learned and deadly. With that object, all holds, throws, etc., that do not merit this description have been rigorously excluded. The syllabus which follows must now be regarded as standard and instructors, therefore, will please not deviate from it in any way whatever. It is plainly undesirable that students should be taught one method in one place and another method somewhere else.

3. The syllabus includes various suggestions by instructors themselves. Further suggestions, if they constitute improvements, will be welcomed. Such suggestions must be put forward through the proper channels and must not be taught to students until sanction has been received.

4. Dummies are essential. Six should be provided, slung irregularly in a space approximately 10 or 12 feet square. In addition, each instructor must make a straw-filled dummy for practice with the knife.

5. Other Equipment. German steel helmets are available and each instructor should have one, for practice in sentry attacks. Dummy knives are useful but care should be taken that they are of some material which will not cause injury. Wood, for that reason, is not permissible. Rubber is unobtainable. The most practical solution appears to be short lengths of suitably thick rope.

6. Kit, etc. Ordinary P.T. kit is best though, at suitable intervals, students should practise in the kit that they are most likely to wear in the field. Students should not always be paired off in equal sizes. Sometimes, small men should be paired with big men.

7. When commencing the course with a class of untrained
   students, the instructor should make a short introduction,
   not necessarily in the same words but to the same effect as
   the following:

"This system of combat is designed for use when you have lost
your firearms, which is something you should not do, or when
the use of firearms is undesirable for fear of raising an
alarm.

"At some time or other, most of you, probably, have been
taught at least the rudiments of boxing, under the Queensbury
rules. That training was useful because it taught you to
think and move quickly and how to hit hard. The Queensbury
rules enumerate, under the heading of "fouls", some good
targets which the boxer is not trained to defend.

"This, however, is <u>WAR</u>, not sport. Your aim is to kill your
opponent as quickly as possible. A prisoner is generally
a handicap and a source of danger, particularly if you are
without weapons. So forget the Queensbury rules; forget
the term "foul methods". That may sound cruel but it is
still more cruel to take longer than necessary to kill your
opponent. "Foul methods" so-called, help you to kill quickly.
Attack your opponent's weakest points, therefore. He will
attack yours if he gets a chance.

"There have been many famous boxers and wrestlers who time
after time have won their contests with their favourite blows
or holds. The reason is that they had so perfected those
particular blows and holds that few could withstand them. The
same applies to you. If you will take the trouble to perfect
one method of attack, you will be far more formidable than if
you only become fairly good at all the methods which you will
be shown.

"Since this course of instruction is meant to teach you to
kill, it will be plain to you that its methods are dangerous.
Your object here is to learn how to kill but it is quite
unnecessary to kill or damage your sparring partner, you
will get no credit if you do. In learning and practising,
therefore, you will avoid taking any risks of that kind. You
must never disregard the submission signal - two taps on your
opponent's body or on your own, or on the floor. It is the
signal to stop instantly and that is a rule which must never
be broken."

8. The syllabus is divided into six progressive sections. This arrangement is to be regarded, however, as elastic. Depending on such considerations as time available, progress made by students or their standard of knowledge, there is no reason, for example, why two or more sections should not be amalgamated.

9. One of the primary objects of the instructor is to make his students attack-minded, and dangerously so. No effort should be spared to realise this object, which should be regarded as one of the instructor's chief responsibilities. No instructor should be satisfied unless his students become thoroughly proficient in the performance of the few simple things enumerated in the syllabus. Dull as it may become, constant repetition is the only road to proficiency and constant repetition there must be, no matter how much students may complain of boredom. Their business is to learn, at any cost. By proficiency is meant the ability to execute all the requirements of the syllabus swiftly, effectively and neatly, without having to stop to think.

CLOSE COMBAT

The Syllabus

Blows with the side of the hand. Explain that the most deadly
blows without the aid of weapons are those with the side of the
hand. To deliver them effectively the fingers must be together,
thumb up, and the whole hand tensed. The blow is struck with the
side of the hand, all the force being concentrated in one small
area, i.e. approximately half-way between the base of the little
finger and the wrist joint, or where the hand is broadest. If
striking sideways, the back of the hand must be uppermost. No
force can be obtained if the palm is uppermost.

Explain that with these blows, it is possible to kill,
temporarily paralyse, break bones or badly hurt, depending upon
the part of the body that is struck. The effect of these blows
is obtained by the speed with which they are delivered rather
than by the weight behind them. They can be made from almost any
position, whether the striker is on balance or not, and thus can
be delivered more quickly than any other blow.

Having explained the blows, the instructor should demonstrate
them on the dummies and get the students to practise after him.
His main point here is to bring out the speed of the blows and
to see that students deliver them correctly.

Students should now be shown where to strike, as follows,
explaining the effect on each particular point:

1. On the back of the neck, immediately on either side of the
   spine.
2. From the bridge of the nose to the base of the throat.
3. On either side of the head and throat, from base of the throat
   to the temple area.
4. On the upper arm.
5. On the fore arm.
6. The kidney region.

Students should practise on the dummies again, keeping in mind
the vulnerable points listed above. Strike with either hand.

SECTION 2.

Other Blows.

How to kick. As a general rule, kick with the side of the foot
and, unless you possess unusually good foot work and balance,

don't kick above knee height. Never kick too foremost unless your opponent has both hands occupied. In that case, it is safe to kick to the fork. Once the opponent is down, kill by kicking the side or back of the head (not the top of the head).

The Boxing Blows.

The open-hand chin jab, fingers held back and apart ready to follow up to the eyes. Utilise the occasion to obtain some improvement in foot-work, explaining that the body must be properly positioned in order to obtain telling effect from either boxing blows or the open-hand chin jab. Explain, too, that neither can secure more than a knock-out, which should be followed up instantly by a killing attack.

Use of the Knee, often in simultaneous combination with other attacks (e.g. with the chin-jab). Show how, while being used for attack, it is an excellent guard for oneself.

Use of the head and elbows, for attack when the opponent is not in position for more effective blows.

Finger-tip jabs, to solar plexus, base of throat, or eyes, when nothing more effective can be done.

All the blows listed should be practised now on the dummies.

Conclude this section by telling students, as emphatically as possible:

a) That they should never go to ground if they can help it. If they have to, they should get up again as soon as they can. While a man is killing his opponent on the ground, the opponent's friends could walk up and kick his brains out. Again, while on the ground, it is difficult to go on attacking.

b) That if their knowledge of the subject is confined to the contents of Sections 1 and 2, they will have made themselves extremely dangerous, even to highly trained adversaries, if only they will attack first and keep on attacking. Don't stop just because an opponent is crippled. If you have broken his arm, for instance, that is only of value because it is then easier to kill.

SECTION 3.

Releases from holds.

Explain first that, in general nobody should be so slow in wits or body as to allow someone else to get a hold on him. In case of misfortune, however, show how to effect release from:

A wrist hold, taken with one hand.
A wrist hold, taken with two hands.
A throat hold, taken with one hand.
A throat hold, taken with two hands.

Show here how, instead of the customary wrist-and-elbow release or one of its variants, it is far simpler, quicker and more effective to attack, e.g. knee to the fork and fingers to the eyes, simultaneously.

A body hold, from front or rear, arms free and arms pinioned.
Police or "come-along" holds.

The whole idea of releasing yourself from a hold is to enable you to attack and kill your adversary. Whenever possible, the disengaging movement should form the commencement of an attack. In any case, there must be an effective and instant follow-up attack after every release. The instructor should demonstrate most carefully every detail to do with this Section and then insist on students practising until not only the mode of release but the subsequent attack becomes a matter of instinct, to be carried out at lightning speed. The instructor should emphasise the importance of footwork, and, where necessary, try to improve it.

SECTION 4.

Crowd Fighting.

One cannot always choose when one will fight and it may sometimes happen that one is faced with several opponents at once. On such occasions, unarmed yourself, your object is not so much to kill your opponents as to get quickly away from them so that you do not get killed. Pride is expensive if it entails defeat and death.

To escape from circumstances like these, a special technique is necessary.

For the technique, balance is essential and the instructor should now demonstrate how to keep on balance when swift movement is necessary in kicking while standing on one foot. Students can be paired off and, standing on one foot, arms folded, they should try to kick each other off balance whilst maintaining their own balance.

Once this is mastered, it should be explained that, surrounded by a crowd, your only chance of escape lies in continual movement. This is so because, after you have taken up a new position it requires a second for an opponent to turn and balance before he is able to strike you with any force. If one moves at least three feet in each second, there is obviously little chance of an opponent scoring an effective hit on you. At the same time, by the use of the blows previously learned, you will be able to do considerable damage while you are moving.

NOTE: 1. In addition to forward, backward and lateral movement, move also at different levels, sometimes with the knees very much bent. It all helps, if done at speed, to bewilder your adversaries.

      2. Of necessity, there will be little room for movement, so make room by moving against one opponent after another, attacking as you do so. Point out the value of the balance and foot work in which the students should have been practised at the beginning of this section.

The information contained in the two above notes should suffice to prepare students for the actual practice, which is now outlined. Six dummies should be suspended as indicated in the preface. One student at a time should enter the ring and, with all the speed of which he is capable, should then attack the dummies at random, using every kind of blow with hand, foot, knee, elbow and head, from any position.

The practice is very exhausting and it is difficult to keep it up for more than a minute.

The instructor must watch carefully for faults so that he can give advice afterwards.

Before the student tires he should be told to leave the ring and he will do so at speed, exactly as if he were actually making an escape.

To derive the maximum benefit from this exercise it should first be done both by the instructor and the student in slow time, paying careful attention to footwork.

It should then be followed by many short periods in the ring and only an occasional longer one. It must always be remembered that the aim is to get out of the place and not to fight any longer than necessary.

SECTION 5.

Knife Fighting.

The knife is a silent and deadly weapon that is easily concealed and against which in the hands of an expert, there is no sure defence, except fire-arms or by running like hell.

Students should be taught how to hold a knife, how to pass it from one hand to another, to thrust and how to use the disengaged hand to feint and parry. It is unnecessary to be ambidextrous to be able to use the knife with either hand.

Show the vulnerable points, emphasising that the abdominal region is the principal target. Show how to make an opening for a thrust in the region, e.g. by slashing across face, hands, wrist and forearms, by flinging gravel, a stone, a hat, a handkerchief, etc., in the opponent's face.

Explain the value of a really sharp point and edge, the latter, particularly with a double-edged knife, being as much to prevent the knife from being seized as for slashing.

Show the hamstring slash at the back of the knee.

Make students now practise thrusts at the straw-filled dummy.

SECTION 6.

For special needs and occasions:

1. <u>Killing a sentry, if you are armed with a knife</u>.
   Attack from the rear. With left fore-arm, strike violently on left side of opponent's neck and instantly transfer the left hand to cover his mouth and nostrils. Simultaneously with the blow on the neck, thrust the knife (held in the right hand) into his kidneys. If equipment interferes with the kidney thrust, bring the hand round to the front and thrust into the abdomen. Note that once the left hand covers mouth and nostrils, the adversary is dragged backwards and downwards.

2. <u>Killing a sentry, if you are un-armed</u>.
   Attack from the rear. With right fore-arm, strike violently on right side of adversary's neck. Go immediately into the head-hold and take him down on to your thigh. Keeping the hold properly (i.e., right hand open and tensed, fore-arm between adversary's jaw and temple, left hand grasping right wrist so as to apply pressure, lifting up and twisting adversary's head), sit down instantly with legs stretched out in front of you. Instructors will see to it that their students, when practising with each other, do <u>not</u> sit down while keeping the hold. With a little ingenuity, it should be possible to adapt one of the dummies for practice. All that is necessary is to sling the dummy on a pulley. The instructor could release the cord and so allow the student to take the dummy to the ground.

369

Needless to say, extreme speed is necessary for both methods of killing a sentry and both methods should be practiced equally on right and left-hand sides.

3. <u>Spinal Dislocator, opponent sitting, or at a much lower level</u>. Approach from rear. Left hand under chin, drag opponent's head back completely under your right arm-pit. Drop your left hand on his left shoulder and, passing your right arm across the back of his neck, grip your left wrist from above. The finishing touch is a quick snap upwards and backwards. A very dangerous hold and requires great care in practising.

4. <u>Disarming, if held up with a pistol</u>.
Explain first that only a fool would hold you up with his pistol within reach of your hands. Nevertheless, it is plainly evident that there are still a lot of such fools about and if you did not know how to deal with them it would be you who would feel a fool.

<u>From the front</u>:
<u>Method A</u>. Hands up, well above your head and wide apart. Don't look at the pistol. Bring your right hand down smartly on to his wrist, gripping it firmly with your thumb, preferably, above. Accompany the movement by a half turn to your left. Simultaneously, your left hand grips the pistol barrel from underneath and presses the pistol backwards. Note that while the pistol is being pressed backwards, its barrel should be parallel with the ground. This will break your opponent's trigger finger and give you possession of the pistol. Turning half right, attack, with foot or knee to the fork, open-hand chin-jab, butt with the top of your head or do anything calculated to knock your opponent out. Each movement has been described separately but, in actual practice, the several movements should be performed so quickly that they appear to be almost one.

<u>Method B</u>. Hands up, well above your head and wide apart. Don't look at the pistol. Bring your left hand down smartly on to his wrist, gripping it firmly with your thumb, preferably, above. Accompany the movement by a half turn to your right. Simultaneously, your right hand grips the pistol barrel from underneath and presses the pistol upwards, backwards and over. This is practically the equivalent of the ordinary wrist throw and will give you possession of the pistol. Turning half left, <u>attack</u>, with foot or knee to the fork, open-hand chin-jab, butt with the top of the head, or do anything calculated to

knock your opponent out. Each movement has been described in detail, but, in actual practice, the several movements should be performed so quickly that they appear to be almost one.

From the rear:

Method A. Hands up, well above your head and wide apart. Make up your mind which way you will turn. If to the left, look over your left shoulder, to make sure that it is the pistol which is touching your back. At the same time as you look over your shoulder, turn your right foot inwards. When you are ready to move, turn right round to the left, at the same time bringing your left arm down in a circular sweep over your opponent's pistol arm, continuing the sweeping motion until your opponent's arm is locked firmly under your left arm-pit. Simultaneously with your turning round, your right hand comes into position for a chin-jab or punch to the jaw and your right knee comes up to your opponent's fork. Finish the matter by turning smartly to your right, re-inforcing the movement with your right hand on the elbow of the arm which is still locked under your left arm-pit. This movement, if continued, will bring him across you, in position for either a smash to his face with your right knee or a side of the hand blow, with your right hand, on the back of his neck. All to be done with lightning speed.

Method B. Hands up, well above your head and wide apart. Look over your right shoulder, turning your left foot inwards as you do so. Turn right round, to your right, locking your opponent's pistol arm, as described above, but under your right arm-pit. Meanwhile your left arm is coming round for a side of the hand blow across his throat or face. You are also in position to use your knee. Finish as described above, by turning to your right, etc.

Disarming a man holding someone else up. If holding the pistol in his right hand, smash down with your left hand on his fore-arm at the elbow joint, simultaneously seizing the pistol from underneath with your right hand. Turn rapidly to your left until you are face to face with him, pressing the pistol upwards, towards him and finally to the left. Use your knee and butt with your head.

Students should become proficient in all these five methods of disarming.

5. Searching a prisoner, if you are armed.
Kill him first. If that is inconvenient, make him lie face to the ground, hands out in front of him. Knock him out, with

rifle butt, side or butt of the pistol or with your boot.
Then search him.

6. <u>Taking a prisoner away, if you are armed with a rifle or other firearm</u>.
Get someone to cut the prisoner's belt or braces, or make him do so himself. March him away, one of his hands above his head, the other holding up his trousers.

7. <u>Securing a prisoner for some time</u>.
Using 15 feet of cord and any effective knot, show the conventional method, i.e. knock him out, place him face down on the ground, tie his hands behind his back, lead the cord round his throat, back to his wrists, round both ankles, back to his wrists. Students should be told not to forget to take the cord with them.

Having shown how to tie him up, show how to gag a prisoner. Almost anything will do to stuff in his mouth - turf, cloth, a forage cap, etc. For something to tie over his mouth, strips can be torn from the prisoner's clothing. It is useful if instructors will let students, once or twice during the course, go through the whole process of tying up and gagging, having handy some cord and strips of cloth for the purpose. It is not enough for students to be told how to do it; they must do it themselves.

8. <u>Defence against a downward or sideways blow</u>.
Presuming that you are utterly unable to get hold of any kind of weapon, no matter how crude, employ one of the following methods:

a) Side-step and attack.
b) Parry with the opposite fore-arm and attack.

Students should know, at this stage of the training, how best to attack.

<u>Various Holds. Throws, etc.</u>
<u>(not to be taught)</u>

This is a selection of holds, blows, throws, attacks, etc., which are known to every instructor. Sooner or later, some of the more knowing students are sure to ask the instructor if he knows this, that or the other hold, etc., and if so, why it is not taught. This list is intended to provide answers to such questions.

CLOSE COMBAT

If obliged by such questions to show some of these holds, etc., the instructor should:

a) Demonstrate the objections,

b) Demonstrate the appropriate releases or counters.

c) Warn students that against a trained adversary, many of these holds, etc., would be difficult, risky or impossible to apply.

d) Warn students of the unwisdom of assuming that their adversaries in this war will be untrained men. If students have mastered the far simpler and quicker methods of the syllabus, all the holds, etc., in the following list are entirely unnecessary. The (unarmed) defences against a rifle and bayonet are possibly the only exceptions.

e) <u>Holds designed to keep a man captive or to take him away as a prisoner.</u>
Point out that the man who attempts to use them for any purpose other than as a means to finish off an opponent should realise that he is running a considerable risk, a risk that is only justified if he has first crippled his opponent or if he possesses a marked and obvious superiority in physique or knowledge.

<u>Defences against a rifle and bayonet.</u>
Show particularly the one which consists of parrying the rifle or bayonet away to your left, using your right hand and making a simultaneous half left turn, stepping in immediately to your opponent's left-hand side and attacking at speed with hand, foot or both. Disregard the rifle once you are past the bayonet point.

Explain that all the defences against a bayonet are apt to be extremely effective if you, unarmed, are exceptionally quick and if your opponent doesn't know his job.

<u>Bent-arm hold, as a defence against a downward blow.</u>
Why waste time? You have got to parry, in any case, so parry with one fore-arm and attack simultaneously with the knee and disengaged hand (chin-jab or punch to the jaw).

<u>Wrist and elbow hold, usually employed as a defence against a throat hold</u>.
Why bother? Attack instead, knee to the fork, fingers to the eyes.

<u>Thumb and elbow hold.</u>
Difficult to apply unless your opponent has lost his senses. Show how to escape from it.

Head hold.
Excellent for dealing with a sentry if carried instantly to its
full conclusion. Don't use it merely as a hold, however, for it
gives your opponent an opportunity for a crotch throw that can
finish you.

Arm and neck hold.
Effective but with a quick opponent you are most unlikely to get it.

Japanese strangle.
When the hand is in the correct position, i.e., almost on top of
the head, you cannot prevent your opponent, if he is quick, from
dragging your hand away. If the hand is held lower down, where
it cannot be seized and dragged away, you are apt to lose the
necessary leverage and the hold becomes ineffective. Also, again
if your opponent is quick, he can sink with his full weight and
the hold cannot be applied. It can only be applied if secured
and taken to its conclusion with extreme speed. A steel helmet
would probably make it very difficult to secure the hold.

Rock-crusher.
Only effective if delivered in exactly the right spot and if
there is no equipment in the way. Why not use one of the other
methods of attack?

Grape-vine.
Useless as a means of keeping a man prisoner. It needs two men
to apply it and if the prisoner does not escape (some men can),
he may die before very long. If you want to kill him, do so, but
don't torture him. If you want to keep him prisoner, tie him up.

Match-box blow.
Good, but you don't always have a match-box at the critical
moment. Why not use the elbow, followed immediately by a chin-
jab, side of the hand blow, or punch to the jaw?

Baton and spring cosh.
Open to the objection common to all forms of attack with the
raised arm, in that they leave the attacker wide open. Directly
the arm goes up (or sooner), step in close and use your knife.
If you have no knife, step in closer and use chin-jab or punch,
and the knee. If you yourself use a spring cosh and you miss your
blow with the extreme end of the weapon, it is likely that you
will only hit harmlessly with the spring. Both the baton and the
spring cosh are a bit clumsy to carry about and it is doubtful
if they are worth the trouble.

Safety-razor blade, or blades, in cap peak.
May be shown, in order that students may know what to expect,
but the use of this device is not to be encouraged.

All the following, good as some of them are, are open to the
objection that while attempting to apply them, you make yourself
very vulnerable to attack. Also if you are in a position to apply
them, you are equally in a position to make a killing attack on
your opponent. Why not do so?

    Handcuff hold
    Handcuff hold for smaller opponent
    Wrist and neck attack
    Police or "come-along" holds
    Flying mare and variations
    Hipe or hip throw
    Wrist throw
    Japanese ankle throw
    Cross buttock

ADDENDUM

GAGGING A PRISONER

The following method should be used:

a) Apply the gag - turf, cloth, handkerchief, forage cap, etc. - in the prisoner's mouth.

b) Similar to the First Aid method of bandaging a broken jaw, place the centre of a piece of cloth over the mouth and round the chin and tie at the back of the head as shown in the diagram.

c) Apply the centre of a second piece of cloth under the jaw, carry it in front of the ears and tie on top of the head.

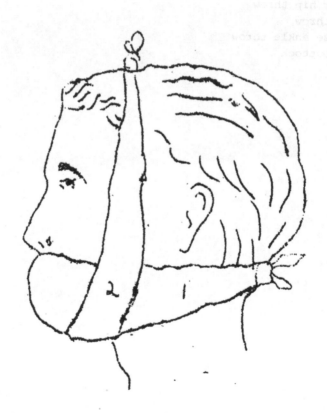

I.4.
February 1944.

ADDENDUM

ATTACKING A SENTRY

Under "Killing a Sentry, with a knife or with hands alone",
(Section 6), the methods there described are designed
exclusively for use by one man acting entirely on his own. Those
methods remain in force and will continue to be taught but it
is necessary now to go further and to teach methods of attack by
two men acting as a team, providing thereby for conditions where
this is possible and preferable.

In making this addition to the training, two distinct sets of
circumstances are envisaged:

a) Merely to disarm, knock out, tie up, gag and, if necessary,
   remove a sentry out of reach of immediate discovery. It is
   extremely unlikely that one man alone could accomplish all
   this. That is why the Syllabus confines itself in this regard
   to the simpler task of killing.

b) To disarm, kill and, if necessary, remove a sentry out of
   reach of immediate discovery. It is thought that one man
   alone is unlikely to do this as efficiently and silently as
   two men.

Essentials of both a) and b) are:

> Extreme speed,
> The utmost silence.

The first essential implies a complete understanding between the
two attackers as to the part which each will play; the second
refers particularly to the avoidance of noise from a dropped
rifle or from the sentry's nailed boots on a stone pavement,
gravel or hard ground.

For the practice of the following methods, the student who acts
as sentry will have on nailed boots, wear a German steel helmet
and carry a rifle. The attackers will wear rubber shoes. The
practices will be carried out on a stone pavement, a gravel path
or on hard ground.

a) <u>When the object is not to kill</u>.

The "sentry", equipped as above, will take up his position, rifle slung over his right shoulder. The attacking team, having agreed upon their respective parts, will make the customary "stalk" approach, one immediately behind the other. The leading man will attack the sentry from the rear, using the fore-arm blow on the side of the neck and simultaneous kidney punch (left forearm and right fist respectively). Instantly, his left hand is transferred to cover the sentry's mouth and nostrils. Using his right arm to help, he now commences to drag the sentry backwards and downwards. The second attacker's job, working as nearly simultaneously as possible with the first attacker, is to secure the rifle, administer a knock-out blow (chin-jab, punch to the jaw or solar plexus) and help to lower the sentry to the ground quietly. Once on the ground, the sentry is turned over on to his face, the first attacker, kneeling astride of the sentry, knees well under the latter's armpits, proceeds with the tying up. The second attacker, working opposite the first, can proceed with the gagging process. Once bound and gagged, the sentry is to be carried away a few yards, as if to put him out of reach of immediate observation by others.

Repeat with the following variations:

- Rifle slung over sentry's left shoulder.
- Rifle carried under one arm or the other.
- Rifle in sentry's right hand, in the "at-ease" position.
- Repeat in the dark.
- Aim at completing the job in two and a half minutes.

b) <u>When the object is to kill (using the knife)</u>.

The first attacker can use the method described in Section 6, the second attacker being responsible for the quiet seizure of the rifle and for helping subsequently to carry the sentry away, presumably into the cover from which the attackers emerged. This may not always be necessary but there is no harm done by practising in as complete a manner as possible so that, if the need really arises, everything will then be carried out with the minimum of fumbling, half-understood whisperings, etc.

Alternatively, the first attacker can be responsible solely for seizing the sentry and keeping him quiet while the second secures the rifle and uses the knife (thrust in the abdominal region).

This method appears to suit some men better than the first and there is no objection to their using it if they prefer.

Repeat in daylight and in the dark, with the sentry's rifle in the different positions referred to under a).

These methods are all based on the supposition that favourable conditions will be encountered, e.g., cover within easy reach of the sentry, darkness, opportunity for prior observation of the sentry's equipment, regularity or otherwise of his beat, etc. They teach what to do when within reach of a sentry but it must be pointed out to students that if they encounter circumstances different from those envisaged, it will be largely up to them to devise ways and means of getting within reach. Presumably, nature endowed them with some sense of strategy. If not, they had better not tackle this particular job. With this proviso, students should be encouraged to think out for themselves, and find means of dealing with, all sorts of different conditions. Such conditions, for instance, might be inadequate cover, two sentries instead of one (in which case two teams of attackers might be employed). It might be better for one man to try to bluff the sentry while another attacks. It might be impossible to attack from the rear, in which case resort might be had to the old dodge of flinging a pebble to distract his attention and make him face the other way. If it is at all possible, time should be given for working out these and other problems which are sure to arise. Time so spent may well mean the difference between success and failure in the field.

It is reported that German Sentries have for some time been in the habit of carrying their rifles in such a way as to make the approved method of silent attack almost impossible. It would appear to be done as a protective measure.

The rifle is carried as though at the "slope" on the left shoulder but the left hand is carried out to the left (to an angle of approximately 45 degrees from the front) and raised slightly. This means that the rifle, while resting on the top of the left shoulder close to the neck, crosses behind the neck, the muzzle being slightly behind and above the right shoulder.

This, combined with the wearing of the German steel helmet effectively precludes the possibility of the forearm blow on the side of the neck, from either side.

It was found, however, that while the kidney punch was delivered, it was possible for the attacker to cover the sentry's mouth and nostrils with his left hand, dragging his head backwards.

In that position the rifle is locked between attacker and attacked and is in no danger of falling to the ground. Attacker No. 2 must, however, simultaneously catch the muzzle of the rifle with his left hand and press forward to prevent it striking the head of No. 1. He can then administer the knockout by punch to the solar plexus, but not chin-jab or punch to the jaw, as the latter is covered by No. 1's left hand.

It was found to be a benefit if No. 1 having adminstered the kidney punch with his right, then uses it to lock the right arm of the sentry, thus keeping it out of the way of No. 2 who can slip his left knee behind the sentry's legs.

As the latter is dragged backwards, his feet are automatically levered off the ground (by No. 2's knee), making a minimum of noise.

The only risk of noise, in this method, would appear to be the sentry's helmet hitting against his rifle at the moment of attack, but this noise must be of frequent occurrence in the course of walking with the rifle in this position.

With a rifle carried in the manner described, it considerably complicates the silent killing of a sentry by one man. Silence is almost an impossibility.

WEAPON TRAINING

INTRODUCTORY NOTES FOR INSTRUCTORS.

It is not possible for every Instructor to be a tried Gunman. But it is possible to teach the Pistol successfully by acquiring a thorough knowledge of the principles involved and applying them in a practical way. The principles are based on natural body movements not unique to gun fighting and for that reason the instruction is simple, providing the imagination is used to the fullest extent to visualise the circumstances of Gun-fighting, to provide a background. Particular attention must be paid to instinctive body movements combined with the speed upon which depends survival.

A large percentage of students have had previous Revolver Training in the old style. It is not advisable to state bluntly that the old method is no good as it is possible that some of them have achieved considerable success using the pistol as a defensive weapon or in competition shooting. It is better to give a proper Introduction in which you paint a picture of the circumstances under which they might be using the pistol and to show them quite clearly that the method you propose to teach them is the only method of firing under these circumstances.

It shows a healthy interest in the subject if students are continually asking questions. Invariably the Instructor can give a satisfactory answer if he asks himself the question: "What would be the natural thing to do?".

With the time and ammunition available the aim is to turn out good, fast, plain shots. Time spent on teaching fancy or trick shooting is not justified

As with every sport, providing the principles taught are sound, practice makes perfect. Every endeavour should be made to build up the enthusiasm so that practice is carried out voluntarily. Dummy practice in front of a mirror is particularly beneficial and should be encouraged.

———————

Instruction in firing the Machine Carbines follows exactly the principles of Pistol Instruction, i.e. Tremendous speed in attack with sufficient accuracy to hit the vital part of a man's body.

The conditions are the same, i.e. Killing at close quarters, demanding agression and extreme concentration.

The principle of firing and manipulation of the weapon is different inasmuch as you are dealing with a two handed weapon having a larger magazine capacity and capable of full automatic fire. Automatic fire is of no use unless it is controlled. In the excitement and stress of close combat fighting it is difficult to fire from "Full Automatic" with complete control and therefore it is better to fire always from "single". With practice, shots are fired very fast and with accuracy in the same way as with the pistol.

The most accurate position for firing a two handed weapon is from the shoulder because the gun is in line with the eyes and you have natural control of your direction. The vital factor which governs the position in which the gun is fired is, of course, the speed with which you can get into the "firing" position from the "carrying" position. With the Thompson the position which gives the maximum speed for the normal man is the "under-arm" position. This is an accurate firing position providing the head is down close to the Gun. There are few people who find the butt of the Thompson suitable for obtaining an equally fast shoulder position but for those it does suit it must be the most accurate position.

The low hip position has been proved to be almost useless for fast close quarter work where you must be able to turn tremendously fast into position. The gun is held so low on the body and is so remote from the head and eyes that you can't control either your position or your elevation and direction.

Because of its weight and design the Sten is an ideal gun for very fast shoulder work. It can be brought into the shoulder as fast or faster than the hip, and, of course, it must be more accurate from the shoulder.

The tendency is to compare the Sten unfavourably with the Thompson. This is wrong, as the Sten is really the better weapon for the type of work with which we are concerned, as it fires Standard Continental Ammunition, it is lighter, more easily concealed and has a much more simple mechanism than the Thompson.

The tendency for stoppages to occur with practice Mark II weapons is to a certain extent exaggerated. Often these are due to bad filling of magazines or faulty manipulation of the Gun.

The Hand Grenade is a very deadly close weapon under certain circumstances. It should be taught as such and every endeavour should be made to make Live Throwing practices as practical as possible.

WEAPON TRAINING

INTRODUCTION TO PISTOL COURSE.

(Given immediately before the first two firing practices)

STORES: .22 Hi-Standard and .32 Colt (or any other Pistol/
Revolver or Pistol Automatic required).

1. Proving. Demonstrate.

   The first thing you do when you handle any weapon is to prove
   to yourself that it is not loaded.

   To prove that an Automatic is not loaded, first remove the
   magazine. The magazine catch is situated at the base of
   the Pistol Grip. Using the thumb of the left hand, press
   the magazine catch to the rear and withdraw the magazine.
   Then, by grasping the slide with the fingers of the left
   hand, elbows close to the body, work the slide backwards and
   forwards two or three times by punching or thrusting forward
   with the right hand.

   The source of food (the magazine) has been removed and any
   round which might be in the breech will be ejected by the
   action of the slide. The weapon is therefore safe.

2. Loading. Demonstrate.

   a) Charge the Magazine.

      Hold the magazine in the palm of the left hand with the
      thumb on the assisting stud. Using the right hand, feed in
      the rounds, base first, depressing the magazine platform by
      means of the assisting stud, to receive each round.

   b) Insert the loaded magazine into the Automatic with the
      left hand, ensuring that it is locked into position by
      giving a final thrust with the thumb.

   c) Cock the action and feed the first round into the breech by
      withdrawing the slide and allowing it to spring forward.

      The weapon is now ready for firing.

3. To Unload. Demonstrate - As for Proving.

   Note:

   Speed in the handling and manipulation of the Automatic
   is essential. This speed is only obtained by handling the
   weapon correctly at all times. Each hand has a definite job
   to do. The right hand holds the weapon, with the forefinger
   inside the trigger guard. The left hand carries out the
   manipulations, i.e. Proving, Loading and Unloading. To assist

the left hand in its work, the Automatic is turned over left or right to allow the magazine base and the slide to come naturally and easily into the left hand.

4. _Firing_. Introduction.

Get out of your mind the idea that the Pistol is a weapon of self-defence. It is not. It is a weapon of attack, in just the same way as the rifle, the machine gun or any other combat weapon.

The difference between the Pistol and these other weapons is that the Pistol has a short barrel; it fires blunt nosed pistol ammunition and is therefore a short range weapon. The normal combat range is not more than 12 - 15 yards. When you are attacking so close to the enemy you must be able to move with extreme speed, you must be able to kill from any position and in any sort of light - even in complete darkness.

Picture in your mind the circumstances under which you might be using the Pistol. Take as an example a raid on an enemy occupied house in darkness. Firstly consider your approach. You will never walk boldly up to the house and stroll in as though you were paying a social call. On the contrary, your approach will be stealthy. You will be keyed up and excited, nervously alert for danger from whichever direction it may come. You will find yourself _instinctively_ crouching; your body balanced on the balls of your feet in a position from which you can move swiftly in any direction. You make your entry into the house and start searching for the enemy moving along passages, perhaps up or down stairs, listening and feeling for any signs of danger. Suddenly, on turning a corner, you come face to face with the enemy. Without a second's hesitation you must fire and kill him before he has a chance to kill you.

From this picture these facts are clear:

a) You will always fire from the crouch position - you will _never_ be in an upright position.

b) You have _no time_ to adopt any fancy stance when killing with speed.

c) You have _no time_ to use the sights.

Any method of firing which does not allow for all these factors is useless. Gun fighting at close quarters is a question of split seconds.

The best method of firing under these circumstances is by what is called "Instinctive Pointing".

5. <u>What is Instinctive Pointing</u>.

It is the natural way that any man points at an object when he is <u>concentrating</u>.

As an example: stand squarely in front of a man and point at the exact centre of his stomach, his right or left foot or his right or left eye. You don't look down your finger and sight - you know you are pointing at the exact spot, instinctively. Analyse what you are doing. Your arm extended, with the finger pointing, comes into <u>the centre of your body</u>. In this position it is also right in the centre of your eyes and therefore what you are doing is to point straight down the centre of your line of sight. This is instinctive and you have natural control over your direction and elevation.

Try pointing quickly from the side of the body. You will find that there is no instinctive control over direction. The reason for this is obvious. Your line of sight and your pointing line are remote. Any fractional variation in your pointing line produces a large error on an object several yards in front of you.

The method we are going to use for firing the pistol is therefore by Instinctive Pointing, the pistol replacing the finger in pointing.

6. <u>Holding</u>.

The correct method of holding the Pistol is as follows:

a) You always hold the Pistol with a tremendously strong grip. Grip it as though you were trying to squash the butt to pulp. This applies to any Pistol, large or small.

b) The trigger finger is always kept inside the trigger guard with the finger nail resting against the front of the trigger guard. The finger is never kept running along the outside of the trigger guard; it reduces your speed in fast action.

c) Try to get the thumb of your right hand running horizontally along the side of the Receiver, i.e. on the same plane as the barrel. This assists you in pointing naturally and also gives **you** lateral control of the Pistol.

7. <u>Firing Position</u> - Demonstrate.

A natural crouch position, the body balanced on the balls of the feet and pressed forward over the forward foot; shoulders square to the target. The right hand, holding the pistol, is brought into the centre of the body and reaches out towards the target until the arm is almost fully extended, in the natural pointing position. The barrel of the pistol is always parallel to the ground. In this position the right hand is turned slightly to the right to allow the barrel to point straight down the centre of the line of the sight.

This is the Firing Position.

It is impossible to hold the actual firing position throughout the approach to the enemy. It is a tense position, where every nerve is concentrated on killing with tremendous speed. In the approach it is necessary to adopt a more relaxed position but it must be possible to come from this relaxed position to the "Firing Position" in a fraction of a second. This relaxed position is known as the "Ready Position" and is adopted from the "Firing Position" as follows:

Imagine there is a groove down the centre of the body. Lock the wrist and the elbow, then allow the arm, pivoting at the shoulder only, to slide down this groove until the pistol is pointing at the ground two or three yards in front of the body. Neither the wrist nor the elbow have relaxed and the downward movement from the shoulder is a minimum one. The return to the "Firing Position" is a fast, smooth movement from the shoulder. No adjustment of the position is necessary as the original correct position has been regained.

8. Practise Squad in Proving, Loading, Unloading and in adopting the "Firing" and "Ready" positions.

NOTE: Practice loading is not carried out with charged magazines. Practice in charging magazines is gained when student is preparing for firing practice. The Instructor is in the best position to check positional faults when standing in front of student, making himself the target. He must ensure that all safety precautions are observed and particularly that each weapon is proved.

FIRING PRACTICES.

PERIOD I.

The Recruit Target.

Recruit Target - Fig. 2 (Full Figure) - Field Grey - White Aiming Mark on Stomach.

Range - 3 yards.

WEAPON TRAINING

Purpose of Recruit Target.

It is a large target very close to the firer. You can't miss it and consequently it is possible to see exactly what happens to each round fired. The aiming mark is the object on which you are concentrating. If you are pointing correctly from the centre of your body and your elevation is 100% correct, then every round fired must be in the aiming mark. If you are pointing from the centre of your body correctly but your elevation is slightly wrong, then your shots will be shown either above or below the aiming mark and they will form a line up the centre of the target. This is what we are looking for. If your shots are shown on the left of the target it is because the barrel is not pointing straight down the line of sight. To remedy – turn the hand slightly to the right.

If shots are shown on the right of the target it is because you are not firing from the centre of your body.

Shots consistently low – either the barrel is not parallel to the ground or you are firing on the way up.

Shots consistently high – barrel not parallel to ground.

To kill a man it is not necessary to put a shot through his heart. The vulnerable part of a man's body is from his crotch up to the top of his head. Two fast shots anywhere into that area are going to dispose of him permanently.

The object of Pistol Training is to obtain maximum speed in attack with sufficient accuracy to hit the vulnerable area.

Firing Practice No. 1. (.22)

Recruit Target.
Range – 3 yards.
No. of Rounds – 6 – fired under control.

Student charges magazine with six rounds and advances to Firing Point.

On Command "Load" he loads and adopts "Ready" Position.

Without firing, practise sliding smoothly up into the "Firing" Position whilst Instructor checks any fault.

Return to "Ready" Position.

On the Command "One" the student comes up to "Firing" Position, fires one round and returns to "Ready" Position.

Repeat.

On the Command "Two" student comes up to "Firing" Position, fires <u>two</u> rounds fast and returns to "Ready" Position.

Repeat.

Unload.

Student, with Instructor, examines position of shots on target, discusses their position in relation to any error in the "Firing" position.

<u>Firing Practice No. 2</u>. (.22)

Targets - Moving and/or bobbing targets at various ranges and elevation.

No. of Rounds - 8.

The Recruit Target represented a man standing at short range in front of you and it has been clearly shown how easy it is to control your shots into a vital part of the body providing you are concentrating, gripping correctly and <u>pointing</u> from the centre of your body.

We are now going to fire at Moving Targets.

Supposing you were asked to point with your <u>finger</u> at any target which appeared on the range in front of you. It would be ridiculous for anybody to suggest that you couldn't do so, with accuracy. It is going to be just as easy to point with the automatic, providing the correct position is adopted and you are concentrating intensely. There is one other thing to be considered and that is the correct method of turning left or right on the target.

It is ridiculous to try to make rules as to how a man should move his feet when turning. In fast close combat fighting, your feet move naturally and instinctively to balance your body, just as a boxer moves his feet. The vital thing in turning is that you must get round on to your target with <u>tremendous speed</u>. How you get round doesn't matter providing your position when you are round is correct, i.e. body balanced, shoulders square to the target and your pistol <u>pointing</u> correctly from the centre of the body.

The common fault in turning is to allow the arm to swing round faster than the body. With practice this tendency is easily cured. The arm does not move independently of the body; it stays in is original position in the centre of the body and is _pulled_ round by the shoulders turning.

You will always fire two fast shots at every target. The reason for this is as follows:

1. You must _kill_ your man. One shot _may_ kill him but it is better to make _absolutely_ certain by putting two shots into him.

2. If a man is advancing to attack you and you put _one_ shot into a vital part of his body it rarely drops him in his tracks immediately; his nerve system doesn't collapse for several seconds. On the other hand, if you put _two_ shots in quick succession into him, he will drop in his tracks because his nerve system breaks up immediately.

3. If you are just about to press the trigger to attack an opponent and you see a flash from his gun, you will instinctively "freeze" for a fraction of a second. Even if his shot misses you he will have a momentary advantage. It is this momentary advantage given to the man who gets the first shot that _you_ must always obtain by training yourself to fire _two_ shots at tremendous speed. Even if you miss with your _first_ you will get him with your second.

Practise Squad in Turning.

In this practice your magazine will be charged with _eight_ rounds; you will fire two fast shots at each target as it appears.

NOTE: Throughout this and every other practice, the Instructor observes closely every detail of body position, movement of the automatic and any effect on the destination of the rounds fired. The position of the shots on the target and the reason why any "misses" have occurred is discussed with the student and errors rectified.

PERIOD II. (1-½ hours)

Firing Practice No. 3. (.22)

Targets - Moving and/or Bobbing - at various ranges and elevations.

No. of Rounds - 8.

This practice is similar to No. 2 Practice. It is a warming up practice in which all that has been taught in the previous period is checked. Speed is again emphasised. Maximum speed comes from a fast, smooth movement into position and a very firm grip with tremendously fast trigger work.

Firing Practice No. 4. (.22)

Targets - Moving and/or Bobbing Targets, as before. No. of Rounds ÷ 8. Fired in the dark.

You must be able to fire equally well in the dark as in the daylight. It is not difficult. Again, you would have no difficulty in pointing with your finger at a shadow in the dark. It is just as easy to point with the automatic. You must, however, be on your toes, concentrating and peering into the darkness so that you will be able to pick out the movement of your target and kill it without a moment's hesitation.

NOTE: The way in which this practice is carried out on the range will depend on the lighting facilities available. Any of the following methods are good.

1. Complete darkness with a flickering dimmed light or alternatively, flicking the black-out curtain to admit flashes of light.

2. Complete darkness with the rays of a dimmed torch moving quickly backwards and forwards over the range area.

3. Using night glasses.

Firing Practice No. 5. (.22)

Targets - Moving and/or Bobbing Targets, as before. No. of Rounds - 8.

In previous practices firing has taken place from a definite Firing Point. In actual combat you will invariably be moving in to the attack. In practising movement, the important thing to remember is that however fast you are moving when you are actually killing the target, you must be in the 100% correct "Firing Position", body crouched and balanced, automatic pointing correctly down the line of sight and every nerve concentrated on forcing your shots deep into the belly of the target.

Imagine the range is a beer cellar containing a number of Germans. You are outside with your automatic loaded and you are going to burst in and kill them ruthlessly.

In the old-style shooting, an attack of this nature involved slow, stealthy movement, relying entirely on the enemy not hearing or seeing anything until the entry had actually been made. This is an impractical and dangerous method when you are dealing with an alert enemy.

The following is the better method as it involves that shock of surprise which freezes into immobility even the most dangerous individual for a few seconds:-

You have reached the doorway of the cellar by a stealthy approach, making no sound whatever. Your automatic is loaded and cocked. Very quietly turn the handle of the door as far as it will go and then, preparing yourself for the effort, you kick the door open and burst into the room with maximum speed and noise and kill your targets before they have a chance to realise what has happened.

NOTE: The old-style and the new methods are demonstrated by the Instructor, showing particularly how the body retains the balanced crouched position and the correct Firing Position irrespective of the movement of the feet. Also emphasise how the loaded automatic is held in the "Ready" position before and during the entry into the cellar.

Magazines are charged with eight rounds - two rounds to be fired at each target.

In the supervision of the firing the Instructor forces the speed of the student in every way possible.

If a student is wild in his movements and loses position altogether, then a slower controlled practice attack should be made which can be speeded up as progress is made.

PERIOD III.

Firing Practice No. 6. (.32 Colt)

Targets - Moving and/or Bobbing as before.

No. of Rounds - 6.

The manipulation of the .32 Colt is the same as the .22 Hi-Standard, except that the magazine has not an assisting stud. The thumb of the left hand assists in the feeding of the rounds into the magazine by depressing the top round to facilitate the entry of the next round.

If you fire one Pistol you can fire any Automatic or Revolver, whether British, American or Foreign. The important thing to remember is that the barrel of your pistol is always parallel to the ground in the normal position.

Before firing a strange automatic always test your position. Get the feel of the weapon, adopt the Firing position, bring the barrel parallel to the ground and lock your wrist so that when you move into the "Ready" position and return to the "Firing" position it is still parallel.

Magazine charged with six rounds. Two shots to be fired at each target.

NOTE: Instructors should again emphasise the tremendously firm grip. When firing the .22 slight relaxing of the grip has probably not taken a shot off the target. With heavier calibre weapons the effect of relaxing the grip is greater and shots will not be "on".

Continue to build up agression in attack. Aggression denotes complete concentration, which is so vital in practice. It also encourages the state of mind which would exist in actual combat.

Firing Practice No. 7. (.32 Colt)

Targets – Moving and/or Bobbing Targets, as before.
No. of rounds – 6.
As for practice No. 4 – with poor lighting.

NOTE: Again emphasise speed and maintaining correct firing position. Speed up the targets.

PERIOD IV.

Firing Practice No. 8. – Outdoors. (.22)

Targets – Full figure – with aiming mark on belly of target.

Range – 20 to 25 yards.
No. of Rounds – 6.

So far we have been dealing with the normal firing position for close combat. There is the occasion, however, when it is necessary to take a long range shot. Firstly, the prone position: this gives you an ideal firing position and at the same time makes you a very difficult target to hit.

Demonstrate.

Lie down square to the target, right hand grasping the pistol, left hand gripping the right fist, thumb forward and clear of the recoiling slide; elbows on the ground and well apart; head well back from the sights.

Secondly, the long range firing position in the open. A position which can be adopted very quickly from the normal position.

<u>Demonstrate</u>.

Feet astride, body balanced and square to the target. Right hand, grasping the pistol, thrust straight out in front of the body. The left hand grips the right fist, thumb clear of the recoiling slide, and pulls back slightly against the fully extended right arm. In this position the pistol is in the centre of the body and held as though in a vice.

<u>Thirdly</u>, the long range firing position from behind cover. Utilising a lamp-post, a tree, the side of a house, the doorway of a house, in fact anything providing cover which presents a high support which will bear your weight. In this position you have an ideal firing position with maximum cover for the vital parts of your body.

<u>Demonstrate</u>.

Using a convenient tree, placing the left toe and left knee against the cover, right foot extended well to the rear until the right leg is straight and rigid. The ball of the thumb of the right hand rests against the right hand side of the cover, left hand grasping the right wrist, back of the hand downwards. The body is now supported at all points and lined-up behind the cover to give maximum protection. The pistol must be gripped very firmly and not canted over to the right.

Practise squad.

Magazine charged 6 rounds. Two aimed or rough aimed shots to be fired from the prone position. Rising quickly, adopt long range standing position in the open and fire two more shots. Then move quickly to a suitable tree and fire the last two shots from the Firing position behind cover.

<u>NOTE</u>: It should be emphasised that these positions will be adopted quickly. Use of the sights is permissible but there will not always be time to use them and necessity for quick rough aiming should be explained and practised.

<u>Firing Practice No. 9</u>. (.22)

Target - "Gallows" Target approx. 20 feet from ground. (See Appendix "A".)

Range from Tree - 8-10 yards.
No. of Rounds - 6.

The difficulty when firing "up" is to control your elevation. Generally you find that your shots are striking either above or below the target. The reason for this is because the arm <u>and</u> the body are elevating quickly and unless the movement of each is 100% correct the aim is not correct.

<u>Demonstrate</u>.

It is better to elevate the pistol by a movement of the body only which can be easily controlled with practice. At the same time as the body is elevating by bending back from the waist over the rear leg, the right arm is extended straight out.

It is impossible to fire in this way when you are right underneath the target, as, for example, if you were suddenly attacked from the top of a flight of stairs as you were going up. Under these circumstances the fastest and best method of dealing with the target is to thrust the right arm out towards the target just as though you were trying to thrust the muzzle into his stomach.

Practise Squad.

Magazine charged 6 rounds.

Adopt the normal firing position as though engaging a target on you own level underneath the "Gallows" target. On the command "Up" engage the "Gallows" target, firing two shots, and return to the normal position. Repeat. On the command "Advance" move quickly in the direction of the target; when you are almost underneath you will get the command "Up". Like a flash you must come up and fire two shots in the method you have been taught, arm straight as though you were thrusting the muzzle into the stomach of the target.

PERIOD V.

<u>Firing Practice No. 10</u>. - Outdoors. (.22)

Target - Fig. 3.

Range - From a platform between two trees 20-25 feet from the ground, or from a suitable cliff or similar ground where the target can be placed almost immediately below the firer.

<u>Demonstrate</u>.

<u>Firing Down</u>. As with firing "up" the difficulty is to control elevation when firing from the normal position.

In addition, to see your target when firing down, it is
necessary to expose a large part of your body. The best
method under these circumstances is to stand sideways,
stretch the right arm out to the fullest extent in the
direction of the target. The automatic is held as though
it was an extension of the right arm, so that by turning
your hand and looking straight down your arm the sights are
lined on to the target.

You will find that it is possible to stand several feet
away from the edge of the platform so that you are almost
invisible to the person at whom you are firing.

This is the best method of sniping at a person below from
the room of a house. If the window sill is high, you can
stand on a table or a box several feet away from the window
and you are getting maximum concealment. Also the flash and
smoke from the discharge of your pistol is absorbed in the
room, making the source of the shooting very difficult to
trace unless it is observed at the exact moment of firing.

Magazine charged with 6 rounds.

NOTE: Before firing, the Instructor should demonstrate the
extent of the concealment offered by this firing position.
Students grouped underneath the platform. Instructor mounts
the platform and adopts the correct position, aiming as
though to fire into chest of each student in turn.

Firing Practice No. 11. - Outdoors. (.32 Colt)

Targets - Three full-figure and two hand and shoulders.
Range - Maximum 35 yards.

No. of Rounds - 6.

Attack in the Open.

The object of this practice is to develop speed in closing
to attack the enemy.

The targets are in view from a distance of approximately 35
yards.

Magazine is loaded with 6 rounds.

The student advances two or three yards, adopts the prone
position and fires one round at a full figure target: he
then rises quickly, runs to 20 yards, deals with another
full figure target, from the standing long range position.
Then, without hesitation, he moves very fast to close

quarters and deals with the remaining two targets from the normal firing position.

NOTE: Speed in attack, shooting and adoption of Firing position must be emphasised throughout.

The sequence of this practice can of course be varied to suit the ground. If possible, the starting point should be in a position where the student can advance to cover for his first shot. The close quarter targets should be wide apart to give maximum right and left turn.

Firing Practice No. 12. - Outdoors. (.32 colt)

Targets - As for Practice No. 11.
No. of rounds - 6.

This practice is a repetition of Firing Practice No. 11.

PERIOD VI.

Firing Practice No. 13. - Outdoors. (.32 Colt)

Stalk Course - 6. Targets

No. of Rounds 14.

NOTE: The object of the Stalk Course is to provide targets at distances which would be involved in actual combat so that the student is forced to decide, immediately, the correct position for dealing with the target. The targets should also be on different levels.

In order to obtain the maximum benefit from the course, an endeavour should be made to present practical problems which will emphasise the principles already stressed throughout the pistol course. If the student deals with the situation presented satisfactorily, his successes will increase his confidence in his ability to overcome other situations. It will teach him to expect them and to find an immediate remedy.

The student who is "caught-out" or who does the wrong thing is shown what he should have done and why. He, also, will have an idea of what to expect and is encouraged to improve his ability.

In proceeding round the course the student will use his knowledge of Fieldcraft. He will have been previously taught the correct method of stalking in a preliminary practice under the Fieldcraft Syllabus.

WEAPON TRAINING

There is a tendency to make the Stalk Course a test of Fieldcraft, where, if the student's powers of observation are not acute, he proceeds round the course without firing a shot. This is **not** the intention. The Stalk Course is a shooting practice where all the emphasis on speed in attack, control of position in wide fast turns, the necessity for alternative positions to deal with middle distance and awkward targets, is shown in a practical way. If necessary, he should be "frightened" on to a target which hasn't been seen so that he reacts almost without thinking. He must be forced to move fast in killing a target and prevented from deliberate aiming.

In the past, a system of scoring was used, where "hits" on the target received so many points. This is of no use in training as it encourages a man to aim deliberately so that he can return a good score.

The targets should be painted to represent Germans. A simple standard design, not involving the services of an artist, is easily obtained and is most practical from a maintenance point of view. After dealing with the first target, the student will know what he is looking for, as he would if he was actually dealing with a German in uniform.

When the students are grouped in the "Waiting Bay" before commencing the course, the object of the practice should be fully explained. It creates interest if a story is evolved around the course with particular emphasis on the imagination being used. They are not shooting at targets but at Germans, who are armed and lying in wait for them. They must kill the enemy before he has a chance to kill them.

Two Magazines charged with seven rounds in each. Two shots to be fired at each target. Reload with fresh magazine after disposing of three targets. Care must be taken when reloading; there is one round still in the breech. Remove empty magazine, insert full one and carry on. After dealing with the sixth target - unload, removing magazine and ejecting the round remaining in breech. When reloading you must get behind cover. For a few seconds you are virtually unarmed. The enemy will take advantage of this if you let him.

After completion of course Instructor discusses with student his performance, particularly the way in which he has attacked the targets and definite Fieldcraft errors which would have been fatal in actual combat.

PERIOD VII.

The balance of 10 Rounds with the .32 Colt is intended to be used on the Street Fighting course. Where this course is not available an additional indoor practice at moving targets should be given or, if _time_ is available, an additional "Stalk".

NOTE: It is proposed to construct an outside Firing Bay in close proximity to all Ranges. The object of this Firing Bay is to cut out the "waiting" period whilst the principal Firing practices are being carried out. After a student has fired a practice he will fire a further practice with a .22 under another Instructor. He will then return to the original range. The Firing practices at the Firing Bay will be based on the practices being fired on the Main Range as shown on the appended list of Practices. In addition, drawing and firing from a shoulder holster will be incorporated.

Firing Bay.

It should be built in a 'safe' place as close as possible to the Main Range. All that is required is a back butt of banked turf or sleepers with side wings about 5 yards long constructed of sandbags or turf extending left and right.

Targets should be moving or bobbing but if this is not practical stationary targets will serve the purpose.

The method of carrying out a practice with Stationary Targets is as follows:-

The targets, head and shoulders and full length, are placed in positions giving as wide a turn left and right as possible. They are numbered from the left, in the presence of the student, either by actually marking the targets or by word of mouth. The targets are engaged on the word of command given by the Instructor. For example, on the command "Two" the student attacks No. 2 Target, firing two fast shots. The command "Four" follows immediately, he engages No. 4 Target, and so on. Whilst this method is not so efficient as a practice with moving or bobbing targets, it does make the student get "on his toes" waiting for the word of command. Another advantage is that the targets can be moved to any position.

In "movement" practices, to make the student familiar with a complete turn, he should be made to stand with his back to the target, charged magazine in the automatic, but not cocked. The Instructor engages him in conversation, trying to take his attention away from the targets. In the middle of conversation suddenly <u>scare</u> the student on to the targets so that he has to turn, cock and engage the targets in one movement. This is also a good practice for shoulder-holster training.

The battle-dress blouse does not allow for the proper use of the shoulder-holster, as it is designed for civilian clothes. In practice it should be worn with the jacket off or over the battle-dress blouse.

The use of Screens.

This is an innovation, contrived by a well known B.O. Instructor, and enables the range to be converted quickly into an alley-way where fast turns and surprise targets are easily arranged. The principle is very simple. Posts are erected at a distance of four or five yards apart on each side of the range up to the firing point. Wires are stretched from post to post across the range on which are hung screens made of split sand bags extending to the ground. By staggering these screens it is possible to form a corridor down which the student attacks. Targets are placed in any surprise position and the student can also be made to surmount obstacles on his way through. This is the most obvious use of the screens but they can also be arranged to form the walls of a room and by incorporating a door frame on two supports you can include practices involving an attack into a room.

Firing Bay Practices.

Period		Practice			No. of Rounds
I	.22	1	Turning Left & Right at Standing Targets, firing under control.		6
II	.22	2	Turning Left & Right at Standing Targets speeding up.		6
III	.22	3	Introducing Movement.		6
		4	Repeat – Using Door and Screens.		6
IV	.22	5	Long Range Firing.		6
		6	Firing Up, Prone and Long Range.		6
V	.22	7	Turning on to targets at wide angles with movement. Drawing from shoulder-holster.		6

There are a number of interesting points regarding care of weapons and Gun Fighting generally which can be incorporated in a short lecture towards the end of the course.

Unorthodox Lubricants.

Automatic weapons with fast moving mechanism and bearing surfaces must be kept slightly oiled to avoid overheating and seizing. It is more than possible that rifle oil will not be available to students on operations. In an emergency the following can be used to oil or grease the weapon:

1. Bacon Fat.
2. Tallow - Candles.
3. Graphite - Pencil Lead.

Holding-up.

Normally, when you are attacking into a room you will immediately kill everybody in it. There is the occasion however when for one reason or another you wish to hold the people under the threat of your gun whilst another member of the raiding party is perhaps obtaining rope to tie them up or the leader of party to interrogate them before they are disposed of.

The normal firing position is a tense position which cannot be held for long without fatigue and consequent relaxing of vigilance. The best way of holding up is to relax from the normal position until the feet are comfortably astride, at the same time bringing the pistol back until it is held in the centre of the body, barrel parallel to the ground with the elbow resting on the right hip. Then, herd the enemy into the far corner of the room on the same side as the door and then back away until you are against the wall opposite the door. In this position you are relaxed and at the same time you can turn your gun on to anybody who makes a move, simply by turning the body until it is square to the target. Also, in this position you can't be surprised from the rear and you have the door in sight all the time.

Attack into a Room against Armed Opposition.

This is the occasion when the enemy is cornered in a room and has locked or barricaded the door. He is also armed. Assuming some of your party are armed with Stens, then two of them take up a position where they can crossfire through the door into opposite corners of the room. You blow the lock off and force the door open, working from the ground, underneath their crossfire. When the door is open make your way in on your stomach, engaging targets as they appear. When you are in the room, the Sten gunners maintaining their fire follow you in, at the same time spreading their fire round to the main part of the room.

In theory, perhaps faults can be found with this technique but it gives you an idea how weapons can be co-ordinated in an attack of this nature.

Escape Hints.

If you are cornered in a room with the enemy forcing an entry and you are armed, it is fatal to stay on floor level. As the enemy burst into the room, their gaze and fire will immediately sweep the floor level before they give their attention to any higher level. If you can get on top of a piano or pile of boxes, as high as possible on the same side of the room as the door, you stand a chance of escaping notice for a few seconds, which will enable you to concentrate accurate fire at the point where it is most likely to break up the attack.

The enemy have cornered you in a room and are forcing the door in. An old ruse was to get behind the door. As the enemy rushed in you were able to take them from the rear if you were armed, or dodge round the door if you were unarmed. This method is more or less worn out now, as police and other agents are often trained to fire through and behind the door as they are rushing in, to prevent anybody surprising them from that direction. A better and more effective ruse is to stand on the other side of the door where it opens. Get as close to the wall as possible. As the door is forced and the enemy rushes in, the force of their rush will carry them right past you and all you have to do is to slip out.

Firing in the Dark.

When firing in the dark never stay in the position from which you fired. The enemy will fire at the flash of your gun. If you are in the prone position "fire" and roll away to the side. Keep on doing this, never stay still.

General.

The methods you have been taught during this course have been proved to be the best methods in Gun Fighting. But it is impossible to give a ready-made solution to every problem which is likely to arise. With your knowledge of Gun Fighting you must use your initiative and, if necessary, vary a general practice to suit a particular situation.

As an example: You have been taught always to fire two shots into a man when you wish to kill. The reasons for this have been explained and are sound, but there is the occasion when you cannot afford to put two shots into a man. If you dive into a room with seven rounds in your magazine and there are five people to kill, obviously you can't give them all two rounds each without changing a magazine. You wouldn't have time for this and you would necessarily have to fire <u>one</u> shot at each man, keeping two to finish them off.

Remember, also, as soon as you have finished firing, before you do anything else, clear your gun and insert a fresh magazine.

You have been taught to ignore the safety catch on the automatic, always carrying a loaded magazine in it but with the action not cocked, so that you draw, cock and fire in one movement. The reasons for this are also sound, but again there is the occasion when to meet particular circumstances it would be better to have the action cocked with the safety catch applied. Again, you must use your initiative.

Always take great care of your magazines. If the magazine is distorted or treated badly the automatic will not function.

Never store your magazines <u>fully</u> loaded. When the spring is under full compression for any length of time it becomes weak.

NOTES FOR INSTRUCTORS ON PISTOL TRAINING

<u>Introducing the Weapons and the Principles of Firing them Instinctively</u>.

1. It must be left to the discretion of the Instructor whether the instruction in the weapons themselves, i.e. stripping, loading, unloading, etc. is carried out at the same time as the introduction to instinctive firing, or whether the

introduction to the weapons and their mechanisms is done first and separately.

An advantage of giving, say, half-an-hour's instruction on the weapons themselves is that the student is familiar with the working parts of the weapon when he first attempts to practice instinctive firing positions, and the instructor is free to concentrate upon these only, and the students will know by that time all such points as correct handling of the pistol while cocking, loading, unloading, etc.

2. The principles of instinctive firing should always be introduced in the form of a short talk - either in a lecture-room or in the range. This talk should draw a picture of a man entering an enemy-occupied house or some similar circumstance, and should point out which of the actions involved in our methods are <u>instinctive</u>. The more amusing and the more dramatic this talk the greater its value, but the instructor must always ensure that while the weapon is in his hand he is practising what he teaches.

Practising the Student in Instinctive Firing Positions.

1. The student will naturally be required to practise the position before firing at the recruit target, and the instructor must make certain that the student has a grasp of what is required before he begins to fire. The instinct of many instructors is to put the student into position by hand. This should be avoided - let him do it himself by verbal instruction and repeated demonstration. Here again, the instructor must make certain that his own position is correct. The only handling of the student which may be necessary is that of the hand holding the pistol and of the left shoulder if the student shows a tendency to let it drop back.

2. At all costs guard against keeping the student in an uncomfortable position while his mistakes are being corrected verbally. Before the student is accustomed to it, the "ready" position is very uncomfortable if prolonged for more than a minute or so. Therefore always allow the student to rest if you have much talking to do.

3. It is unnecessary to dance round the student searching for mistakes. In the early stages of instruction always get in front of the student, and see him from the "target's eye" point of view.

4. The instructor should have a certain definite sequence in which he looks at a student whenever he has a weapon in his hands -just as an officer is taught to have a sequence when inspecting troops. Each instructor may have his own individual sequence which suits him best – but see that nothing is missed. Feet (balanced position), body (Crouch and shoulders square), firing arm (whether too bent or too straight), wrist (whether correct amount of cocking and correction and whether remaining rigid when the arm is moved), other arm (whether resting heavily upon the knee and thus making it difficult to turn the upper half of the body), hand (whether in the centre of the body and whether fingers and thumb in correct position) – is a specimen sequence.

Early Firing Practices.

1. Do not let a student fire while making an obvious error in position – unless you wish to prove to him that this particular error causes a certain inaccuracy. With the small amount of ammunition at disposal, every shot fired incorrectly is a waste. Therefore, if you see some fault when the student is in the "ready" position, correct if before he begins to fire. Do not be afraid to stop the practice in order to correct a fault at once, but correct the fault quickly and do not go into a lengthy discussion. Every time a fault is made it becomes more difficult to eradicate.

2. When the student is firing, always stand on his right (unless he is left-handed) and slightly to the rear. Don't crowd him, and on no account shout in his ear – this is a common fault which flusters a nervous student.

3. ALWAYS WATCH THE STUDENT AND NOT THE TARGET AT THE MOMENT OF FIRING. By watching the student the instructor should be able to tell automatically where the shots have gone. If, instead, the instructor watches the target and it is missed, he is not in a position to tell the student the reason.

Analysis of Faults causing Consistent Error on the Recruit Target.

Right Error.

1. Hand not in centre of body at the moment of firing.
2. Hand in centre but over-correction with the wrist.
3. Elbow of firing arm pushed under and into the centre.
4. Hand and pistol canted over to the left.

Left Error.

1. Lack of correction with the wrist.
2. Elbow bent upwards and outwards.
3. Hand and pistol canted to the right.

Low Error.

1. Firing on the way up.
2. Wrist turned too much down.
3. The same, with the pistol brought so high that the pistol hand obscures the target.

High Error (Unusual)

1. Wrist turned too much up.
2. Pistol comes up too high.
3. Jerking from "ready" position to firing position - movement should be smooth and fast.
4. Jerking the body back, or raising the body as the pistol hand comes up.

Analysis of Faults causing Inconsistent Error on the Recruit Target.

1. Loose grip of the pistol.
2. Flinching, with closure of the eyes.
3. Feet off balance, causing staggering.
4. Hand not kept in centre of body.
5. A different hand elevation is reached each time.
6. The pistol is "punched" towards the target with a movement of the elbow.
7. Pistol arm not straight enough - the arm should be almost fully extended, so that the bend is only just perceptible.

If a student shows an error which cannot be immediately traced to its cause, the points under the above analyses should be eliminated one by one until the instructor is certain of the reason.

Faults in Firing at Moving Targets, and at Targets in Varying Directions.

1. When changing direction from one target to another, the whole of the upper half of the body must be turned squarely to face the new target. In the majority of cases this requires a slight alteration in the position of the feet. This alteration should be a smooth natural action - "jumping" round should be discouraged at all costs.

2. Both the footwork and the movement of the upper half of the body are seriously handicapped when the left hand is rested heavily upon the knee, as this is tending to lock the body in the direction in which it was originally facing.

3. Most students feel that it is necessary to "aim off" a moving target. At instinctive firing ranges this is entirely unnecessary and will cause a miss in front of the target. The pistol should be pointed at the centre of the target as if it were stationary.

4. A miss is also almost certain if the pistol is pointed in front of the target and the firer waits to pull the trigger until the target has reached that point. Apart from other considerations, a live target might change direction and never reach that point.

Faults in Handling.

Magazines should be inserted with the fingers and thrust home with the thumb - it should not be banged into place with the base of the hand.

General.

1. Unteachables do exist, but they are one in a thousand. An instructor should never allow a student to leave his school as a bad shot - his life will probably depend upon how well he has been taught this subject. If the student is getting consistently bad results, first ascertain whether his fault is consistently in one direction. Then go through in your mind the errors causing that deviation, and eliminate them one by one until the cause is determined.

2. Upon the atmosphere which an instructor creates in his teaching of this subject will largely depend the amount of interest which a student will take in it. If an instructor is not himself aggressive, he cannot expect his students to show aggression. If he himself is obviously not interested in the subject, he cannot expect his students to be keyed up to the desirable pitch. An instructor should try to create in the student's mind the impression that he is actually "killing" the targets, and should force him to shoot as though his life depended upon it.

3. An instructor should try to dispel the atmosphere of "Range Practices" where it is incumbent upon every man to try to get a good score, and should impress upon the students that

during instruction it is the application of fast, instinctive methods that matters, and not the number of hits upon the target achieved by slower or less practical methods.

APPENDIX "A"

MACHINE CARBINE COURSE

PERIOD I.   A. Introduction to Thompson Sub-Machine Gun.

Stores: Thompson Sub-Machine Gun. 2 Magazines.

A. 1. INTRODUCTION.

The Gun is known as the Thompson Sub-Machine Gun. Calibre .45. Rate of fire – 700 Rounds per minute and it weighs approximately 10 lbs.

There are two types of magazines: The Drum type holding 50 Rounds and the Box type holding 20 Rounds. You can forget about the Drum type. This is of no use for fast close combat work for the following reasons:

a) It is too heavy.
b) It is difficult to fill quickly and filling is noisy.
c) The magazines are an awkward shape, making them difficult to carry without some special carrier.
d) Attachment to the gun is insecure.

The box type of magazine is ideally suited for our purpose. It is light, easily filled and can be conveniently carried in the pockets or inside the blouse. You can carry eight or nine filled magazines distributed in your clothing without being inconvenienced in any way.

2. MAGAZINE FILLING.

To fill or charge the magazine, grasp it in the left hand with the ribbed side at the base of the fingers. Assisting with the thumb of the left hand, feed in the rounds with the right hand by pressing the base of the round on the magazine platform and thrusting downwards and forwards.

3. CHARACTERISTICS.

The "Tommy Gun" has a short barrel and fires blunt nosed pistol ammunition. It is therefore a short range weapon and by reason of the heavy calibre of the bullets and the high rate of fire it is a valuable weapon for any type of close combat fighting, such as Street and House Fighting, etc.

It is fired, from the hip up to a distance of 12 yards;
from the shoulder standing up to 50 yards; the maximum
effective range of the Gun is 175 yards fired from the
shoulder in the prone position.

4. <u>MANIPULATION</u>. Demonstrate.

<u>Proving</u>: As you have been taught, the first thing you do
with any weapon is to prove to yourself that it is <u>not</u>
loaded. To 'prove' the Tommy Gun, firstly turn the Gun
over on to its right-hand side and grasp the magazine with
the fingers of the left hand. Then place the thumb of the
left hand on the magazine catch, press upwards and withdraw
the magazine. Turn the gun upright. Grasp the knob of
the cocking handle with the fingers of the left hand and
work the bolt backwards and forwards two or three times,
keeping the trigger pressed throughout. Leave the knob of
the cocking handle in the forward position. The gun is now
"safe".

<u>To Load</u>: Hold the gun at the "carry", i.e. gun under
the arm, right hand grasping the rear claw grip, muzzle
pointing to the ground directly forward, at an angle of
about 45 degrees.

See that the bolt is forward or, in other words, that the
breech is closed.

Turn the gun over to the right, so that its left side is
uppermost, and verify the positions of the change and safety
levers. The former must be at "single-shot" and the latter
in the firing position. If they are not in these positions,
they are to be altered at once, without waiting for orders.
The bolt must be pulled back until it locks before the
alterations can be effected. The alterations effected, <u>ease</u>
the bolt forward until the breech is closed again.

Left side of the gun still uppermost, lay the right
forefinger along the right-hand side of the trigger
guard. Take a 20-shot magazine in the left hand and
using as a guide the tip of the right forefinger, which
should protrude a little beyond the trigger guard, enter
the magazine in its grooves and send it smartly home.
<u>Invariably</u>, pull down on the magazine (with the left hand)
to ensure that it is locked in position.

Turn the gun into the upright position. As there is nothing
in the breech, the gun is perfectly safe and may be carried
for an indefinite period without risk.

Note that in all the operations described so far, the gun muzzle remains pointed at an angle of 45 degrees, at the ground directly to the front. To prepare for firing, draw the bolt back until it locks.

Unloading: On the cessation of firing, magazine wholly or partially exhausted, the bolt remains in the rearward or firing position. If firing is not to be resumed, remove magazine and ease the bolt forward. Work it back and forth two or three times and leave in the forward, or closed, position.

If the magazine is exhausted and it is desired to resume firing at once, remove the empty magazine and insert a filled one. The bolt being in the rear, or firing, position, firing can be resumed instantly.

Note: All operations described under Manipulation must be practised until they can be performed, in daylight or in the dark, smartly and without the slightest suspicion of fumbling. Instructors should show how to verify by touch, in the dark, the positions of the bolt, change-lever and safety-catch. Students should be shown and practised in the charging and uncharging of magazines. They should be informed also that while it is possible to put 21 rounds in a magazine intended for 20, a magazine so charged will sometimes not lock in position when inserted in the gun. Their attention should be drawn, therefore, to the necessity, before going into action, of testing each charged magazine in the gun to make absolutely sure that it will lock in position. If it is not noticed, as might be the case in a hurry, that the magazine is not locked, either it will drop out or the bolt will fail to take the cartridges into the breech.

5. THE FIRING POSITION. Demonstrate.

The 'Low Hip' Position.

A natural crouched position of the body, left foot forward. From the "Carry" position the gun is raised until the barrel is parallel to the ground, the butt pressed into and held in the hip by the right arm. The left hand grasps the foregrip, all the fingers engaged in the grooves provided, thumb to the rear; the left elbow is now brought inwards until it is locked in position, as far underneath the gun as possible. The body is then over the gun with the head well down in an aggressive attacking position. This position is known as the "Low Hip" position. It is not a satisfactory position for fast close combat work as it has been proved that you cannot maintain the forward elevation of the gun when turning tremendously fast on to a target. It is also such a low position that it is very difficult to deal effectively and quickly with high targets.

The 'Under Arm' Position.

The position of the body is the same as with the 'Low Hip' position. The gun, instead of being held into the hip, is held underneath the arm, left hand grasping the foregrip, left elbow underneath the gun barrel parallel to the ground. Head in an aggressive position close to the gun. In this position the gun is much higher in the body so that the left elbow can easily "lock" under the gun. This enables you to maintain the forward elevation of the gun when turning fast on to a target. The head and eyes are much closer to the gun and you have naturally more control over your direction and elevation.

In the approach to the target the butt can be held "ready" underneath the arm, with barrel pointing towards the ground at an angle of 30 degrees, left hand grasping the foregrip. To go into "Action" all you have to do is to "snap" the barrel up until it is directed at the target, at the same time bringing the head down to the gun. Alternatively, if the butt permanently under the arm is an uncomfortable position to carry the gun, the gun can be held in the most comfortable two-handed position and "snapped" into position when "action" is required. This requires practice. The left elbow and right arm "lock" the gun simultaneously.

The Shoulder Position.

In this position the gun is used exactly as you would use a shot-gun. As the gun is brought into the shoulder the body is pressed forward towards the target. It is not fired from the upright position.

This position is ideal for the man who is used to a shot-gun or the man with very long arms. With practice the gun can be brought into the shoulder very fast and as the gun is in line with the eyes, it is the most accurate position. For a frontal shot it is slightly slower than the hip position but, with practice, it is just as fast when turning on to a target.

A variation of this method which allows the man with short arms to use the gun from the shoulder quickly, for close quarter targets, is as follows:

Butt in the shoulder, left hand grasping the foregrip, barrel pointing to the ground in front at an angle of 30 degrees, left foot forward. To fire, raise the gun into the shoulder until it is pointing at the target. This is a very quick and accurate snap shooting method and if need to the sights can be used conveniently. Its one disadvantage is that it is an uncomfortable way of carrying the gun for any length of time.

Note: Having demonstrated the various firing positions, the Instructor should assist the students in choosing the position which suits them best. All the positions should be practised but the low hip position should be discouraged as it has been proved to be an impractical position. It should be pointed out to those students who choose the Under Arm position that in normal combat they must be able to combine this position with a fast shoulder position to deal with targets at over 12 yards distance.

B. FIRING PRACTICE NO. 1.

The Recruit Target - Fig. 2 (Full figure) Field Grey - white aiming mark on belly.

Range - 3 yards.
No. of Rounds fired - 10

The Purpose of the Recruit Target.

The target is at close range so that you can't miss it. You will see exactly what happens to every shot fired and you should endeavour to control all your shots on to the aiming mark. The gun is not moved independently of the body. In the correct position it is locked, so that you depress your body to depress your shots. Similarly, when you wish to elevate, you ease your body slightly back. Shots right or left of the aiming mark are corrected by pressing inwards slightly with the left or right shoulder.

Student charges magazine with ten rounds and advances to Firing Point. On command "Load" he loads and adopts the "Ready" position. (Gun muzzle at 45 degrees to ground). Without firing, practise coming quickly into the Firing Position whilst the Instructor checks faults. On command "One" come quickly into the "Firing" position, fire one shot without hesitating and return to the "Ready" position.

<u>Note</u>: This is repeated until six shots have been fired.

On the command "Two" come quickly into position and fire a burst of two rounds and return to the "Ready" position.

Repeat.

Student, with Instructor, examines position of shots on the target and discusses their position in relation to any error in the "Firing" position.

<u>Note</u>: Concentration on the aiming mark should be emphasised as the principal aid to instinctive firing. Any attempt to aim must be discouraged immediately.

FIRING PRACTICE NO. 2.

<u>Period I</u>

<u>Targets</u> - Moving and/or Bobbing Targets at varying ranges and elevations.

No. of Rounds - 5

In this practice we are going to fire at Moving or Bobbing Targets. It is not difficult to hit them providing you are concentrating, adopting the correct position with the left elbow well under the gun, the head down and the body pressed in towards the target in an aggressive attacking position.

In turning on to the targets, the gun does not move independently of the body. It is brought on to the target by the body and feet moving. The feet move naturally to balance the body and the principal point is that you must get round on to your target with <u>tremendous speed</u> and when you are round your "Firing Position" must be correct.

<u>Note</u>: Jumping round is a poor substitute for neat, precise footwork and Instructors should not permit it.

Magazine charged with five rounds. One shot to be fired at each target as it is exposed.

<u>Note</u>: Throughout the practice the Instructor observes closely every detail of the student's actions in attacking the target so that he will know the reason why 'misses' occur and will be able to remedy faults.

<u>Period II</u>. 1-½ Hours.

FIRING PRACTICE NO. 3.

> Targets - Moving and/or Bobbing - at varying ranges and
> elevations.

> No. of Rounds - 5

FIRING PRACTICE NO. 4 - in dark.

> Targets - As for Practice No. 3.

> No. of Rounds - 5

FIRING PRACTICE NO. 5.

> Targets - As for Practice No. 3.

> No. of Rounds - 5.

Note: Practices Nos. 3, 4 and 5 are concerned with speeding
up and teaching the students to attack fast and maintain
their correct firing position although turning at wide
angles. Practice No. 5 should involve an attack into the
Range as used in the Pistol Instruction.

The most common faults are loose holding, failing to obtain
position with the left elbow under the gun, keeping the
head up and not forcing the body into the target. These
points must be continually emphasised, also the necessity
of aggression and concentration in attack.

The balance of 5 Rounds will be utilised as follows:

> > Assault course - 4 Rounds
> > Aerodrome Scheme - 1 Round

MACHINE CARBINE COURSE

STEN GUN

Period III.

Stores - Sten Gun - 2 Magazines.

A. 1. INTRODUCTION.

This gun is known as the Sten Machine Carbine. Calibre -
9mm. Rate of Fire - 500 rounds per minute; it weighs
approximately 7 lbs.

The magazine is of the box type holding 32 rounds. The
magazine is difficult to fill by hand but there is a simple
magazine filler which allows the rounds to be fed quickly
and easily into the magazine.

Demonstrate.

It is natural that you will compare the Sten with the
"Tommy Gun" and principally because of the rough appearance
of the Sten, your comparison will not be favourable.

This is wrong for the following reasons:

a) It fires 9 mm. Luger (Parabellum) Ammunition.
b) It is approximately 3 lbs. lighter than the Thompson.
c) It has a very simple mechanism and the design allows for
   simple stripping.
d) When stripped it is easily concealed.
e) The Gun is fired dry. You do not have to keep the
   working parts oiled.
f) Immersion in water, mud or sand does not interfere with
   the firing of the gun.

The advantages of all these points are obvious.

2. CHARACTERISTICS.

The Sten is ideally suited for all types of close combat
fighting. The lightness and design of the gun enable
it to be used with extreme speed from the shoulder at all
ranges. The maximum effective range is approximately 175
yards.

3. <u>MANIPULATION</u>.

<u>To Prove</u>:
Hold the Gun at the "carry", i.e. gun under the arm, right hand round the pistol grip, muzzle pointing to the ground directly forward at an angle of about 45 degrees. Remove the magazine by grasping it with the fingers of the left hand and at the same time pressing the magazine catch which is on the top of the magazine housing. Then, turning the gun over to the left, work the bolt backwards and forwards two or three times and leave it in the forward position.

<u>To Load</u>:
Gun in "carry" position. With the left hand draw back the bolt and engage the cocking handle in the safety notch. Then turn the gun over to the right so that the left side is uppermost and verify the position of the change stud. This should be at single shot. See that it is, by pressing the stud inwards from left to right. Turn the gun upright. With the left hand insert the loaded magazine into the magazine housing, sending it smartly home and <u>invariably pull away to make sure it is locked in position</u>. To prepare for firing, disengage the cocking handle from the safety notch and ease the bolt forward until it stops in the cocked or firing position.

<u>Unloading</u>:
As for Proving.

<u>Stoppages</u>:
Should a stoppage occur during firing, the first thing to do is to withdraw the bolt and engage the cocking handle in the safety notch. Then, remove the magazine and examine the breech to see the cause of stoppage. If there is an empty case or any other obstruction, shake it out, replace your magazine, ease the bolt into the cocked position and carry on firing.

<u>Note</u>: Before replacing magazine make sure that the top round is correctly positioned, otherwise another stoppage will immediately occur.

<u>Firing Position</u>:
Owing to the light weight and the design of the Gun the normal man can engage targets efficiently, at close quarters, firing from the shoulder. With practice the gun

can be brought into the shoulder firing position as fast as into the hip and as it is the more accurate position, it should be used for firing at all ranges, except at very close quarters, when a fast hip position is the most convenient.

The shoulder position is adopted in the same way as the Thompson except that, as the Sten possesses no front grip, the left hand should grasp the cooling cylinder, taking care that thumb and forefinger are definitely in contact with the front edge of the cylinder or that the little finger bears hard up against the foresight. With any other grip the ejector cut is liable to be blocked by the hand, causing a stoppage and most probably damaged fingers. In prone shooting the left hand may be placed in front of the trigger guard but great care must be taken to keep the fingers below the line of travel of the recoiling cocking handle. On no account must this gun be grasped by the magazine during firing.

Practise Firing Position

Firing Practice No.1.

Targets - Moving and/or Bobbing Targets at various ranges and levels.

No. of Rounds - 6.

In this practice one round will be fired at each target as it appears.

Student charges magazine and advances to Firing Point.

On command "Load" he loads and adopts the "ready" position.

Targets are attacked with extreme speed as they appear.

Note: Emphasise speed in attack. The body must be pressed towards the target so that shots drive deep into the target.

Period IV.

Firing Practice No. 2.

Targets - As for Practice No. 1, in darkness.
No. of Rounds - 6.

This practice is carried out in the same way as Practice No. 1 except that it is fired in darkness, as in Pistol Practices.

<u>Firing Practice No. 3</u>.

<u>Targets</u> - As for Practice No. 1.
<u>No. of Rounds</u> - 6.

In this practice introduce movement by attacking into the range.

<u>Period V</u>.

<u>Firing Practice No. 4</u>.

<u>Targets</u> - Stalk Course, and Spraying Target.
<u>No. of Rounds</u> - Stalking - 8
                   Spraying - 7

The Stalk with the Sten is carried out in the same way as with the Pistol, emphasising fast attack and avoiding any attempt to take deliberate aim.

Two magazines are carried, one charged with 8 rounds and one with 7 rounds. The eight round magazine is used on the Stalk, on completion of which the student immediately gets down behind cover and changes his magazine, inserting the second one holding seven rounds. He then engages the Spraying Target.

<u>Note</u>: <u>Spraying Practice</u>.

The object of this is to practise the secondary purpose of the gun. Firing is to be done standing up, from the shoulder, at a plain white stream of painted canvas 7 yards long, 5 feet high, without aiming mark. The gun is traversed back and forth from one extremity of the screen to the other. Students should be warned of the tendency to shoot low at either extremity of the traverse and firing should be done as rapidly as possible.

<u>Period VI</u>.

<u>Firing Practice No. 5.</u>

<u>Targets</u> - Stalk Course.
<u>No. of Rounds</u> - 12

This is a further Stalking practice. Targets should be in a different position from the previous Stalk and students will be told to fire two fast shots at the close range targets in the same way as they fire double shots with the Pistol.

After a student has fired a practice he will proceed immediately to the Lecture Room or other convenient place, where he will carry out the following practice under another Instructor:

Period II.

Practice. Loading and Unloading with speed.
               Magazine Filling Tests.

Note: Stripping will be demonstrated and practised during the general stripping period. Special worn springs will be kept and used solely for this purpose and on no account will good condition springs be used. Our own method of assembling should be taught and practised. It is faster and does not rely on the use of any tools or implements and is therefore the most practical method to teach students. As a secondary method only, for those students who are unable to cope with our own method, the use of a nail to assist the spring into position should be shown.

Period III.

Stripping and Assembling Tasks.

Note: As a variation and a test of knowledge, two or three weapons can be stripped by the Instructor and the parts mixed together. Student reassembles.

Period IV.

Further study of Foreign Weapons and spotting faults in sabotaged weapons.

Note: Instructor interferes with gun in some way so that it will not operate. For example, remove firing pin or assemble incorrectly.

Period V.

Spare for expenditure of balance of .22 Ammunition if necessary.

WEAPON TRAINING

FOREIGN WEAPONS

This subject is of great importance, and in view of the large number of weapons and the difficulty of housing them, a special establishment has been opened at which a course is run designed to suit the particular nationality of the students. All students receive instruction in German Weapons and in the Weapons of their particular country, and in addition are taught how to recognise the various types of ammunition used on the Continent.

The object of the course is to teach students enough about the weapons which they are most likely to encounter in the field so that they can recognise them, select the correct ammunition, and put them into use immediately.

It is not intended to make students into Armourers.

During the course, students are given the opportunity of firing a number of the more common weapons.

419

FOREIGN WEAPON TRAINING SYLLABUS

PERIOD NO. 1 - 1-¼ Hours

Introductory Talk to Students.

a) Object of Foreign Weapons Training.
b) Safety Precautions to be observed.

Lecture and Practical.

Foreign Automatic Pistol Calibres and Ammunition.

Recognition, characteristics, location and weapons using the following types of S.L. pistol ammunition.

a)
  i) .22" or FLOBERT, long and short.
  ii) .25" or 6.35 mm.
  iii) .32" a.c.p. or 7.65 mm.
  iv) 7.65 Parabellum.
  v) 9 mm. Parabellum.
  vi) .30" or 7.63 mm. Mauser.
  vii) 9 mm. Mauser Magnum.
  viii) .380" a.c.p. or 9 mm. Short.
  ix) 9 mm. Long or 9 mm. Browning.
  x) .45" a.c.p. or 11 mm.
  xi) .38" a.c.p.
  xii) Any particular type peculiar to the nationality of the students.

b) Methods of distinguishing from certain common obsolescent types.

c) Continental commercial ammunition in 2 qualities; first quality and export quality - export quality often defective or unreliable - examples and general recognition.

PERIOD NO. 2 - 45 Minutes

Lecture and Practical.

German Army Pistols.

Characteristics, location, stripping and handling of:

  i) German Imperial Service Revolver.
  ii) Mauser Military Model, 7.63 mm. and 9 mm. Parabellum.
  iii) Lugers, all models.

420

WEAPON TRAINING

PERIOD NO. 3 - 30 Minutes

Lecture and Practical.

Other German Pistols.

      i) Government issues to Luftwaffe, Gestapo, etc.
    ii) Commercial types common to the Continent.
        (Specimens of almost all types available.)

PERIOD NO. 4 - 45 Minutes

Firing Practice - German Pistols.

  i) Army Pistols.
 ii) Representatives commercial and issue pistols as selected by
     students.
iii) Demonstration by Instructor of effect of sawn-off shot gun
     as an emergency weapon.

PERIOD NO. 5 - 45 Minutes

Lectures and Practical.

German Machine Carbines.

Characteristics, location, stripping and handling of:

      i) Bergmann M.P. 18 I.
     ii) Schmeisser M.P. 28 II.
    iii) Mauser M.P.
    iv) Steyr-Solothurn M.P.
     v) Neuhausen M.P.
    vi) Erma M.P.
   vii) M.P. 38.

PERIOD NO. 6 - 30 Minutes

Lecture and Practical.

a) German Army Rifles.

    Characteristics, location and handling of:

      i) Mannlicher Model '88.
     ii) Mauser Model '98 (rifle and carbine).
    iii) Mauser Einheitsgewehr.

b) Garand S.L. Rifle.

    (As example of Military S.L. Rifle.)

PERIOD NO. 7 - 45 Minutes

Firing Practice - German Army Rifles.

 i) Model '98.
 ii) Einheitsgewehr.
iii) Garand S.L. Rifle.
 iv) M.P. 38 Machine Carbine.

PERIOD NO. 8 - 30 Minutes

Lecture and Practical.

German Grenades.

PERIOD NO. 9 - 30 Minutes

Lectures and Practical.

German A/T Rifle PZ b 39.

PERIOD NO. 10 - 1 Hour

Lecture and Practical.

German Machine Guns.

 i) Spandau Maxim '08.
 ii) Spandau Maxim '08/'15.
iii) M.G. 34.
 iv) M.G. 15.

PERIOD NO. 11 - 4 Hours

Lecture and Practical.

National Weapons of Students.

Specimen collections available for the following countries:

Belgium, France, Holland, Spain, Russia, Scandinavia, Poland, Balkans and Greece, Austria, Italy and Japan.

PERIOD NO. 12 - 30 Minutes

General Revision.

 i) Weapon Assembling Tasks.
 ii) Mounting and handling M.G.'s under practical conditions in the open.
iii) Recognition of weapons and equivalent ammunition from assorted pile (carried out under supervision on Range).

Total No. of Hours - 11¾

CONSTRUCTION OF FIGHTING HOUSES

The houses are built of rough timber as near to scale as possible and are not normally of more than one storey in height owing to the shortage of material and labour. The situation is important as it must be possible for students to fire in any direction or at least through 270 degrees. It is an advantage if there is high ground overlooking the site or high trees adjacent so that a suitable control tower can be constructed.

Three houses are generally sufficient and they are placed as though forming a cul-de-sac. The impression of a street is achieved by building fences, gardens to houses, marking the roadway with sidewalks and erecting dummy lamp-posts, etc.

Targets are made to be either automatic in action or controlled from the adjoining tower. By using automatic devices the aim is to achieve as much realism as possible and particularly to force the student to use the technique of gunfighting that he has been taught. Incidents can be created which will show him in a practical way the advantage of this technique.

As an example of the foregoing, the following series of targets might be used:

HOUSE "A"

This house comprises one large room with two doors.

Three targets represent Nazi officers sitting round a table. The table is situated in the corner farthest away from the main door. All the targets are hinged so that they can fall backwards out of sight. In front of the main door there is a partition extending into the centre of the room and a wire is stretched from the wall behind the partition around the end of it to a position on the wall on the right of the main doorway. A running target is attached to this wire.

The operation of all the targets is by means of a series of weights actuated by a 'master' weight on a shelf behind the door.

As the student attacks into the room through the main door he sees the three targets sitting round the table and he proceeds to 'kill' them. As he is in the process of doing this, the running target races round the corner of the partition straight towards him and simultaneously the three targets at the table disappear from view.

The whole action from the time of entry has taken approximately 3-½ seconds and the student has had the task of 'killing' four targets during that period.

The lessons brought out are: firstly, the necessity for sheer speed, and secondly, the necessity to utilise to the fullest those first few seconds when your opponent is motionless through shock of surprise.

HOUSE "B".

This house also comprises one room, divided by a partition facing the door. There is a 'charging man' target which runs on a wire straight through the doorway into the street. This is weight-operated and controlled from the control tower. When the student is about to approach the door, the target is released and the door opened so that the target rushes out with considerable force straight at the student.

Having dealt with this target the student enters the house. The partition faces him and on his right is a doorway which he has been told to investigate. This doorway leads to an underground tunnel which in turn leads to an underground chamber. There is a steep stairway leading down and in the tunnel there are various 'horror' devices: see-saw flooring, spring flooring, objects hanging from the roof, etc. As the student goes down the stairs the door behind him automatically closes, leaving him in almost complete darkness. The depth of the tunnel varies so that there is the impression of going deeper underground. As the student moves along the tunnel a glimmer of light discloses a man standing at the end. He fires at him and the target disappears through the roof, leaving the student in darkness again. At the end of the tunnel, steps lead to the chamber. As he proceeds up these a trap door about ten feet above his head opens and a man looks down. As the student fires the man disappears and the trapdoor slams back into the place.

The chamber is dimly lit by a hurricane lamp, and as the student pulls aside a curtain at the entrance he sees a 'prisoner' bound to a chair, with a Nazi standing beside him. He 'kills' the Nazi and releases the prisoner. (The prisoner is an S.K. dummy.)

There are steep steps leading out of the chamber, and the student, carrying the dummy over his shoulder, makes his way

up these and eventually arrives back on the ground floor of
the house through a narrow doorway. As he is coming though
this doorway he finds two Nazis waiting for him and it is
necessary to 'kill' them immediately despite his burden and
his cramped position. Having dealt with these opponents he
deposits the 'prisoner' and prepares to attack the third
house.

This brings out the student's ability to handle the pistol or
Sten efficiently although scared and in complete darkness and
the ability to shoot effectively under all circumstances even
when he is carrying a heavy object and in a cramped position.

HOUSE "C".

This house also comprises one room with one door. Upon entering
the door there is a full-length target standing beside an
armchair against the opposite wall. The target is hinged to a
post so that it can swivel. The chair is attached to a pulley
overhead which is mounted on an inclined wire, which runs across
the room to the wall on the right of the doorway.

Against the right hand wall there is a double tier bunk
containing two figures as though asleep. When a central control
is released the bottom figure throws back the bedclothes and the
top figure sits up.

There is also a trap-door in the floor. To the underside of the
trap a head and shoulder figure is attached so that it appears
when the trap is raised.

On the left of the doorway there is the entrance to an enclosed
staircase. From this two control wires run to the control tower.
One when pulled causes a noise, as though somebody was running
downstairs, the other causes a head-and-shoulder figure to look
round the corner of the entrance to the staircase.

All the targets, with the exception of the staircase figure, are
controlled automatically from a release on the door.

As the student attacks into the room he is confronted by the
figure standing by the armchair. He kills this figure and then
turns to deal with the men in bed; as he turns, the chair is
thrown violently across the room in his direction and at the same
time the trap-door is raised to disclose the figure underneath.
After several seconds the noise of somebody running down the
stairs is heard and the figure of a Nazi is momentarily shown at
the foot of the stairs.

Here the student is required to get right inside the room and fight fast, using his footwork to dodge missiles and at the same time to shoot efficiently whilst turning fast and engaging targets at different levels.

STREET TARGETS.

Whilst crossing from house to house the student is called upon to deal with running targets representing men escaping and running across his front or running away from him. He also gets a momentary glimpse of targets looking out of windows. As he is leaving a house he might find a man waiting on the other side of the door. All the running targets are operated by weights controlled from the control tower.

GENERAL.

To add realism to the exercise and at the same time to practise the students in forming a proper plan of attack, a short narrative is generally given in which the houses are represented to form an enemy Battle H.Q. House "A" becomes Staff H.Q., House "B" partly disused -full occupation unknown but to be investigated, House "C" the Guardroom.

The plan of attack is discussed and possible faults to be avoided brought out, e.g. forgetting to change magazines, attacking into a house with a half-empty magazine, standing in the doorway and not getting right inside, etc.

From the control tower the behaviour of the student can be watched and his faults noted. After having fired, students are allowed to watch and criticise other students from the control tower.